Money for Life

*The 20 Factor Plan
for Accumulating Wealth
While You're Young*

Robert Sheard

📖 HarperBusiness
An Imprint of HarperCollinsPublishers

HarperCollins books may be purchased for educational, business,
or sales promotional use. For information please write:
Special Markets Department, HarperCollins Publishers, Inc.,
10 East 53rd Street, New York, NY 10022.

FIRST EDITION

Library of Congress Cataloging-in-Publication Data

Sheard, Robert.
    Money for life : the 20 factor plan for accumulating
wealth while you're young / [Robert Sheard].
        p. cm.
    Includes index.
    ISBN 0-06-662043-0
    1. Finance, Personal.   2. Retirement income—Planning.
3. Financial security.   4. Investments.   I. Title.

HG179 .S454 2000
332.024'01—dc21
                                                00-038927

00 01 02 03 04   10 9 8 7 6 5 4 3 2 1

CONTENTS

For Cyndi and Brenden

INTRODUCTION

Every individual who has given any thought to his or her financial future (and you wouldn't be reading *Money for Life* if you weren't among that group) is looking for guidance. What's the magic formula that will allow me to walk away from my job and remain financially secure for the rest of my life? How will I know when I've got enough money to quit the corporate game and take on that Peace Corps challenge I was too poor to accept when I was right out of college? How will I know when I'm financially secure enough to leave my job and start my life? How will I know when I can quit working for someone else and open that business of my own without worrying about my paycheck every week?

The whole point of the American economic system and cultural work ethic is that we work hard to accomplish our financial goals. Too often, however, we don't even have those goals very clearly defined; nor do we have the tools to accomplish them once they are defined. *Money for Life* will help you with both tasks: defining what your financial goals are, and then determining how to accomplish them. The pathways I'll advocate toward those goals are likely to be ones you've never considered before. Most financial planning books have one model in mind and gear all of their advice toward that model—the traditional retirement scenario. But *Money for Life* is *not* a retirement book. If you're planning to work until you're 65 and then sit on the porch looking at your gold watch (does anyone even get one of those any more?), this book probably isn't what you want.

Money for Life is a *financial freedom* book. You may be 30 years old and be thinking about how to quit your mundane job and go to a culinary school to become a chef. You may be 40 years old and be thinking about heading back to your workshop to finish those inventions you started a decade ago but put down because of your job's demands. You may be 20 years old and already be thinking about how you want to spend your life after you've amassed enough money to quit working. It doesn't matter how old you are or what you currently do. Don't wait until retirement to start your life; that's a long way off, and if you do things right today, retirement won't ever be an issue. *Money for Life* will show you, first, what's required to live your dream life, and second, how to start making it happen now.

Fear of the Unknown

Americans today have every right to be fearful about their financial futures. Study after study tells us that Americans have one of the lowest savings rates among all industrial nations. Credit card debt continues to plague consumers, eating away every dime most people could be putting to work elsewhere. Even though the job market is healthy today, there's still no real job security because companies and employees alike have moved away from a lifetime-commitment model to one based on free agency. To get a promotion today, you don't climb your company's corporate ladder, you change firms. In other words, uncertainty is a fixed component of our financial lives today and we have to learn to use that to our advantage. The days of lifetime pensions after a full career of service to a single company have gone the way of the dime telephone call and civility in the big city. But even worse is that financial education is so appallingly absent in our public schools that the average citizen is all but illiterate when it comes to his or her own money. The typical adult American today has precious little saved for the future, and instead of becoming financially independent, too many Americans are looking at bankruptcy as a way to escape their debts. It should be the reverse, with twice as many self-made millionaires as bankrupts, but it's not. We *should* be frightened.

To make matters worse, the bulk of personal finance advice available today (and you're probably wondering how this book can be any different from the spate of others on similar topics) is terribly old-fashioned, shortsighted, or downright silly. Even those few people who really want to take control over their financial destinies are so confused by what they read in books and magazines or see on the several financial cable networks that they become paralyzed.

One of the labels being plastered on this generation is the "Age of Information," and the benefits of global and instantaneous communication are too many to attempt to list here. But free and immediate access to all that is available carries a curse with it as well. Trying to wade through the sea of information, and keeping that which is worthy and discarding that which falls short, are far more difficult tasks than many people want to undertake. And even though the financial part of our lives is so crucial, we all too often let it slip from our attention because it's so daunting.

America has long stood firmly on the principle of self-reliance. From our governmental structures, where the people choose their representatives and change them often when they prove unsatisfactory, to our economic system, where hard work and risk-taking in a meritocracy are presumably rewarded, even to our current infatuation with self-help books (in which category, alas, this book may be cast), Americans have an enduring desire to "go it alone."

Somehow, however, we've completely forgotten those ideals when it comes to preparing for our financial futures. Pull average workers off the street and ask them what their financial plans are, and they're likely not to have any idea beyond a vague notion that they should be saving more. Too many of us seem to believe that the future will never become the present, and we put off planning indefinitely. All the dreams we could fulfill if we just set up our finances the right way don't have to become shattered. Financial independence is not just for those fortunate few who inherit wealth. It's within the grasp of all of us. All it takes is a little knowledge, a little tenacity, and a little time. If you can provide the latter two, I'll provide the first.

I realize I've begun on a somewhat apocalyptic note. And believe me when I claim that I'm not generally a gloom-and-doom type of writer. But the state of America's personal finances is deplorable, and the only way to wake up to some of the problems is to be smacked in the face by them a few times. We'll need to trample on the toes of some cherished beliefs you no doubt hold as unassailable before we can start over with new definitions, new methods, and new goals.

It's time for Americans to regain control of this most crucial area of their lives and stop trusting to the system to be there when it's needed. It's time for us all to understand, first, what we really need to accomplish during our earning years, and second, how to become good stewards of our own fortunes, whether they be massive or modest. To accomplish that, we need to tear down a great many misconceptions about money, investing, and risk. That's what *Money for Life* will help you do.

Light at the End of the Tunnel

The best news, though, to close this introduction on a much-needed bright note, is that what I propose we all need so desperately is wonderfully easy to understand and virtually as easy to put into practice. The principles I will outline here can be grasped without any special training in finance. You don't need to dread being pulled back through your long-forgotten calculus courses. In fact, any well-schooled seventh grader with a basic calculator will be able to do all the mathematics you'll find in this book.

In other words, I'm making no claims that what I'll discuss in *Money for Life* is rocket science or genius; it's decidedly not. And that's precisely my point. What we *don't* need is lots of academic theory and muck about risk tolerance and portfolio allocation that no one understands and can't possibly implement for him- or herself. What we all need is a concrete plan that defines the correct goals, is simple to understand, is easy to put in place (and to keep in place when the investment world seems scary), and will actually get us to the goals we've identified. So much of what's out there today under the vague umbrella of "financial planning" fails on one or several of these criteria.

Money for Life will:

- Show you why financial independence has nothing to do with age
- Give you a simple formula (The 20 Factor) to define your financial freedom target
- Teach you how and when to save, and then how to invest those savings to reach your target as quickly as possible

- Show you, once you've arrived, how to stay financially independent indefinitely

So forget about waiting until retirement age to begin living. Learn now how you can set up your finances so that they can begin taking care of you and providing you the freedom to enjoy your life. If you've got the desire to change your financial destiny, *Money for Life* will show you how.

A NEW FINANCIAL BLUEPRINT

Money for Life is not a retirement book. As I've already said, it's a personal freedom book, a financial independence book, a book about a voyage that you define for yourself. And then once you've launched the ship, you're given the drawing tools to create a clear map for getting to your destination. Anyone with full-time employment, the right set of tools, and time can amass enough money to live an independent life. That's not the financial model we typically picture today, where you work until age 65 and then sit on the porch, looking at the gold watch your employer honored you with at your retirement party. Far from it. Retirement in that sense is a long way off, and that's not our concern. In fact, if you do things right today while you're young, retirement is not even an issue that you need be concerned with at all.

I'm talking about a 40-year-old businesswoman who has made enough in commerce that she can afford to walk away from the proverbial rat race and write poetry in her cabin by the sea for as long as she likes. I'm talking about the 30-year-old who wants to start his own company instead of working for someone else. I'm talking about the 50-year-old who wants to learn a new language, study archeology, and work on the sites surrounding the pyramids at Giza. I'm talking about people who have dreams about how they'd like to spend their time if the daily task of making a living were removed.

Believe it or not, that kind of freedom could be within the reach of most of us if we only knew how to reach for it in the right way. I'm not promising to make you a Rockefeller. I'm not telling you that you can build a house that will rival Bill Gates's. But I can show you how to define your own ideal vision of financial freedom and then show you the ways to get there. What most Americans lack isn't financial power; it's simply the proper tools to take advantage of the financial power they possess. Let's put yours to work.

Challenging Archaic Ideas

Anytime one plans to establish a new set of definitions or paradigms (to use one of today's favorite buzzwords), the dismantling of previously held beliefs is required. Copernicus had to challenge the idea of an Earth-centered universe in order to establish our current view of the solar system. Darwin challenged the notion that the world's current state is somewhat how it has always been, in developing his theories of evolution and natural selection. And Tiger Woods rewrote the old theory that one needs a long iron to hit a golf ball 200 yards. (Please, a 180-yard pitching wedge?)

Any such redefinition enterprise, however, will face skeptics. There are still people who believe the Earth is flat, that we never put an astronaut on the moon, and that Elvis is alive and well. Heaven help them; I can't. But for rational people, when an old notion is proved to have outlived its usefulness, or is simply proved false, it is time to accept an alternative vision of the issue. On a much more modest scale than

Copernicus or Darwin, that is precisely what I'm suggesting must occur when we think of preparing for a self-reliant financial future.

I'm going to banish the term *retirement* altogether, because that's not at all what our goal should be. The old model suggests the end of something, and in an era where we used to work until age 65, and then had 5 to 10 years of life left, that may have been an appropriate concept. It's fine to spend a few years rocking on the porch or puttering around in the garden. But can you imagine doing it for several decades?

Our society has changed too drastically for that old view of working until 65 and then enjoying a few golden years. First of all, there is no typical age where one stops working today. It's a rarity when a worker begins a career in his or her twenties and ends it at age 65, all with the same company. The typical American adult today will change not just *jobs*, but *careers*, no less than three times.

For example, I'm not sure how typical I am, but my personal experience follows this pattern. I began college as a music education major, took my first degree in business administration, opted to remain in school for a second undergraduate degree in English, then taught as a college lecturer in English while pursuing a master's degree and a PhD. Just before finishing my PhD dissertation (on confessional narratives in contemporary British and Commonwealth fiction, if anyone's dying to know), I left academics to join the staff of The Motley Fool, an Internet forum dedicated to teaching individuals how to manage their own stock portfolios. After five years writing for The Fool about managing money, I was given the opportunity to manage money professionally for a group of private clients, which is my profession today. I've gone from music to business to English literature to business writing to money management—and I'm not anywhere near the end of my working years yet. While I don't currently anticipate changing careers again (my 12 handicap just won't make many cuts on the PGA Tour), I've already met the average before I've reached 40 years old.

Some would say that I just can't keep a job—but I prefer to think of it as having seized on a series of good opportunities that meshed together very well. And this is more and more typical today as our economy has changed from a provincial one to a national one and ultimately to a global web of economic interconnections.

With these major shifts in the way Americans work, the old financial planning models are outmoded. We can see this perhaps most clearly in the way American companies now typically pay "retirement" compensation. A generation or two ago, it was fairly typical for an employee to work until a prescribed age (65 perhaps) and then receive a pension for the rest of his or her life. It was the company's way of rewarding worker loyalty and providing a safety net for its employees.

Today workers no longer climb the corporate ladder within a single company. The path to advancement is by changing positions frequently, sometimes within the same company, moving from department to department to acquire new skills, sometimes changing companies regularly. In fact, today it's often seen as a sign of a career on the slow track for an employee *not* to change positions regularly.

Since that lifetime commitment between company and employee no longer exists (and it's not just the workers who have changed attitudes; companies stopped being loyal to employees when corporate downsizing became the management technique *du jour*), the pension model had to be changed. Today the vast majority of such compensation comes in the form of portable investment accounts like 401(k) or 403(b) plans. The company will contribute money to the employee's account, and the employee may often contribute his or her own money as well, but it's the employee who controls the account, not the company. The employee faces the decision regarding how the money is to be invested, and when the employee leaves the company, he or she takes the account along, rolling it over either into the new company's plan or into an Individual Retirement Account (IRA).

This presents today's workers with a lot more opportunities, but it also puts an added burden on them by requiring that they be responsible for the management of that money. It's an enormous responsibility that most people aren't prepared to undertake.

Financial Independence Is Not a Function of Age

Even the age at which we typically stop working is being called into question. With the number of Americans involved in entrepreneurial enterprises today, fortunes are often made at relatively young ages. A businessperson who builds a small company from scratch into a successful venture may well sell out at age 45 or 50 and be financially able to live comfortably on the growth of his or her investment portfolio. Corporate executives frequently receive handsome severance packages when they step down, leaving them able to pursue personal dreams rather than other jobs. Anyone inheriting wealth from a parent or grandparent may suddenly be in a changed financial position. Or an individual who simply has saved and invested well throughout his or her working career may decide to change courses at an earlier age than the standard 65. Financial independence isn't a function of age, but of accumulated wealth, and that can occur much sooner than many of us believe.

In my investment advisory firm, for example, we work with a number of professional athletes (my business partner, Don Davey, is a former professional football player) and we

see young men—in their late 20s or early 30s—who are in the
enviable position of having enough money to live on their
portfolio proceeds indefinitely. I realize that very few of us
will be in such a wonderful position so young, but whether
it's through business success, investing success, inheritance,
or whatever, more and more Americans are becoming financially independent at younger and younger ages. Keep in
mind that it's not necessary to have millions in order to
achieve financial freedom. I'm not writing this book to create
the next generation of financial moguls. Your needs may be
an annual income today of only $30,000 or $40,000. If that's all
you require to live the life you want, it's not that far out of
reach. But we need to get you to the place where you can
afford to spend that much each year without having to work
from 9:00 to 5:00. If the life you want to live is more costly, it
may take a little longer. The point is, *you're* in charge of defining what kind of life you want. Once you have a destination,
much of the hard work is done. Then it's just a matter of
putting a solid trip plan together to get you there.

In other words, we shouldn't really be concerned at all
about what age we can stop working and sit on the porch.
Age doesn't matter in the least, in fact. What we should really
be focusing on is the point in our lives at which we become
financially independent. Whether that achievement comes at
age 30, or 50, or 70, or perhaps in some unfortunate cases not
at all, that is the real goal. When you can say to yourself, "If I
am a careful steward of my finances, I have enough money
now to last me the rest of my life—*no matter how long I live,*"
you've won the game. That's financial independence.

The Goal Is Financial Independence

At the point of financial independence, it doesn't matter what
career decisions you make. You may decide you want to con-

tinue working as you are. Great; you'll just be in an even more secure position as the years pass. You may decide to take that Peace Corps job you didn't feel you could afford to take earlier in your life. Now you can do it without worrying about what you're not earning. Maybe your lifelong dream has been to take up a musical instrument, but you never felt you could give it the time and dedication you know it would take. Now you can. Or perhaps you have the greatest ambition of all, traveling to the world's finest golf courses and trying to break 90, or 80, on each one. (Is it clear yet that I'm an avid golfer? Does it become any clearer when I tell you that I live in Pinehurst, North Carolina, America's golf mecca?)

The point of all this is that financial independence is the goal, and it's not a function of age. It's a function of two factors I'll spend a great deal of time discussing later: (1) how much you need in income each year to maintain your chosen lifestyle (and it is a choice), and (2) how much you must have saved and how it must be invested in order to generate that level of income indefinitely. That's *all* the decision comes down to. A lot of the other factors you will have heard about in conventional treatments of financial planning are either red herrings (and can be ignored) or will be accounted for when I explain the details of the 20 Factor Plan guidelines.

So the first cherished myth we have to abandon before we can go any further is that our goal is retirement. It's not; the goal is *financial independence,* and that can come at any age depending upon a number of factors. What I'm going to help you discover is what that magic target is for you personally and how to get there. And then once you're there, I'll help you discover how to make sure you manage your assets the right way to sustain your financial independence as long as necessary.

Another issue complicating our planning for financial independence is that of the terrific advances in healthcare in recent generations. Americans enjoy an ever-expanding life expectancy, as well as an advancing quality of life as we age. If we're becoming financially independent at earlier ages and living much longer lives, that creates a very real dilemma—how can we be sure that we won't outlive our money? In the past it was always a concern, but if a typical worker left the workforce at age 65 and died at age 72, one only needed to generate income for seven years. In many cases, it was possible even to live in part on one's principal.

This kind of thinking is one of the major flaws in traditional financial planning even today. Pick up any book or article or software package designed to help you plan for retirement, and one of the first variables you're likely to be asked to supply is your life expectancy. Everything else in the plan will be calculated based on that figure. How absurd! If you're young when you start planning for financial independence—and you should be—there's no possible way you can enter an intelligent response to that question. Heaven help you if you're working from such a plan and you live 20 years longer than you anticipated.

What about a young corporate wizard, age 40, who decides she's had enough of the grind and wants to spend more time with her children? Even if she's amassed quite a portfolio, she's looking at a potential time frame measuring some four to six decades. It simply isn't possible to live on the money she's accumulated unless she invests well and has a feasible plan that will work indefinitely. Whether she lives another 10 years or another 70, she needs to be able to live on the growth of the money she's invested, not on the principal itself. The plan I'm proposing, then, is one where you don't need to be clairvoyant about your own demise. Once you reach financial independence, it won't matter if you live another six months or 60 years. Your assets will sustain you. Anything short of that isn't really financial independence at all; it's gambling on a race between your last dollar and your last breath. That's a race I'd just as soon skip.

Myth: Get Your Income from Bonds

As bad as gambling on your date with the grim reaper is, the advice typically presented by traditional financial planning on how to invest to get to financial independence, and how to stay financially secure once there, is even worse. If you've read anything at all about this type of financial planning you've heard the rule of thumb that you should diversify, diversify, diversify. Take your age and subtract from 100, the formula tells you. The result is the percentage of your investments that should be in equities (common stocks). The rest should be in bonds, according to this theory. For example, a 40-year-old should have 60 percent of his or her money in stocks and 40 percent in bonds. Conversely, a 60-year-old should have only 40 percent invested in stocks and 60 percent in fixed-income securities (bonds).

The theory behind this scheme is that bonds are perceived to be safer investments than are common stocks, and as one gets older, it's desirable to reduce the risks one takes. But there are a number of things wrong with this theory.

First, it's an illusion that bonds are somehow *safe.* Yes, it's true that if one buys a government bond and holds the bond to the final maturity date, one's principal and annual yield are safe so long as our government remains in business and solvent. (The risk of our government defaulting on these bonds is so minimal, I'm prepared to consider that a nonrisk altogether.) So in that limited regard, yes, bonds are safe. But there's much more to the equation than that.

The vast majority of bond investors in America don't buy bonds directly and hold them to maturity. Typically, if a financial planner convinces you to buy bonds, you'll be steered toward a *bond mutual fund.* (Mutual funds, whether they invest in bonds or stocks or both, are organizations that allow unlimited numbers of investors to pool their money and have a professional manager make the investment decisions for them.)

Bond mutual funds, however, very rarely hold their bonds to maturity. There would be no good reason for you to pay them a fund management fee if all they did was buy bonds and sit on them until they matured; you could do that for yourself and save the fee. Instead, these fund managers try to improve the returns by trading the bonds on the open market, buying and selling them to other bond traders. The minute they begin buying and selling bonds on the open market, however, your supposedly safe investment takes on the same risk as any common stock traded on the open market. Just as with stocks, the price of any given bond fluctuates, and supply and demand make it more or less attractive to investors. When the price rises, the bondholder can sell it at a profit, and when the price falls, selling it generates a loss. So bond funds aren't at all safe in that guaranteed sense of a given return. Just ask anyone who was invested in bond mutual funds in 1994 how safe their money was. Bond fund holders lost a bundle, nearly an 8 percent loss of principal in long-term government bonds. So if that safety is just an illusion, why settle for traditionally lower returns in bonds compared to stocks? (I'll compare the historical returns of the two investment vehicles more fully later.)

So to invest in bonds safely—that is, to eliminate the securities risk associated with trading bonds—we have to revert to the original option of buying bonds and holding them to maturity. But there are hidden risks associated with that strategy that may be even more damaging in the long run to the investor who is living on the proceeds of his or her investments for many years.

Let's look at a current scenario to see what risks lie hidden for the bond investor. Suppose Fran Fearful quit her job today and bought the idea that bonds will generate a nice safe income stream for her and that stocks are just too risky. She's 55 years old and has accumulated $1 million in cash over the years of her career as a shop owner. She's sold the shop now and wants to live on the proceeds for the rest of her life while she launches a graphic arts design business.

To gain that desired safety, Fran has decided to forego bond mutual funds and simply buy 30-year U.S. Treasury bonds and hold them. As of the time of this writing, the 30-year bond carries a yield of 6 percent per year. That is, once a year the U.S. government will pay Fran $60,000 for the right to use her $1 million as Congress and the president see fit. Fran feels she can live on $60,000 a year easily, so she's ready to sign up.

Not so fast! Let's look at two factors that could make Fran regret her decision down the road. First of all, Uncle Sam is only going to give Fran part of that $60,000. He is going to pull some of it back in income taxes. And to make it worse, the yield on bonds is taxed as ordinary income, at whatever Fran's marginal tax rate happens to be. (The current tax brackets range from 15 to 39.6 percent.) Let's assume Fran is in the lowest tax bracket—15 percent. So, of her $60,000 bond yield for the year, $9,000 will go to taxes, leaving her $51,000 she can actually use to live on.

"That's not so bad," I hear Fran saying. "I can still live well enough on $51,000 [a 5.1 percent yield now]." But the dismal news doesn't stop there, I'm afraid. Taxes are probably the least of Fran's worries. They're at least limited to a percentage of what Fran is making. The real risk—and this is the risk bond advocates often conveniently overlook in their pitches about safety—is *inflation*.

There's a good reason bonds are called *fixed-income* securities. That yield the government will pay Fran for the next 30 years isn't going to change. Every year she'll get $60,000 regardless of how well the economy is doing (the government's or Fran's personal economy), and at the end of the 30 years, she'll get her original $1 million back. But each year, that $60,000 becomes worth less and less in terms of what Fran can buy with it. And 30 years later, how much will Fran's $1 million be worth in today's buying power?

Unfortunately, that's a question no one can answer. There's a perennial joke on Wall Street that the only reason market forecasters exist is to make weather forecasters look good. Predicting the economy over the next 12 months has proven an almost fruitless exercise. Imagine the futility of extending such a forecast over the next three decades. We have to face the fact that no one can predict what inflation will be in the future, but whatever the rate turns out to be, it will eat away a little more of Fran's ability to sustain her lifestyle each year because her income is fixed at $60,000 ($51,000 after taxes).

Right now inflation is very modest, and we're enjoying a wonderfully robust economic expansion. But even the most optimistic dreamer wouldn't suggest that such will be the case for the next three decades. What happens when inflation creeps up from today's levels of around 2 or 3 percent a year and reaches 8 or 9 percent, or even double-digit numbers as it did in 1974 (12.20 percent) and again in 1979 and 1980 (13.31 percent and 12.40 percent)? If or when that happens, Fran's $60,000 a year will become worth significantly less and less, and she'll be powerless to do anything about it short of selling her bonds and beginning to invest another way, which brings the risks she was trying to avoid right back into the mix.

Even if inflation remains very modest, though, 30 years' worth of constant chipping away at her fixed income's value will ruin Fran's plans of living indefinitely on her $1 million fund. Let's say the tax rate remains constant at 15 percent a year and the inflation rate also remains constant at 3 percent per year. After one year, that inflation rate would reduce the buying power of Fran's $60,000 check from the government to $58,200. After paying the 15 percent tax ($9,000) on the $60,000, Fran would really be left with $49,200 to live on. That's a significant dent in her original plan, based on an annual income of $60,000. And we've only begun.

The next year that money is reduced in value another 3 percent, down to $56,454. After paying the $9,000 in taxes, Fran will really be left with only $47,454. After five years of this progressive march of inflation, Fran's $60,000 income will be worth only $42,524 after inflation and taxes. After 10 years? $35,245. Twenty years? $23,628. At the end of the full 30 years, Fran will really get only got $15,060 a year to live on in today's dollars, and her financial security will have long since fallen apart in this supposedly safe investment (see Table 1.1). To make things worse, her original $1 million, which she will then get back from the government, will be worth only $401,007 in today's dollars! At this date, Fran will be 85 years old. What happens if she lives another 15 years or more? She won't have nearly enough principal to generate the income she'll need to live on and no reasonable way to increase it fast enough to do her any good. If she turns to living on the principal, it will last only seven or eight years at most at prices 30 years from now. Remember, by the time she gets that principal back from the government, she will already have been reduced to penury for many years. In other words, by investing for safety, Fran will have effectively locked in a guarantee that she'll outlive her money's buying power unless she dies prematurely. Now there's a cheery alternative: Die young or end up poor.

Does Fran have any other alternatives without having to accept the risks associated with investing in stocks? Perhaps,

TABLE 1.1 *The Effect of Inflation and Taxes on Fearful Fran's $1 Million Bond Investment*

Year	Bond Yield	After 3% Inflation	After Taxes	Value of Principal
1	$60,000	$58,200	$49,200	$970,000
2	60,000	56,454	47,454	940,900
3	60,000	54,760	45,760	912,673
4	60,000	53,118	44,118	885,293
5	60,000	51,524	42,524	858,734
6	60,000	49,978	40,978	832,972
7	60,000	48,479	39,479	807,983
8	60,000	47,025	38,025	783,743
9	60,000	45,614	36,614	760,231
10	60,000	44,245	35,245	737,424
11	60,000	42,918	33,918	715,301
12	60,000	41,631	32,631	693,842
13	60,000	40,382	31,382	673,027
14	60,000	39,170	30,170	652,836
15	60,000	37,995	28,995	633,251
16	60,000	36,855	27,855	614,254
17	60,000	35,750	26,750	595,826
18	60,000	34,677	25,677	577,951
19	60,000	33,637	24,637	560,613
20	60,000	32,628	23,628	543,794
21	60,000	31,649	22,649	527,481
22	60,000	30,699	21,699	511,656
23	60,000	29,778	20,778	496,306
24	60,000	28,885	19,885	481,417
25	60,000	28,018	19,018	466,975
26	60,000	27,178	18,178	452,965
27	60,000	26,363	17,363	439,377
28	60,000	25,572	16,572	426,195
29	60,000	24,805	15,805	413,409
30	60,000	24,060	15,060	401,007

but they're not particularly attractive. One way to generate a slightly better income stream from bonds is to turn away from government bonds, which are guaranteed by the nation's security, and toward corporate bonds. These are bonds floated by America's individual companies when they wish to raise capital for growth or the acquisition of other companies. Since the risk of a bond default is greater with an individual company than with the federal government, corporate bonds generally pay a somewhat higher yield to attract investors. (Over the last seven decades, long-term corporate bonds have averaged a yield of 5.7 percent per year, versus the 5.2 percent rate averaged by long-term government bonds.) And it's still possible to minimize the default risk by investing solely in very stable companies. Buying an IBM or General Electric bond is relatively safe.

But there is a catch. Corporations don't want to pay out a penny more in bond yields than they have to. Every penny they pay to their financial backers is one less penny in profits. So corporations ideally like to float new bond issues when the interest-rate environment is fairly benign and they can pay modest yields. As an investor you want the highest yields possible, so you and the corporations are working at opposite purposes. Occasionally, of course, corporations will have to float a new bond issue when rates are high because they can't afford a delay in raising new capital. When this happens corporate bond investors make a very nice return—but only temporarily. What's the first thing a homeowner does when mortgage rates fall significantly? That's right—refinance. Corporations do exactly the same thing. If you've bought a 15-year corporate bond with a yield of 9 or 10 percent and then interest rates come back down a year or two later, the corporation isn't going to keep paying that high yield. It will immediately refinance that debt and call your bond back in. Then you're stuck trying to find a new bond to buy, and it will come with a much lower yield, reflective of the current interest rate environment.

So there's no long-term way to win in corporate bonds without playing the bond-trading game (accepting those very same security risks you were hoping to avoid in buying bonds in the first place). When rates are low, bonds won't pay you much. When rates are high, and you lock in an attractive yield, it doesn't last. Companies call the bonds in as soon as they can refinance at lower rates. You're stuck with mediocre returns either way.

The Only Long-Term Investment Is Common Stock

Where does this leave Fran (and us)? The only reasonable alternative for a long-term investor (and someone trying to live four or five decades on an investment portfolio is about as long term as one can get) is an investment strategy in common stocks. Of all the alternative investment vehicles available, common stocks have provided by far the best returns over very long periods of time. Sure, there are periods where stocks go down. In the last 30 years, there are two memorable periods that tend to stick in most investors' minds, perhaps clouding the larger picture regarding the successes of the stock market. In 1973 and 1974, the stock market suffered two dramatic losing years in succession. Dropping 14.66 percent in 1973 and another 26.47 percent in 1974, the Standard & Poor's 500 Stock Index (an index including 500 of America's largest companies) lost 37 percent of its value. There's no denying that such a drop is painful (but not catastrophic, as the fear-mongers would have us believe). But what the doom-and-gloom crowd doesn't seem to remember is that in 1975 the S&P 500 climbed back 37.20 percent and then tacked on an additional 23.84 percent in 1976, recovering all of the lost ground of the great bear market of 1973–1974 and then a touch more.

I'm not trying to argue that bear markets don't happen or that they don't matter; they certainly do. But with the right kind of planning and strategy, they're not a sufficient reason to forego the growth available to the long-term investor in stocks. The plan in *Money for Life* will show you how to survive the next 1973–1974 if and when we face it in our lifetimes.

What about the great crash in October 1987? After all, in percentage terms it was the single worst crash in the stock market's history. In one day, the Dow Jones Industrial Average (the most famous stock index, including 30 of America's premier industrial giants) dropped 508 points, a loss of 22.6 percent! The S&P 500's loss was a similar 20.5 percent. Isn't such a meltdown enough to keep sensible investors out of stocks? To borrow from Paul Harvey, let's look at the rest of the story. For the entire *year* of 1987, despite the October crash, the S&P 500 Index recorded a *gain* of 5.23 percent. That's right, investors in stocks in 1987 *made money*.

The stock market had risen so dramatically in early 1987 that the crash in October did nothing more than take away the year's profits already recorded. The Rip van Winkles who bought stocks in January 1987 and slept until January 1988 simply awoke to discover they'd made a slightly below-average profit, but a profit nonetheless. It was only the short-term investor, ruled by emotions (fear and greed), who panicked during the crash and locked in those dramatic losses by selling at the worst possible moment. The long-term investor simply grimaced and rode out the crash and went on to new gains in 1988 and 1989.

There you have it, the two worst events for the stock market in my lifetime, and neither one was as devastating for the long-term stock investor as the bears want us to think. Sure, skeptics will say I'm being selective in starting my history with my own birth in 1960. What about the Great Depression, they will ask? Without getting into too much of a technical economic discussion, let me state two very general reasons why I think there's nothing profitable in comparing today's stock market to the market in the 1920s and 1930s. First of all, today's stock market is much more of an investor's market than a speculator's market. Millions of individuals are involved in today's stock market through investment plans at work, adding billions of dollars in new money every month and never even looking at their holdings. This provides an amazing level of liquidity that didn't exist in the 1930s. Despite all that one hears about day traders (90 percent of whom lose money regularly, incidentally), our stock market today is primarily driven by long-term investment money. Second—and this is the real difference—the stock market rules leading into the Depression allowed speculators to buy stocks with as little as 10 percent down. They could borrow up to 90 percent of their stakes on *margin*—a loan from a broker to allow the buyer to lock up more shares than the buyer had actual cash for. With that kind of loose margin requirement, speculation ran rampant in a much less liquid and less stable market. Today's margin requirements are far stricter (50 percent of one's purchase must be covered by one's investment) and the stock market regulations are far greater to prevent the kind of calamity the market suffered in 1929–1932, when in a four-year span large-company stocks lost 64 percent of their value. Bear markets, recessions, and corrections will always be with us, but this is not your grandfather's stock market!

By now you've figured out that I'm an advocate of common stocks for the long-term investor. And when I say *long-term investor* I'm referring to someone who is planning in decades, not months or quarters or even just a few years. Far too many investors I've corresponded with or worked with, however, claim to be long-term investors but are anything but. They're just like fair-weather sports fans. They're as loud and boisterous in celebration of their team's victories as anyone, but let the team hit a small slump and they're out for blood. Stock investors who sour on a proven strategy the minute a correction hits are the same way. They're convinced they can outsmart the stock market's short-term chaos. They can't; neither can you; neither can I. They jump out of stocks at the first sign of trouble, only to watch the market go back up without them. They end up doing everything exactly wrong—they sell low and buy high. It's no wonder so many individual investors are scared of the stock market. So many investors are ruled by their emotions that they can't possibly succeed.

A true long-term investor rides out corrections (even long ugly ones), holding on to the knowledge that, historically, stocks have always come back strongly and surpassed their old levels.

Fundamentally, what's required is a faith in American business. As long as you believe America's businesses will continue to be competitive and grow, stocks are the place to be. The nervous investors who jump in and out when they think they see the next apocalypse (and if you listen to the media, there's one around every corner) are the ones who end up as road kill (Wall Street kill?).

The Record

So just how good a record does the stock market really have? At this point, I should step back and define *stock market*. When most people talk about the stock market in generic terms, they really mean one of the two major market indices rather than the entire market: either the Dow Jones Industrial Average or the S&P 500 Index. Neither, of course, is the entire stock market. Thousands of stocks are traded on the major American exchanges (the New York Stock Exchange and the Nasdaq-AMEX market). Both of the popular indices only take into account America's largest stocks and exclude small and medium-sized companies. That said, however, these major indices do give us a measure of the stock market's temperament, and they track the stocks most Americans are familiar with, the giants that represent the bulk of the trading volume on any given day. As a large-company stock investor, this is the universe I follow exclusively. There are lots of ways to invest in stocks, but sticking with very large, very widely followed industry giants has proven a successful way for the individual investor to narrow the seemingly endless array of options to a manageable field of opportunities.

Fortunately for market historians, these major indices also have the longest records, dating back more than seven decades. As I've said before, I'm not sure how relevant a comparison between the 1920s and today is, but it is comforting to see the long and consistent outperformance of stocks over all other investment vehicles. Since the end of 1925, for example, large-company common stocks like those included in the S&P 500 Index have returned an average of 11 percent per year. Obviously it hasn't been 11 percent each and every year, but taking into account the ups and downs, stocks have a 75-year track record of 11 percent a year. That's roughly double the returns recorded by long-term government bonds over the same period.

In more recent history, stocks have performed even better. In my lifetime (since 1960), stocks have returned an annualized gain of 12.0 percent a year. Since 1970, the return has been 13.3 percent. Since 1980, the return has been 16.0 percent. And in the 1990s, the return has been 18.3 percent. (All of these calculations are through the end of 1998. See Table 1.2 for a year-by-year listing of common stock gains.) Obviously, the last several decades have been increasingly strong ones for common stocks. There are many reasons to count for this progress, and I'll leave it to more-qualified economists to

TABLE 1.2   Large-Company Annual Stock Returns (Percentage)

Year	Gain	Year	Gain
1926	11.62	1963	22.80
1927	37.49	1964	16.48
1928	43.61	1965	12.45
1929	−8.42	1966	−10.06
1930	−24.90	1967	23.98
1931	−43.34	1968	11.06
1932	−8.19	1969	−8.50
1933	53.99	1970	4.01
1934	−1.44	1971	14.31
1935	47.67	1972	18.98
1936	33.92	1973	−14.66
1937	−35.03	1974	−26.47
1938	31.12	1975	37.20
1939	−0.41	1976	23.84
1940	−9.78	1977	−7.18
1941	−11.59	1978	6.56
1942	20.34	1979	18.44
1943	25.90	1980	32.42
1944	19.75	1981	−4.91
1945	36.44	1982	21.41
1946	−8.07	1983	22.51
1947	5.71	1984	6.27
1948	5.50	1985	32.16
1949	18.79	1986	18.47
1950	31.71	1987	5.23
1951	24.02	1988	16.81
1952	18.37	1989	31.49
1953	−0.99	1990	−3.17
1954	52.62	1991	30.55
1955	31.56	1992	7.67
1956	6.56	1993	9.99
1957	−10.78	1994	1.31
1958	43.36	1995	37.43
1959	11.96	1996	23.07
1960	0.47	1997	33.36
1961	26.89	1998	28.58
1962	−8.73	1999*	8.33

*Partial year, through August 31, 1999.

enumerate them. But suffice it to say that the American economy, if anything, has strengthened its position as a global power, and the advances in American businesses bode well for continued gains in common stocks.

True to my belief that no one can predict the market over the short run, I won't hazard a guess (and a wild guess is all that it could be) regarding the returns for the stock market over the next year, or even the next few years. But I have a much higher degree of confidence that over the next several decades—the period you and I should really be concerned with—common stocks will continue to record annual average gains between the very long-term historical average of 11 percent a year and the more recent average of 14 or 15 percent a year.

The Magical Power of Compound Growth

On the surface, two or three percentage points per year may not seem like much, but time has a phenomenal power to compound those seemingly small differences into massive ones. Let's look at a simple compounding example to demonstrate why I get so excited about the long-term investor's prospects. Pick any round number to make the calculations easy. Let's say $100,000. And now let's compound the growth of that $100,000 over four decades at 10, 13, and 15 percent to show how slight increases in the annual rate can grow into an accumulated wealth far beyond your expectations.

In the first year at 10 percent per year, the $100,000 grows to $110,000. But the beauty of compounding is that in the next year, the entire new total of $110,000 grows by another 10 percent. So instead of another $10,000 gain as in the first year, the second year enjoys an $11,000 profit, for a total of $121,000. The following year the gain creeps up even further, bringing the grand total to $133,100, and so on (see Table 1.3). This is

TABLE 1.3   *Compounded Growth of $100,000 over 40 Years*

Year	10%	13%	15%
1	$110,000	$113,000	$115,000
2	121,000	127,690	132,250
3	133,100	144,290	152,088
4	146,410	163,047	174,901
5	161,051	184,244	201,136
6	177,156	208,195	231,306
7	194,872	235,261	266,002
8	214,359	265,844	305,902
9	235,795	300,404	351,788
10	259,374	339,457	404,556
11	285,312	383,586	465,239
12	313,843	433,452	535,025
13	345,227	489,801	615,279
14	379,750	553,475	707,571
15	417,725	625,427	813,706
16	459,497	706,733	935,762
17	505,447	798,608	1,076,126
18	555,992	902,427	1,237,545
19	611,591	1,019,742	1,423,177
20	672,750	1,152,309	1,636,654
21	740,025	1,302,109	1,882,152
22	814,027	1,471,383	2,164,475
23	895,430	1,662,663	2,489,146
24	984,973	1,878,809	2,862,518
25	1,083,471	2,123,054	3,291,895
26	1,191,818	2,399,051	3,785,680
27	1,310,999	2,710,928	4,353,531
28	1,442,099	3,063,349	5,006,561
29	1,586,309	3,461,584	5,757,545
30	1,744,940	3,911,590	6,621,177
31	1,919,434	4,420,096	7,614,354
32	2,111,378	4,994,709	8,756,507
33	2,322,515	5,644,021	10,069,983
34	2,554,767	6,377,744	11,580,480
35	2,810,244	7,206,851	13,317,552
36	3,091,268	8,143,741	15,315,185
37	3,400,395	9,202,428	17,612,463
38	3,740,434	10,398,743	20,254,332
39	4,114,478	11,750,580	23,292,482
40	4,525,926	13,278,155	26,786,355

the big power that stocks have over long-term bonds. With a bond, you get the same yield year after year and your principal remains fixed. Bonds are simply not growth vehicles.

At first the incremental compounded gains each year seem minimal, but as time and compounding effect their magic, the gains become increasingly significant. By the end of the first decade, for example, the annual increases have jumped from the $10,000 a year we saw in year 1 to $25,938 between years 10 and 11. After 25 years, the annual increase is nearly $100,000. And between years 39 and 40, the annual increase is over $400,000!

What about the total dollar value? Before you read the answer, jot down what you think $100,000 would grow to at 10 percent over 40 years. $1 million? Maybe $2 million? Believe it or not, it would grow to more than $4.5 million! And that's without saving an additional penny beyond the initial investment.

Even more exciting is the fact that this example was at a growth rate lower than the actual rate for stocks over the last seven decades. Take that same $100,000 for 40 years and look what it does at 13 percent instead of 10 percent. Instead of the already impressive $4,525,926 we just discussed, our hypothetical long-term investor would be sitting on a fund worth $13,278,155! That's right, an additional $8.7 million (nearly three times our previous total) after 40 years as the result of three little percentage points a year. Compounding is amazing, isn't it?

Let's go a giddy step further. While I'm always hesitant to make predictions, I'm nevertheless willing to crawl slightly out on a limb and suggest that a long-term investor with a sound strategy for investing in common stocks might reasonably expect to earn a compounded average return in the neighborhood of 15 percent. (I actually think that figure is slightly understated, and I'll tell you why shortly, but for now let's stick with a round, modest number.) Imagine now what that extra two percentage points per year will do to our compounding model. We've already seen $100,000 turn into more than $13 million at 13 percent per year. So at 15 percent a year we should be looking at $15 million after 40 years, right? (*BUZZ*—Wrong, but thanks for playing!)

Keep in mind the principle of compounding. After each year's gain, the entire new total grows the following year. It's a geometric progression that baffles the mind. In fact, of all the world-changing ideas that ran through Albert Einstein's mind, the power of compounding was one of the concepts that continually excited him.

Let's see what it does to our $100,000. After 10 years, the growth at 15 percent per year brings us to $404,556. After 20 years, to $1,636,654. After 30 years, to $6,621,177 (already significantly more than our original example at 10 percent reached after the entire 40 years). And after four decades at 15 percent a year, the $100,000 starting value has been transformed into—are you sitting down?—$26,786,355!

Now I know the skeptics among you are champing at the bit to ask about things like taxes and inflation. You're right, this simple model was only to show the power of time and compounded growth. We'll get into more real-life scenarios later and include inflation and the like. But keep this in mind: I also believe you can do better than 15 percent growth. Imagine the possibilities!

The Investor's Real Foe—Inflation

So let's recap the real issues facing an investor who's heading toward financial independence as well as one who has made it and wants to remain there safely. Your real challenge over many years is keeping ahead of inflation so that your assets last indefinitely. Too many financial plans put you in a race with death to see if your money will last long enough. Why take that chance? Why not just establish a plan that will sustain you no matter how long you live? If that means passing a lot of money on to children, grandchildren, or charity upon your death—well, much worse things have happened, don't you agree?

To stay ahead of inflation, you must be thinking in terms of long-term growth. And the only reasonable investment vehicle to achieve that growth on a consistent basis is common stocks. Bonds provide steady and secure income, but they lose every year to inflation, so that by the time you've held a bond 15 or 20 years, you've lost the bulk of your buying power, and your financial independence is gone. To make things worse, the income on bonds is taxed at a higher rate than the capital gains on stocks. (Bond income is ordinary income which is taxed more heavily than long-term capital gains on stocks, no matter what your tax bracket.)

If you're serious, then, about living for decades on your investment portfolio, you must be in the stock market. But at the same time, you need a plan that will allow you to ride out the bad patches every stock-market investor will experience. Your plan can't afford to be so fragile that a bear market will wipe you out. And your personal discipline needs to be rock solid so that you don't end up a de facto market timer, letting your emotions scare you out of stocks at precisely the wrong moment.

In order to make the *Money for Life* plan work, you will have to relinquish some of the old investment ideas you've had drilled into you for decades. In fact, you'll still hear the old-fashioned ideas long after you've abandoned them, but you'll be in a position to know better.

The Wall Street Accountability Sham

You see, the professional investors on Wall Street are driven by emotions, too. They are just as prone to fear and greed as the average investor on Main Street. But their fear comes from a somewhat different source—job security. Professional investors are afraid of the short-term comparisons the industry makes. Every quarter Wall Street posts its score card, and professional investors know that if they're trailing behind their competitors in virtually any short period, fickle investors will move their money to whichever manager is hot that month. So professional investors take untoward chances in an effort to make their efforts match up. They buy and sell positions frequently; they turn to options; and they try to time the markets—all of which increases the costs for the individual investors and, in the long run, lowers the returns of most investment funds.

In my first book, *The Unemotional Investor* (Simon & Schuster, 1998), I did a survey of thousands of actively managed stock mutual funds over the previous decade. And regardless of the period one looks at (3, 5, or 10 years), 8 or 9 out of every 10 stock mutual funds lose to the S&P 500 Index. (The situation hasn't changed since my first book was published; most mutual funds continue to trail the market indices.) In a market that includes the best mutual fund managers money can buy, supported by the best staffs, using the best resources available, only 1 or 2 out of 10 can keep pace with a mechanical index of America's largest companies. Investors would be better served buying into an index fund and forgetting the hassles than investing in actively managed funds.

Don't get me wrong; I'm not claiming mutual fund managers are somehow stupid or lousy investors. They're just playing the wrong game. Mutual fund managers are more interested in how much money they manage than in how well those assets do. The funds are generally too large to manage efficiently. And the managers are too concerned with short-term results to focus clearly on long-term results. They make the investment process seem so intimidating, they convince the individual investor that one can't possibly succeed on one's own. And quite frankly, their peers perform dismally enough that they thrive even with mediocre track records.

As an example of just how poorly the industry performs and yet gets away with it, there are actually stock mutual funds in business today that have lost money over the last five years—a period in which the S&P 500 Index has returned an average annual gain of 24 percent. And yet these funds still have millions of dollars under management! People either don't understand what's happening to their money or don't bother to check. Either way, the industry is getting away with a monumental rip-off.

Yet ask any certified financial planner where individual investors should put their money, and they'll sing the praises of mutual funds. To make matters worse, they'll trot out the other favorite act in their pony show: diversification. The theory is that you should spread your money around among all asset classes so that you're not as subject to the swings of individual segments of the market. So you'd have money in large-company stocks, medium-company stocks, small-company stocks, emerging markets, bond funds with different maturity horizons, perhaps even some gold funds, and heaven knows what else. The whole goal for this type of approach is not to lose too much. And *safety, risk,* and *diversification* are the buzzwords such planners will throw at you. What they ignore, however, is that such a plan is almost a guarantee of subpar long-term performance. (And the benchmark against which you should measure all your returns is that of the S&P 500 Index.)

A perfect example of this kind of planning is one of our current advisory clients. I'll call him Sam to preserve his anonymity. Sam is a former professional football player who's roughly 30 years old. He asked my partner and me to analyze his current portfolio to see how he was set up for his future after football. Sam had done everything right in his career—spent money modestly, saved regularly, always with an eye toward the day when he would leave sports. The size of Sam's portfolio was indeed impressive, but the actual story of his investment performance was dismal.

Sam's advisor had him split between bonds and stock mutual funds—no real surprise there. My problem with bonds for someone like Sam, who might be looking at six or seven decades of income from this portfolio, is obvious. They're just not going to keep up with inflation. But the stock mutual funds in his portfolio were even more depressing. Sam had between 30 and 40 different mutual funds, spanning the range of equity classes. Foreign, domestic, small company, large company, growth, value—you name it, Sam owned it. Every single one of the mutual funds he owned, however, charged a front-end load (or sales commission) of 5 to 6 percent. That's money skimmed right off the amount invested on day one. The mutual funds believe if they charge such a load, investors won't be so quick to pull out because they lose that money. They're right, of course, but what a racket. If the funds perform well, they'll keep their investors. They shouldn't have to keep investors through extortion.

But even worse than the gross overdiversification and high fees that Sam was paying was the fact that the performance of the funds was atrocious. As my business partner and I sorted through his list of holdings, fund after fund proved to be underperforming the S&P 500 Index. In fact, by the time we finished analyzing Sam's list, not a single one of his mutual funds had a record that bested the S&P 500 Index over any long-term period. Not one!

It turns out that the only real growth in Sam's portfolio in recent years had been the money he was adding regularly from his salary. Again, here's a man who did everything right, but between the fees the mutual funds charged him and the fees his advisor got for choosing those funds, Sam's growth was nonexistent in one of the best bull market periods in decades. His advisor and the fund companies made out wonderfully, though. And what's more disheartening is that Sam's story, except perhaps for the dollar amounts involved, is typical.

I receive hundreds of e-mails each month as a result of my first book and the columns I've written in the past for The Motley Fool (www.fool.com) and Microsoft Investor (www.investor.msn.com), and one of the consistent themes is how disappointed the correspondents are with the results their previous advisors achieved. But mutual fund managers and advisors see the world differently. If they don't lose their clients a lot of money and if they manage to stay somewhere in the pack compared to their peers, they'll keep their jobs forever, even if they never outperform the S&P 500 Index. They're conditioned to do what everyone else is doing because standing out is risky. To be different from everyone else means you'll either be branded a genius when you succeed or you'll be packing your bags and heading away from Wall Street when you fail. And with so much money to be made by being mediocre, human nature dictates that mediocre wins the day most of the time.

In our investment advisory firm (Sheard & Davey Advisors, LLC—sheard-davey.com), we tell all of our clients that we have only one goal, and that's to beat the S&P 500 Index over long periods of time. We don't claim we'll do it every quarter, or even every year. But we're very up front about the fact that if we aren't beating the S&P 500 over multiyear stretches, they should fire us and at least put their money into an S&P 500 Index fund. Why pay advisory fees to a professional manager or an investment advisor if you'd be getting better performance in an index fund?

Now beating the index doesn't necessarily mean one will never lose money. If the S&P 500 Index gains 10 percent, for example, we want to gain 15 percent. But when the Index loses 10 percent, it's still a victory in our eyes if we've lost only 5 percent. In other words, there's no magical number every year that you can use as a solid benchmark. Instead, watch your returns against the indices. If you're beating the S&P 500 consistently, you're accomplishing what the vast majority of professional money managers are not doing. And what's remarkable is that it's not as difficult to accomplish as you might suspect, especially for an individual investor.

Summary

It's time for me to summarize the crucial ideas that serve as a foundation for the 20 Factor planning strategies before we move on to the formula itself.

- Our ultimate goal shouldn't be the traditional notion of retirement, but rather we should be thinking in terms of financial independence—and now, not at some distant date in the future. By *financial independence* I mean the ability to live indefinitely on the growth of one's investment portfolio. This gives the investor the freedom to pursue life in whatever direction he or she chooses. And it's not a function of age at all, but is tied to the level of assets one has accumulated and the income one needs to generate from those assets.
- To become financially independent and remain there, one has to abandon the old-fashioned notion that investing in bonds is

the best and safest source of income. In fact, bonds can be very risky despite their safety of principal. Over long periods of time inflation can simply destroy the buying power of the seemingly safe income stream bonds can produce.

- The only sensible vehicle for long-term investors (read decades, not quarters or years) is the American equity markets. For seven decades, large-company common stocks have virtually doubled the returns of the other possible investment vehicles. Better than bonds, better than real estate, better than gold, and certainly better than cash equivalents, stocks have provided the long-term investor with returns that consistently remain ahead of inflation.

- Despite the brilliant marketing campaigns of most investment companies, stock mutual funds are not the individual investor's savior. In fact, if history serves as an accurate measure, only one in five of the actively managed stock mutual funds will keep pace with the S&P 500 Index. If the individual investor isn't going to choose particular stocks directly (and I firmly believe one should), then he or she should at least invest in an S&P 500 index mutual fund and keep pace with the benchmark the vast majority of professional fund managers lose to. That's a no-brainer, no-effort investment strategy.

- Diversification is widely overrated by the financial planning community. Buying into every asset class and every style of stock fund in the name of asset protection does little more than cost you a wad of unnecessary fees and is likely to weaken your long-term returns. After all, the S&P 500 Index already would have you invested in 500 of America's largest corporations, virtually all of which have a global presence. How much diversification does one portfolio need? Keep in mind that if you own everything in the market (and the type of diversification we saw in Sam's herd of mutual funds covered the spectrum), there's no way you can beat the market. You *are* the market, then, and by the time you've paid all those fees, you've lost to the index again. One can set up a reasonably diverse stock portfolio with approximately 20 holdings, which makes administration of a strategy and total investing costs reasonable. By focusing on 20 top stock ideas rather than investing a tiny portion in every stock available, your odds of outperforming the index improve dramatically.

- Don't ever try to time the market's short-term swings. If you're invested for the long run, what happens this month, this quarter, even this year isn't nearly as vital as what happens over the next 20, 30, or 40 years. And while I have no idea whether the Dow Jones Industrial Average will hit 9,000 or 13,000 next, I'm reasonably sure it will be significantly higher in two, three, or four decades than it is today. Even if the index slows back down from its pace over the last two decades to its seven-decade-long average return of 11 percent a year, that would take us from today's level of approximately 11,000 to a Dow of over 250,000 in 30 years! Do you really care which direction the next 1,000 points goes if you're still going to be invested when the Dow hits 250,000? I don't.

- Measure all of your returns against an objective benchmark like the S&P 500 Index. If your mutual funds gained 15 percent last year while the S&P 500 gained nearly 29 percent, you lost money in one sense. A simple investment in an index fund would have nearly doubled your profit last year. Return numbers in isolation don't help us very much; they must be compared to an industry measure to put them in a meaningful context. And don't have a preconceived return figure in mind. If the S&P 500 Index loses 12 percent one year and you lose only 7 percent, that's a winning year because you've beaten the average. Be objective about your portfolio's progress, and watch your entire portfolio as a single unit. Don't get caught up in how each individual stock is performing today. Every portfolio is likely to have some winners and losers; the only number that really matters is the grand total. It's just like the golf cliché: It's not how; it's how many. It doesn't matter if you had a handful of super performers, a couple of losers, and a selection of mediocre performers, or whether all of your stocks perform about the same. If you've beaten the index, you've won. And if you find that over time, you're consistently trailing the index, it's comforting to know that a very simple option exists to mirror the index, a low-cost index fund.

2

THE 20 FACTOR
FORMULA

I've spent a lot of time so far trying to dismantle some of the conventional wisdom regarding saving for and investing during "retirement," even challenging the whole notion of retirement itself. You'd probably demand a refund of the price of this book, though, if all I did was criticize and complain about what's out there, without providing you with an alternative approach to the problems we've already examined. It's time, then, to look at an amazingly simple formula. The ideas that support the formula will require some questioning and explanations, of course (which will make up the bulk of the rest of this book), but the formula itself is simple enough that you'll understand and remember it always.

Defining Financial Independence

The first element of the formula harkens back to our earlier discussion of financial independence not being in any way a function of age. As you make your financial plans, what you should be searching for instead is a dollar figure at which you would be able to stop working and saving (assuming that's the choice you wish to make) and live strictly off of your investment portfolios for an indefinite period. I've seen some professional athletes and businesspeople reach such a level at astoundingly young ages. And unfortunately, I know all too many people who will never reach that level in time to enjoy it, simply because they didn't know how to prepare for it. But don't for a minute think that you either have to be a hot-shot professional athlete or the president of a multinational corporation to get there, either. Anyone with a full-time job and the right kind of planning can make it. The only difference, perhaps, will be in how quickly one person makes it compared to another. This book isn't written with the superstars in mind, however, although they can certainly benefit from learning how to keep what they have for the future. Rather, I'm writing for all the people who want to control their own financial destinies instead of hoping against hope that someone else will take care of them (Social Security, family, mutual funds, or company pensions).

So the first element of the equation is simply your ultimate goal: *financial independence*. Measured in dollars rather than in years, this is the size your investment portfolio must reach in order to sustain you for the rest of your life, whether that turns out to be 8 more years or 80. You can't afford to enter a race against your last dollars. With medical technology advancing at a quicker and quicker pace each year, with healthier lifestyles becoming the norm, with simple advances in the human species' evolution, we're living longer and longer. Even if you leave the workforce at the traditional age of 65 today, it's not unusual to expect to live another three or four decades. That's a long time to live on the wrong kind of investment portfolio. The plan in *Money for Life* is set up to help you ensure that your assets will live longer than you do.

What I *won't* do in this book, however, is set a specific target value on financial independence. For one thing, any raw dollar amount I might pull out of a hat could be ludicrous in 10 years, and then where will I be? It can't very well become a classic financial book if it's obsolete by the second printing. But more important, of course, each person will have to derive his or her own target value based on the rest of the formula. No two individuals will have exactly the same requirements or the same ultimate goal. *Money for Life,* however, will take into account those differences and allow each investor to develop the right strategy for his or her situation. The plan, then, is one size fits all, but the results aren't.

For Bill, for example, financial independence may come at a portfolio level of $400,000. On the other hand, Kelly might require $1.4 million to reach financial independence. And as more and more time passes, investors working toward financial independence may change their attitudes about life, which can require a revision in their ultimate goals. The beauty of the 20 Factor plan is that it's extremely flexible as a planning tool and allows the investor to look at a variety of scenarios before settling on a plan. And even once a plan is in place, you can alter it as your goals change (to reflect a changing family, perhaps, or a second home, or even a different lifestyle choice altogether). That's entirely dependent on the individual investor's needs, goals, and choices (all of which I'll cover).

Annual Income Requirement

The second of the three elements in the 20 Factor formula is the most complicated and most variable factor. It is simply the financially independent investor's *annual income requirement*. Short and sweet, how much do you need your portfolio to generate in income today for you to sustain the life you want for one year? That's your annual income requirement.

It is in calculating this amount that you have to take serious stock of a great number of issues. And only you can be the final judge of which numbers are appropriate for your goals. I'll guide you through the decisions you'll need to make, but for this section to help, you've got to be brutally honest with yourself. Let's look at the variety of elements you'll need to consider when deriving this total.

Among the first items to look at is whether you have any guaranteed income from other sources. What will your Social Security benefit be (if you're of age to qualify for one)? Do you have any guaranteed pension income from the government, the military, or a previous employer? Don't include income you hope might be forthcoming but isn't guaranteed. My belief is that unless the income is guaranteed to you, assume you won't get it and plan to make up that income on your own. Then if it does come to you, it's a bonus. If it doesn't, your plan won't be ruined.

Look at all the sources of guaranteed income (and use realistic figures; now is not the time to be overly optimistic) and total them in one column of your planning sheet. Every dollar you have coming in on this side of the ledger is one less dollar your portfolio will have to generate for you.

Even if you don't have any such guaranteed income coming in (and most of us won't), don't despair. I'd rather plan on supporting myself fully so that I'll be in control of my financial independence and won't have to watch some government agency or corporate whim alter my critical planning. It's probably even a good idea to assume that Social Security will pay you nothing and then calculate your annual income requirement both ways to get a clear picture of what the difference will be in your savings planning. At my age (soon to be 40), I'm assuming Social Security won't pay me a penny because it's simply too far away to count on. Congress could save the system, or it might bankrupt it; who knows? But I don't want my future jeopardized by that crowd. I'll support myself, thank you!

Now that you've got your guaranteed income calculated, even if it's a goose egg, it's time to take a realistic assessment of what you need to spend for an entire year. The best way to generate realistic numbers here is to keep accurate and detailed records of what you have been spending for the last several years and start analyzing those records. If you haven't kept the most complete records in the past, start now with a simple financial software package like Quicken® or Microsoft Money®. Both have good bank account–tracking features with which you can record your expenditures in whatever categories are appropriate for you and then generate a wonderful variety of reports at the end of any period you wish to examine. (It's also a quick and accurate way to keep your checking account balanced, for those of you who still think that the printing on the back of your bank statement is an advertisement. You know who you are!)

Analyze Your Spending Needs

In your spending analysis, start with the big-ticket items:

- What do you spend on housing? Will your mortgage be paid off before you start living on your portfolio growth? If not, is it a fixed-rate mortgage in which the payments will remain the same or a variable-rate mortgage in which interest rates can fluctuate? Are the property taxes and insurance included in your mortgage payment? If your mortgage will be paid off, still account for the ongoing insurance and property taxes. Do you pay regular dues to a homeowners' association? Total all of the expenses associated with the maintenance of your home.
- What will you have to pay in income taxes? This is often a difficult category to judge until you're through with this whole planning process because you may need to determine your tax liability after you've determined how much income you're planning to generate. So it's a good idea not to estimate yet. Instead, leave a big TBDL (to be determined later) in this

space. I'll show you how we can account for income taxes in another part of the planning process.

- What kind of healthcare costs will you have to prepare for? This is the time to look into health insurance costs if you're responsible for your own premiums. Depending upon your age, examine what's available through Medicare, or if you're not eligible, through private insurance. Be sure to consider the costs of prescriptions for which you'll pay out of pocket. A good review of your current healthcare coverage would be appropriate at this stage to get a realistic view of what you are likely to pay in a year's time.

- Evaluate your transportation costs and expectations. Is that 10-year-old Suburban going to last much longer, or are you likely to need a new vehicle in a few years? In fact, now's a good time to think about how often you plan to buy a new car in the future. Is the extra expense of buying or leasing a new car every three or four years worth delaying your financial independence a few years? Or would you be just as happy getting to your goal several years sooner because you're content with a new car every 8 to 10 years? These are the decisions you must make (and some of them are agonizing choices, no doubt) before you can set up a realistic and lasting plan for financial independence. Don't forget to include the cost of insurance, auto taxes, routine maintenance and upkeep, and fuel. (Again, accurate records for your current spending habits may prove an invaluable planning tool for the future.)

After these big-ticket items are accounted for, it's time to consider the rest of the costs associated with running a household.

- What do you spend on groceries? Utilities? Clothing? Laundry and housecleaning? Dining out? Entertainment? Home repair and lawn maintenance? Do you eat at home most of the time or do you hit the fast-food joints four days a week? Do you rent movies at Blockbuster or spend the weekend in the city taking in the latest play? (Track your likely habits now for the best guide to the way you're likely to live in the future.)

- Include plans for regular charitable contributions you plan to continue making.

- Evaluate your long-term plans regarding furniture and home furnishings. Do you tend to keep the same decor for a decade at a time, or do you redecorate one room each year until your house is finished and then begin the cycle again? You're probably going to want to continue the patterns you've always enjoyed, so make allowances for them.

- Include an amount for hobbies or sporting activities and events. Do you replace your driver every time a new infomercial hits the Golf Channel? Do you have a closet full of 20 different putters and find yourself still browsing the pro shop displays? Don't forget the cost of your club dues and all those golf balls you'll slice into the woods. What about season tickets to the Mets (or for that matter, to the Met)? Include them in your plan, too.

- Include a dollar amount for vacations, holidays, and birthdays. If you run to the beach once a month for a long weekend, add in a reasonable amount for each trip. If you go to Europe once a year, figure in an amount so that you can keep going.

- If you have any other special items that are recurring, include them as well: child support, alimony, tuition for yourself or your children (or grandchildren)—anything you need to pay for regularly that's not already covered elsewhere.

- And finally (as if this list doesn't look long enough already), everyone needs some walking-around money. I don't know anyone who likes working from a strict budget, except the most anal-retentive person in the crowd, so leave yourself some slippage room. We all have expenses we simply can't (or shouldn't have to) plan for in advance. Plan for them anyway, but do it indirectly by including a slush fund amount to cover them.

There, what did you come up with as your grand total? (Remember, we'll take care of the issue of income taxes later.) Once you have a realistic value for each of these items (and any unusual ones I haven't accounted for but that apply to you), you've determined your annual income requirement.

This is how much income you would need to generate in today's dollars in order to be financially independent for one year. Once you've come up with this figure, you're through the hard part. Now we just have to make sure you can generate enough income for these needs every year. (There is a sample annual income requirement worksheet in the appendix. Use it as a rough template for setting up your own calculations, and be sure to include any items in your plan that aren't covered in these general categories.)

Two Scenarios

Let's look at a couple of examples to show how different individuals will develop very different plans. As I mentioned earlier, this is the portion of the 20 Factor plan that will be the most variable, and because of that, it's the portion of the plan that will require the most thought on your part. If you're not careful or not honest with yourself in this section of the planning phase, your entire financial independence may be put in jeopardy years down the road. Always err on the side of caution rather than being overly optimistic.

In our first scenario, Alice is a 58-year-old widow. She's the mother of three adult children, all of whom are independent, so she's not responsible for them (or their children) financially. Currently, Alice works full-time as a public school administrator, earning $45,000 a year, but would like to leave in order to spend more time with her family and as a volunteer with her local literacy council. Between her own investments, her retirement account through the school system, and what she inherited from her husband's retirement account, Alice has an investment portfolio of $800,000.

She's lived in her current home since she was married 40 years ago, so she carries no mortgage debt on the house. Her car was purchased with cash three years ago, and she doesn't anticipate replacing it for another six or seven years. She has no outstanding debts of any kind (not even a credit card balance). In other words, Alice is a hero. But does she have enough invested so that she'll be financially independent should she live another 40 years?

Let's look at what Alice spends. While she doesn't have any significant guaranteed income, Alice's spending needs are also very modest. Her property taxes on her home and car run less than $2,000 a year. Her home and auto insurance are less than $1,000. In fact, with no dependents and no debts, Alice no longer even carries any life insurance. She spends in the neighborhood of $300 a week running her household (food, household items, and discretionary shopping). Her utilities and regular monthly bills run $300 a month. While she has excellent healthcare insurance, Alice still budgets $3,000 a year for her deductible, her copayments on office visits and prescriptions, and visits to the dentist and optometrist (which aren't covered by her plan). She likes to visit her children's families three or four times a year, so she has to budget $3,000 or $4,000 a year for travel costs and gifts. And she likes to add roughly $5,000 a year to her slush fund, which she'll use for any emergencies, replacements for her home furnishings when needed or wanted, as well as that new car down the road.

Altogether, then, Alice needs to generate an annual after-tax income (in today's dollars) of just over $34,000. For the sake of round numbers, let's round Alice's total annual income requirement up to $35,000. By most measures Alice lives very modestly. By not having any debts (including owning her home outright), Alice has eliminated the biggest chunks of most Americans' household budgets. In fact, that's one of the biggest obstacles to financial independence—the amount you spend on buying your home. Once you're over that hurdle, the amount you need each year to sustain your chosen lifestyles drops considerably.

In our second example, we'll see a very different scenario. Alex is 44 and Ginger, a full-time homemaker, is 37 years old. They have three children ranging in age from 10 to 15. Alex also is the father of a 17-year-old child from a previous marriage. Currently Alex is a partner in a chain of regional retail stores, but he's been involved in small-business ventures most of his adult life. Several of them have prospered, but a number of them have gone under, taking much of Alex's savings with them.

Alex's current venture is thriving, however, and he's bringing home nearly $250,000 a year. In addition, his portfolio has enjoyed the fruits of the 1990s gains in the stock market, and his wealth has grown to $2.5 million. The bad news is that his health is weakening, and the doctors have warned him to slow his pace considerably or he may face severe consequences. Alex wants to know if he can live on his portfolio and give up the long hours at the stores.

Over the years, Alex and Ginger have changed cities as business opportunities opened up. They moved into their fourth home last year, beginning a new 30-year mortgage. Currently their mortgage payments run $3,500 a month. In addition, they own a small lake home which has another 20 years on its mortgage, running another $1,200 a month. They each lease new cars every three years, and these expenses total about $1,000 a month. And between Alex's antique gun collection and Ginger's out-of-control shoe fetish, they've racked up nearly $15,000 in credit card debts.

Between running two households and routine monthly bills, Alex and Ginger spend roughly $6,000 a month. Add in their debts (homes, cars, and credit cards) and they spend another $7,000. Alex also sends $1,500 a month in child support to his first wife and is facing out-of-pocket college tuition costs (at least in part after scholarships) for all four of his children over the next 12 years. To begin preparing for these extra expenses, Alex and Ginger are putting away $4,000 a month. Altogether, then, Alex and Ginger spend approximately $18,500 per month, or $222,000 per year. To sustain that lifestyle indefinitely, their annual income requirement in today's dollars (let's round off) is $225,000. Is Alex's stock portfolio, now worth $2.5 million, sufficient for him to stop working and live indefinitely off of his investments?

Your Annual Income Requirement

What is *your* annual income requirement today? If you've worked through all the items in this section and have been honest and realistic with yourself, you've done the hard part. You will now be able to complete the calculations in the 20 Factor formula very easily. How easily?

Remember what we're looking for. The answer we're seeking is the amount of money you must have invested to live indefinitely on the proceeds of your stock portfolio. To calculate that dollar amount (in today's dollars; we'll deal with inflation later), simply take your annual income requirement and multiply by 20. (Now, you saw that coming, didn't you?)

The 20 Factor Formula:

Financial independence = annual income requirement × 20

In this simple formula you have the entire basis for solid financial planning once you've decided to live on your investment portfolio. So if your annual income requirement is $40,000 (after taxes), your stock portfolio must be a minimum of $800,000. (Remember, too, that this assumes investment in common stocks over long periods of time. The formula won't work with other investment vehicles like bonds.) If you need to generate $60,000 a year, your portfolio must be at least $1.2

million. If you need income of $150,000 a year, then your minimum portfolio value must be $3 million.

The math couldn't be simpler, although the reasons behind the simple formula will require some explanation. Now that you've seen the formula, though, you will better understand my contention that the factor that requires the most attention is the annual income requirement. How you decide precisely how much income you need your portfolio to generate each year will determine when (or even *if* in some cases) you will become financially independent.

Let's say, for example, that you've determined that you could live today on $50,000 per year in after-tax income, but your investment portfolio isn't quite the $1 million you would need ($50,000 × 20 = $1,000,000). You essentially have only two options: (1) you can recalculate your annual income requirement and scale back your lifestyle, or (2) you can continue working and saving to reach your goal. As I mentioned several times earlier, the goal of reaching financial independence isn't tied to your age, but rather to your wealth and the income that wealth can generate.

Keep in mind as you're planning, also, that your annual income requirement will change over time as inflation eats away at the dollar's buying power. Assuming the components of your $50,000 goal don't change over a five-year period—that is, you haven't changed the formula and added new expenses, but are simply recalculating for the inflation over five years—your annual income requirement after five years might have increased to $58,000. That means your target portfolio value has also increased, from $1 million to $1.16 million. This increase in costs due solely to inflation is the reason that it's so vital that you invest for growth in common stocks both before and after you reach financial independence. Over those five years, you've presumably continued to save regularly and have invested in a proven stock strategy, so your returns have kept ahead of that inflation creep. So even though your target is trying to slip further away from you, you've continued to close the gap on your magic goal of financial independence by investing in a vehicle that outpaces inflation.

Back to Our Examples

Let's return to the sagas of Alice, Alex, and Ginger and plug their numbers into our formula. If you recall, Alice's annual income requirement was $35,000 per year (after taxes). If we multiply that by 20, her financial independence target portfolio value is $700,000. That's the magic number Alice needs to have invested to sustain her income indefinitely. With $800,000 in her stock portfolio already, Alice has reached her goal. She has enough saved and invested properly in order to live on the income her stock portfolio can generate for the rest of her life. She'll be able to stay ahead of taxes and inflation by using the right stock strategies, and she'll be able to ride out the market's inevitable weak periods without sacrificing her lifestyle. In short, Alice has made it to Easy Street (at least as she's defined it). She can quit her job with the school district, become a full-time grandmother and literacy council volunteer, and enjoy her financial independence; she's earned it.

What about Alex and Ginger? Alex's stock portfolio, remember, is $2.5 million, more than three times as large as Alice's. But their annual income requirement is significantly larger, too—$225,000. If we run that income number through the 20 Factor formula, Alex and Ginger's portfolio should be $4.5 million. Ouch! They're not really even close to financial independence, even though they have what most of us would consider a wonderful portfolio. With their debt load and spending habits, though, they fall a full $2 million short of their necessary goal. Sure, they can live on the $2.5 million they have saved now, but they have no cushion to keep them ahead of inflation or to keep them afloat when the next market downswing occurs. They'll end up living primarily on their principal each year—which, of course, lessens the amount their portfolio can earn each year in new growth. It becomes a vicious cycle that will result in their eventual bankruptcy if something significant doesn't change.

What options do Alex and Ginger have? They really have only two real options. One is to greatly scale back their lifestyle (often the hardest task for anyone to accomplish). Human nature being what it is, it's very difficult to grow accustomed to something comfortable and then give it up for a more spartan existence. It's almost as if the more money we make, the more our spending has to keep pace with our income. If we then try to cut our income, we find it nearly impossible to make the equivalent cuts in our spending. Our wants suddenly feel like needs, and we can't imagine giving them up. But with a portfolio of $2.5 million, if Alex and Ginger really want to stop working and live the independent life, they can only spend $125,000 a year, not the $225,000 their original plan calls for ($2,500,000 ÷ 20 = $125,000). So to make it on their current portfolio, they're going to have to slash (this isn't a trim; it's a major haircut) $100,000 a year from their spending list. Whether they can do it, of course, is entirely up to them.

Their other option is to continue working and saving (even if they have to limit their work for Alex's health) in order to eliminate some of their massive debt, thereby lowering their annual income requirement. Once they get out from under some of their debts, a lot of their cash flow will be freed. There are only two variables in this formula: how much one's portfolio is and how much one can spend. The factor of 20 remains fixed. So if you want to increase the amount you can spend each year, you must increase the investment portfolio amount proportionally. There's no shortcut around the 20 factor.

The Power of Simplicity

I told you from the beginning that what I'm proposing isn't rocket science, nor is it particularly new. (It's amazing sometimes that what's old becomes new again.) In fact, what I'm proposing is so simple it can be ascribed to good old-fashioned common sense. Unfortunately, common sense in the financial community is often frowned upon as far too simplistic. It can't work, the financial gurus bark, unless it's chock full of academic theories and modern portfolio risk analysis and whatever the latest fashionable exercise is. Trust me, though; simplicity is the only answer that gets full marks. If there's one good rule in financial planning, it's *keep it simple*. Every added twist or moving part, just as with any machine, is simply one more element that can break down. Who needs it? In Charles Dickens's *David Copperfield*, Mr. Micawber tells young David the secret to financial well-being: "Annual income twenty pounds, annual expenditure nineteen nineteen six, result happiness. Annual income twenty pounds, annual expenditure twenty pounds ought and six, result misery."

It's really that simple. All I'm proposing (the horror, the horror) is that to be financially independent, you must live within your means rather than living on credit or racing death for your last penny. The tricks, of course, are building up your means so that you can live within them comfortably for an indefinite length of time and then knowing how to marshal them within the complexities of the stock market to generate the consistent income you'll need if you plan to leave the work force. This is what the rest of this book will help you learn.

But Why Does the Formula Work?

I've thrown a formula at you now, but I've yet to discuss why this particular formula, simple and elegant as it is, is all you need to know about planning for financial independence. The time has come.

The elements that lie hidden in this particular formula I've already introduced to you, but I haven't pulled them together in a single place, so let's start to look behind the curtain at the little man throwing the levers. What the 20 Factor plan really suggests is that you're financially independent when you can live on 5 percent of your portfolio a year. (Your whole portfolio divided by 20 equals 5 percent.) So if your portfolio is $2 million, your annual spending can't exceed 5 percent of that, or $100,000. Why 5 percent? Five percent is a reasonable expectation, based on the very long-term history of the stock market, of what you can make each year after taxes and inflation. And those are the two huge pursuers you must stay ahead of in order to remain financially independent.

If you recall our earlier discussion of the stock market's history, the average annual gain for large-company stocks since 1925 has been 11 percent. So if you have $1 million invested, an 11 percent gain would mean a profit of $110,000. Assuming you're investing in a strategy that is tax friendly, this profit should be a long-term capital gain (with some dividends thrown in). Let's say $80,000 of the profit is a capital gain and the remaining $30,000 is from dividends. (Again, this is based on historical averages. Your strategy may generate much different breakdowns.)

Right now, the lowest tax bracket is 15 percent. So let's tax those dividends at such a rate. Your tax on the dividends would be $4,500. The long-term capital gains tax rate for those in the 15 percent tax bracket is only 10 percent, so let's tax that $80,000 capital gain at such a rate ($8,000). Your total taxes are $12,500, leaving an after-tax profit of $97,500 (total profit of $110,000 minus taxes of $12,500 equals $97,500). After you've paid taxes, then, your portfolio has still grown from $1,000,000 to $1,097,500. But don't forget inflation. If inflation runs an average of 3 percent per year, the buying power of each dollar loses ground a bit. If last year we spent $50,000, this year we'll need to spend $51,500 to keep even with inflation. But even after taxes and inflation, the portfolio would have generated a gain (in today's dollars) of more than what we needed to spend. Remember our original target? That's right; we need to generate a 5 percent gain after taxes and inflation to live on our portfolio. Based on long-term market averages, we actually generated a bigger profit than we needed. This allows the portfolio to grow even faster because we won't spend all the income we generated.

Table 2.1 shows this average progression over 30 years. Each year, we'll assume an 11 percent profit (8 percent from capital gains and 3 percent from dividends) and then taxes at 10 and 15 percent for the two categories, respectively. (Keep in mind that I'm calculating taxes on the entire gain. In reality, the taxpayer has a number of deductions that will reduce the amount of taxable income. But as I've said before, it's better to err on the side of conservatism rather than optimism.) The next column accounts for the annual income requirement. It's in this column that I'll account for inflation, raising the amount withdrawn each year by 3 percent. The final column is the total portfolio value after taxes and spending.

So, the first year generated a profit of $110,000 (an 11 percent gain). We paid $12,500 in taxes, and we increased our annual spending from $50,000 to $51,500 to keep pace with 3 percent inflation. After taxes and spending, then, our portfolio is worth $1,046,000. That's a gain, mind you, even *after*

Money for Life

TABLE 2.1 Portfolio Growth after Taxes and Inflation

Year	Starting Value	11% Profit	Taxes	Spending	Final Value
1	$1,000,000	$110,000	$12,500	$51,500	$1,046,000
2	1,046,000	115,060	13,075	53,045	1,094,940
3	1,094,940	120,443	13,687	54,636	1,147,060
4	1,147,060	126,177	14,338	56,275	1,202,623
5	1,202,623	132,289	15,033	57,964	1,261,915
6	1,261,915	138,811	15,774	59,703	1,325,249
7	1,325,249	145,777	16,566	61,494	1,392,968
8	1,392,968	153,226	17,412	63,339	1,465,443
9	1,465,443	161,199	18,318	65,239	1,543,085
10	1,543,085	169,739	19,289	67,196	1,626,340
11	1,626,340	178,897	20,329	69,212	1,715,697
12	1,715,697	188,727	21,446	71,288	1,811,689
13	1,811,689	199,286	22,646	73,427	1,914,902
14	1,914,902	210,639	23,936	75,629	2,025,976
15	2,025,976	222,857	25,325	77,898	2,145,610
16	2,145,610	236,017	26,820	80,235	2,274,572
17	2,274,572	250,203	28,432	82,642	2,413,700
18	2,413,700	265,507	30,171	85,122	2,563,914
19	2,563,914	282,031	32,049	87,675	2,726,221
20	2,726,221	299,884	34,078	90,306	2,901,722
21	2,901,722	319,189	36,272	93,015	3,091,625
22	3,091,625	340,079	38,645	95,805	3,297,253
23	3,297,253	362,698	41,216	98,679	3,520,056
24	3,520,056	387,206	44,001	101,640	3,761,622
25	3,761,622	413,778	47,020	104,689	4,023,691
26	4,023,691	442,606	50,296	107,830	4,308,171
27	4,308,171	473,899	53,852	111,064	4,617,153
28	4,617,153	507,887	57,714	114,396	4,952,929
29	4,952,929	544,822	61,912	117,828	5,318,012
30	5,318,012	584,981	66,475	121,363	5,715,155

taxes and inflation. In the second year, that ending amount from the first year goes to work, earning another 11 percent ($115,050). We'd pay $13,075 in taxes. And we'd increase the salary that we're paying ourselves to $53,045 to keep pace with inflation, and we'd end the year with $1,094,940.

Let's jump ahead to the fifteenth year. We'd start that year with a portfolio value of $2,025,976. Our 11 percent profit would be $222,857. We'd owe Uncle Sam $25,325 in taxes. We'd pay ourselves a salary of $77,898, and we'd end the year with a total value of $2,145,610.

What about after 30 years? At the end of 30 years of average gains, taxes, and inflation, we'd be making a profit of $584,981 a year, paying $66,475 in taxes, paying ourselves $121,363, and ending with a portfolio value of $5,715,155. Remember that bond investor we discussed earlier? His $1 million investment paid him $60,000 every year. So for the first couple of years he'd feel flush compared to the stock investor who would only be spending $50,000 or $55,000. But after a few years, his $60,000 a year wouldn't be enough to keep up with inflation, and his $1 million original investment would be losing value as well. By the end of 30 years, he'd still only be able to pay himself $60,000 a year, whereas the stock investor would be paying himself more than twice that amount. And the bond investor would still have only his original $1 million, while the stock investor's portfolio would have grown to nearly $6 million.

What About Real-World Conditions?

Obviously there are two flies in our ointment, though. The first is that with a portfolio profit so large, our investor wouldn't remain in the lowest tax bracket. The second (and more dangerous) factor is that the stock market and our economy never remain on such a steady *average* pace. Does this model work in real conditions?

Let's deal with the easier problem first (see Table 2.2). Even if we deduct taxes right from the start of this 30-year progression at the very highest tax rates (39.6 percent for dividends and 20 percent for long-term capital gains), the port-

TABLE 2.2 Portfolio Growth after Worst-Case Taxes

Year	Starting Value	11% Profit	Taxes	Spending	Final Value
1	$1,000,000	$110,000	$27,880	$51,500	$1,030,620
2	1,030,620	113,368	28,734	53,045	1,062,210
3	1,062,210	116,843	29,614	54,636	1,094,802
4	1,094,802	120,428	30,523	56,275	1,128,431
5	1,128,431	124,127	31,461	57,964	1,163,135
6	1,163,135	127,945	32,428	59,703	1,198,949
7	1,198,949	131,884	33,427	61,494	1,235,913
8	1,235,913	135,950	34,457	63,339	1,274,067
9	1,274,067	140,147	35,521	65,239	1,313,455
10	1,313,455	144,480	36,619	67,196	1,354,120
11	1,354,120	148,953	37,753	69,212	1,396,109
12	1,396,109	153,572	38,924	71,288	1,439,469
13	1,439,469	158,342	40,132	73,427	1,484,252
14	1,484,252	163,268	41,381	75,629	1,530,509
15	1,530,509	168,356	42,671	77,898	1,578,296
16	1,578,296	173,613	44,003	80,235	1,627,670
17	1,627,670	179,044	45,379	82,642	1,678,692
18	1,678,692	184,656	46,802	85,122	1,731,425
19	1,731,425	190,457	48,272	87,675	1,785,934
20	1,785,934	196,453	49,792	90,306	1,842,289
21	1,842,289	202,652	51,363	93,015	1,900,563
22	1,900,563	209,062	52,988	95,805	1,960,832
23	1,960,832	215,692	54,668	98,679	2,023,177
24	2,023,177	222,549	56,406	101,640	2,087,680
25	2,087,680	229,645	58,205	104,689	2,154,432
26	2,154,432	236,987	60,066	107,830	2,223,524
27	2,223,524	244,588	61,992	111,064	2,295,055
28	2,295,055	252,456	63,986	114,396	2,369,129
29	2,369,129	260,604	66,051	117,828	2,445,853
30	2,445,853	269,044	68,190	121,363	2,525,344

folio earns more than enough to stay ahead of taxes and inflation. Again, I'm accounting for taxes on every penny of the
profit, which doesn't account for any deductions. In other
words, this is the worst-case scenario under our current tax
code. We can only hope Congress and the White House will
come together some day in a joint resolution of sanity and

stop punishing saving and investment and do away with capital gains taxes altogether. But I digress.

Taxes are the easy part. To account for the vagaries of the stock market is more difficult. What we should really be concerned with is whether *any* theory works in the real world. So let's look back at the last 40 years' worth of market history and assume, just for once, that history will repeat itself. What would happen, for example, if the market repeated the returns and inflation rates over the next 40 years that we saw from 1960 to 1998?

Let's suppose Index Ishmael started in 1960 with $1 million and invested it in the S&P 500 Index. He didn't want to bother with picking individual stocks but was aware that the majority of mutual funds don't even keep pace with the index. Logically, he felt his best alternative was keeping pace with the market. So into the index fund he went. His annual spending need at the beginning of this sequence equals our target of 5 percent (or $50,000), and he plans to adjust that annual withdrawal from his portfolio by each year's inflation number (measured by the Consumer Price Index). Since an index fund is a very tax-efficient strategy (very low turnover among the stocks), we'll use 20 percent as his overall tax rate (the maximum long-term capital gains rate).

So in 1960, for example, the index returned only 0.47 percent, generating a profit of only $4,700. Taxes on that gain would be $940. Meanwhile prices rose by a modest 1.48 percent, so Ishmael's spending allowance rose from $50,000 to $50,740. With such a small gain in the market, Ishmael's portfolio lost ground a bit because of his spending withdrawal, but not to worry; there's a cushion built into the approach. His portfolio ended the year worth $953,020 (see Table 2.3).

In 1961, however, the market was back on track, and Ishmael's portfolio gained a very nice 26.89 percent ($256,267). He owed Uncle Sam $51,253 and himself $51,080 (inflation

TABLE 2.3 *Actual Index and Inflation Performance from 1960 to Present*

Year	Starting Value	Return	Gain/Loss	Taxes	Inflation	Spending	Final Value
1960	$1,000,000	0.47%	$ 4,700	$ 940	1.48%	$ 50,740	$ 953,020
1961	953,020	26.89	256,267	51,253	0.67	51,080	1,106,954
1962	1,106,954	-8.73	(96,637)	0	1.22	51,703	958,614
1963	958,614	22.80	218,564	43,713	1.65	52,556	1,080,908
1964	1,080,908	16.48	178,134	35,627	1.19	53,182	1,170,234
1965	1,170,234	12.45	145,694	29,139	1.92	54,203	1,232,586
1966	1,232,586	-10.06	(123,998)	0	3.35	56,019	1,052,570
1967	1,052,570	23.98	252,406	50,481	3.04	57,721	1,196,773
1968	1,196,773	11.06	132,363	26,473	4.72	60,446	1,242,217
1969	1,242,217	-8.50	(105,588)	0	6.11	64,139	1,072,490
1970	1,072,490	4.01	43,007	8,601	5.49	67,660	1,039,235
1971	1,039,235	14.31	148,715	29,743	3.36	69,934	1,088,273
1972	1,088,273	18.98	206,554	41,311	3.41	72,319	1,181,197
1973	1,181,197	-14.66	(173,164)	0	8.80	78,683	929,351
1974	929,351	-26.47	(245,999)	0	12.20	88,282	595,070
1975	595,070	37.20	221,366	44,273	7.01	94,470	677,692
1976	677,692	23.84	161,562	32,312	4.81	99,014	707,927
1977	707,927	-7.18	(50,829)	0	6.77	105,718	551,380
1978	551,380	6.56	36,171	7,234	9.03	115,264	465,053
1979	465,053	18.44	85,756	17,151	13.31	130,606	403,052
1980	403,052	32.42	130,669	26,134	12.40	146,801	360,786
1981	360,786	-4.91	(17,715)	0	8.94	159,925	183,147
1982	183,147	21.41	39,212	7,842	3.87	166,114	48,402
1983	48,402	22.51	10,895	2,179	3.80	172,426	(115,307)

was virtually nonexistent at 0.67 percent). And he ended the year with $1,106,954. In other words, he was back ahead of inflation and taxes, despite the hiccup in the first year.

In 1962, Ishmael lost money again, and then recovered in 1963. (Are you getting the impression that the 1960s weren't terrific for index investors?) In fact, his portfolio wavered a bit throughout the rest of the 1960s, but he still kept ahead of inflation and taxes—and that was his main objective.

And then the bear market hit. Ishmael started 1973 with $1,181,197—more than he began with in 1960, even after paying himself an increased allowance each year. In other words, he had done just fine up till 1973 without thinking about his investments. But that year, the chink in the armor became apparent. In 1973, Ishmael's portfolio lost 14.66 percent of its value (or $173,164). And even though he owed nothing in taxes because of the loss, he still had to pay himself another $78,683 to maintain his style of living. Inflation created a double whammy by jumping to 8.80 percent. He ended 1973 back under his original $1 million investment ($929,351). But this had happened before, and Ishmael's index fund had always bounced right back.

The market, however, wasn't through with Ishmael yet. 1973 was simply a prelude to the carnage of 1974. On top of a 14.66 percent loss the year before, 1974 brought its own loss of a whopping 26.47 percent (or $245,999). And to make the ugly more hideous, inflation soared an additional 12.20 percent. Suddenly Ishmael needed to withdraw $88,282 to meet his spending needs, and the damage was done. By the end of 1974, Ishmael's investment in the index fund was down to $595,070. And because of relatively high inflation for the rest of the 1970s, peaking at double-digit increases in 1979 and 1980, Ishmael no longer had enough capital to generate the kind of income he needed to keep pace with inflation. He made a modest comeback in 1975 and 1976 as the market rebounded, but when inflation began to creep back up in the following years, he was done for. His portfolio declined every year after that until he finally went completely bust in 1983.

If you were simply mirroring the market index, then, from 1960 to the present, it was a grim picture. Between the awful bear market in 1973 and 1974 and the massive jump in prices (inflation), an index investor wouldn't have been able to maintain financial independence. Ouch! So, doesn't this ruin my entire theory that the financially independent investor should be in stocks?

No! (As you probably guessed by the number of pages remaining under your right thumb.) No one can forget the 1970s and the damage that decade did to a lot of investors. But that's not the end of the story. Good news awaits. Who said you had to be an index investor and simply mirror the market? Oh, I know. Wall Street and the academic community tell you that you can't possibly beat the market. After all, if *they* can't, how can *you?* They want you to believe that the best you can hope for is to keep pace with the market (an index fund), so why bother picking individual stocks? You *need* them, they want you to believe.

The Individual Investor versus Wall Street

But the fact is that Wall Street and the professors are dead wrong. Even if you've never bought a stock before and don't know a balance sheet from a P/E (price/earnings) ratio, you can follow a very simple strategy that has consistently beaten the market for seven decades. If you've read my first book, *The Unemotional Investor,* you know that I'm talking about a strategy called the *Dogs of the Dow* (or the *Dow Dividend* approach, or several other similar names). I won't spend a lot of time discussing the actual strategy here, since I'm more interested in discussing overall financial planning approaches than individual stock picking, but if you'd like a full treatment of the Dogs of the Dow, please check out my first book and *Beating the Dow,* by Michael O'Higgins (rev. 2000, Harper Business). And I'll also include a summary version of the approach in Chapter 3 of this book. (If you can't wait to see the details, skip ahead now, but make sure you mark your spot here. I'd hate for you to miss what comes next!)

The beauty of the Dogs of the Dow approach is that it's virtually maintenance free, and more important, it works. This approach does what the vast majority of professional money managers fail to accomplish year after year—it consistently beats the market indices over long periods of time. Just how well does it do? If you recall, the average annual return for the S&P 500 from 1960 through 1998 was a fraction under 12 percent. The Dogs of the Dow approach, over the identical stretch (which includes the up-and-down 1960s as well as the miserable bear market of 1973–1974 and the crash of 1987) returned an annual average gain of 14.56 percent. Now what's two-and-a-half percentage points a year? Over a long time, you'd be amazed. For instance, compare two investments of $10,000 over 40 years; the first grows at 11.99 percent a year and the other grows at 14.56 percent. Care to guess the difference in total value? The first investment swells to $927,192. The second— with its seemingly paltry two-and-a-half percentage-point advantage—balloons to an incredible $2,297,842, nearly two-and-a-half times as much as the first investment. Never scoff at a couple of percentage points over a long period of time. As you're about to see, it's the difference between going broke and thriving in our scenario from 1960 to 1998.

In Table 2.4 I've compiled the same history from Table 2.3 that we examined for poor Ishmael, including a starting investment of $1 million in 1960, a beginning withdrawal of $50,000 a year (which will be adjusted each year based on the

TABLE 2.4 Actual Dow Dogs and Inflation Performance from 1960 to Present

Year	Starting Value	Return	Gain/Loss	Taxes	Inflation	Spending	Final Value
1960	$1,000,000	−0.10%	($ 1,000)	$ 0	1.48%	$ 50,740	$ 948,260
1961	948,260	26.91	255,177	51,035	0.67	51,080	1,101,321
1962	1,101,321	0.15	1,652	330	1.22	51,703	1,050,940
1963	1,050,940	21.06	221,328	44,266	1.65	52,556	1,175,446
1964	1,175,446	20.28	238,380	47,676	1.19	53,182	1,312,969
1965	1,312,969	19.34	253,928	50,786	1.92	54,203	1,461,909
1966	1,461,909	−17.90	(261,682)	0	3.35	56,019	1,144,208
1967	1,144,208	25.68	293,833	58,767	3.04	57,721	1,321,553
1968	1,321,553	14.68	194,004	38,801	4.72	60,446	1,416,310
1969	1,416,310	−12.77	(180,863)	0	6.11	64,139	1,171,308
1970	1,171,308	4.73	55,403	11,081	5.49	67,660	1,147,970
1971	1,147,970	5.71	65,549	13,110	3.36	69,934	1,130,476
1972	1,130,476	23.79	268,940	53,788	3.41	72,319	1,273,309
1973	1,273,309	3.89	49,532	9,906	8.80	78,683	1,234,252
1974	1,234,252	1.04	12,836	2,567	12.20	88,282	1,156,239
1975	1,156,239	52.17	603,210	120,642	7.01	94,470	1,544,336
1976	1,544,336	33.24	513,337	102,667	4.81	99,014	1,855,992
1977	1,855,992	1.17	21,715	4,343	6.77	105,718	1,767,646

1978	1,767,646	2.44	43,131	8,626	9.03	115,264	1,686,887
1979	1,686,887	14.21	239,707	47,941	13.31	130,606	1,748,046
1980	1,748,046	27.95	488,579	97,716	12.40	146,801	1,992,108
1981	1,992,108	4.87	97,016	19,403	8.94	159,925	1,909,796
1982	1,909,796	20.87	398,574	79,715	3.87	166,114	2,062,542
1983	2,062,542	38.43	792,635	158,527	3.80	172,426	2,524,223
1984	2,524,223	7.45	188,055	37,611	3.95	179,237	2,495,430
1985	2,495,430	30.61	763,851	152,770	3.77	185,994	2,920,516
1986	2,920,516	29.43	859,508	171,902	1.13	188,096	3,420,027
1987	3,420,027	8.56	292,754	58,551	4.41	196,391	3,457,839
1988	3,457,839	17.96	621,028	124,206	4.42	205,072	3,749,590
1989	3,749,590	29.64	1,111,378	222,276	4.65	214,607	4,424,085
1990	4,424,085	-10.01	(442,851)	0	6.11	227,720	3,753,514
1991	3,753,514	35.24	1,322,738	264,548	3.06	234,688	4,577,017
1992	4,577,017	6.35	290,641	58,128	2.90	241,494	4,568,035
1993	4,568,035	23.54	1,075,315	215,063	2.75	248,135	5,180,152
1994	5,180,152	2.43	125,878	25,176	2.67	254,760	5,026,094
1995	5,026,094	37.10	1,864,681	372,936	2.54	261,231	6,256,608
1996	6,256,608	27.47	1,718,690	343,738	3.32	269,904	7,361,655
1997	7,361,655	20.39	1,501,042	300,208	1.70	274,493	8,287,996
1998	8,287,996	9.67	801,449	160,290	1.61	278,912	8,650,244

Consumer Price Index), and a long-term capital gains tax rate of 20 percent. The only difference is that instead of the returns from the S&P 500 Index each year, I've substituted the actual returns generated by the Dogs of the Dow strategy. Let's look at the difference in performance.

The first year started a little roughly as 1960 generated a loss of 0.7 percent ($1,000). After withdrawing the inflation-adjusted amount of $50,740, the first year closed below the initial investment value of $1 million with a total of $948,260. But just as with the index portfolio, 1961 brought a big recovery. The gain of 26.91 percent ($255,177) pushed the portfolio back onto the correct side of the ledger, and after taxes and the annual withdrawal, the total net value was $1,101,321.

Just as with the index portfolio, the Dogs of the Dow portfolio had some ups and downs throughout the 1960s. In 1962, the portfolio gain wasn't as large as the annual withdrawal, so the overall value of the portfolio dropped a bit. But the next three years were such fine ones that the portfolio built up a little cushion of profit. Then in 1966 the Dow Dogs strategy had its worst year in the entire four-decade history, a loss of 17.90 percent. But even after this setback, the portfolio still had more than the original $1 million investment because of its previous three years' worth of gains. And the strong two years that followed the disappointing result in 1966 built the cushion right back up. In 1969, the portfolio again suffered a loss, this time 12.77 percent. And then the following two years it recorded small gains so that the overall portfolio value dropped slightly for those three consecutive years. Yet by the end of 1971, the total value was still over $1.1 million, even after all those years of increased spending because of inflation. In other words, it was keeping ahead of inflation and taxes despite a rocky era for common stocks. That's all anyone can ask of an investment strategy. And the Dow Dogs delivered.

What about the bear market, though? Isn't that what did in the index investor? Well, let's see. In 1972, the Dogs of the Dow recorded a strong gain of 23.79 percent. After taxes and withdrawals, the total portfolio value heading into the bear market of 1973 and 1974 was $1,273,309. Would that extra quarter-million-plus be enough to withstand the ravages of the bear market? As you recall, in 1973–1974, the S&P 500 Index lost 40 percent of its value—a devastating hit. Combine that with double-digit inflation, and Ishmael's financial independence was shattered. But in that same two-year bear market, the Dogs of the Dow actually *made a profit* of just under 5 percent! In 1973 the portfolio gained 3.89 percent, and then in 1974 it eked out a gain of 1.04 percent.

Normally, no one's going to cheer gains of less than 5 percent per year, but look at the alternative. At a time when the major indices were getting hammered and the media were proclaiming the death of equities and the end of the stock market as we knew it, this simple 30-minute-a-year approach actually recorded a modest profit. So even though the portfolio lost slightly to inflation for those two years, the losses were minimal because of the stable performance of the Dow Dogs, and by the end of the bear market, the total portfolio value was still over the original $1 million mark ($1,156,239 at the end of 1974).

In the ensuing recovery, of course, the Dow Dogs enjoyed tremendous profits. In 1975, they gained 52.17 percent and then another 33.24 percent in 1976. So by the time the double-digit inflation took hold again at the end of the decade, the Dogs of the Dow portfolio had increased its total value to $1,686,887 (at the end of 1978). In 1979, when inflation hit its peak at 13.31 percent, the portfolio still advanced because the portfolio gained better than 14 percent. And then in 1980, with inflation still soaring at 12.40 percent, the portfolio advanced yet again with a gain of 27.95 percent. The great enemies of the investor who is living on the proceeds of a portfolio—inflation and taxes—were met and defeated by an approach so simple that junior high students roll their eyes at it in boredom.

Since that economic crunch ending in 1980, the Dogs of the Dow approach has only suffered one additional losing year, a loss of 10.01 percent in the recession of 1990. In addition, it's lost ground to inflation on only five other brief occasions, all of them very minor discrepancies. In between those subpar years, the strategy recorded such strong gains that the value after taxes and inflation over the years continued to soar. By the end of 1990, the total portfolio value was $3,753,514. And at the end of 1998, it was an astounding $8,650,244.

Instead of going totally broke in 1983 (as Ishmael would have in the index fund), the Dogs of the Dow investor continued to pay himself a higher withdrawal every year to keep pace with inflation, and watched his overall portfolio grow to more than eight times its original size in just under 40 years. Of course, once a portfolio like this gets a safety cushion where it is generating far more each year in profits than is needed to pay for the inflation increases in spending, the power of compounded growth kicks in even faster, and the total value increases exponentially. That's the beauty of a stable and powerful stock strategy like the Dogs of the Dow. It allowed our hypothetical investor to increase his annual spending withdrawal from $50,000 at the beginning of 1960 to $278,912 a year at the end of 1998, as well as continue to grow the entire asset base used to generate such income. That's impossible with a fixed-income bond investment.

The Long-Term Perspective

This last example, then, is how I intend for you to see your portfolio once you reach financial independence. With the right kind of investment strategy, you'll be able to increase the amount you spend each year to keep up with inflation. You'll be able to ride out market downturns (like the great bear market of 1973–1974 and the crash of 1987) without having to sacrifice your budget plans. You'll be able to continue to grow your asset base so that it will generate income for you indefinitely. If you live a long and healthy life after you leave the workforce, and I'm going out on a limb here in assuming that's what most of us want, such an investment strategy is the only way to keep from running out of money. No one wants to end up counting coupons or eating cat food. It isn't pretty. So prepare now for your own financial independence and then, regardless of how the government mucks up Social Security or Medicare, you'll be responsible for your own comfortable life.

I'm not suggesting necessarily that you adopt the Dogs of the Dow strategy as your portfolio plan. While it's proven a terrific strategy for decades, there are a number of fruitful ways to set up a portfolio plan. My point here is just to demonstrate that with a sound investment strategy, the kind of financial independence I've been advocating is within your grasp. I'll discuss further some of your portfolio management options in Chapter 7.

Summary

Let's go over the critical elements you must examine in your own long-term planning for financial independence:

- To calculate your ultimate goal—the portfolio value you'll need to have invested before you can live on your portfolio indefinitely—use The 20 Factor formula:

Financial independence = annual income requirement × 20

- The annual income requirement is the amount you will need to generate each year (in today's dollars) in order to maintain the lifestyle you've chosen. Included in the annual income requirement are all the costs (except income taxes) you face in today's dollars if you are to live comfortably on the growth of your investments. Be realistic and honest about the life you'll be living at this stage. Don't assume lifelong habits in spending are suddenly going to change unless you make a tremendous effort to change them. Plan for the unexpected expenses and long-term replacement of big-ticket items like cars and home furnishings.

- Remember to subtract from your annual income requirement any guaranteed income you are assured of having, whether it is from Social Security or a company pension plan. But only subtract guaranteed income, not just income you hope will come your way. The idea here is to calculate how much income you absolutely must generate over the years from your own investments. If you're not sure about an income stream, don't count it. It's better to underestimate your guaranteed income from other sources than to overestimate it.

- Once you have the final dollar amount your portfolio must generate right now if you were to leave the workforce forever, multiply it by 20. This will give you the dollar amount necessary to be financially independent as you've defined it in your planning. That dollar amount may be wildly different from the next person's. If you are comfortable living on $40,000 per year, you only need a portfolio of $800,000. But if you require $100,000 a year, your portfolio will need to be a minimum of $2 million. You make the choices and determine the consequences.

- Limiting yourself to an annual withdrawal of just 5 percent of your total portfolio value gives you a cushion against declines in the stock market, but more important, it allows your portfolio to grow faster than inflation. The primary danger to a long-term investor who relies on investment income isn't a stock-market decline as most financial planners would have us believe; it's inflation. Over 30 years, inflation would destroy any plan based on a fixed-income return such as one gets with bonds. The right kind of strategy in the stock market, however, provides the long-term growth necessary to remain in front of taxes and inflation.

- Choose a stock-market strategy that is reasonably stable and tax efficient, yet one that provides consistent market out-performance over many years. You must use a strategy that will survive the inevitable shifts in investor psychology. One year a value approach may be in favor; the next year a growth approach may fare better. It's impossible to know and to successfully switch back and forth rapidly, but a swarm of nervous investors will try. Your best alternative is to find one approach you can follow through any market period and stick with it. The Dogs of the Dow, for example, is a simple large-company value approach that has worked remarkably well for seven decades and requires all of 30 minutes a year. Low maintenance, high performance, reasonably stable (remember that it made a *profit* during the bear market of 1973 and 1974), it's the kind of strategy you can use for a long-term plan.
- And the most radical point of all (at least it appears to be radical given America's love affair with credit card debt) is Mr. Micawber's advice to David Copperfield: *Live within your means.* If what you make isn't enough to support the lifestyle you feel you deserve, then go earn more. It's that simple. Spending first and hoping to pay for it later is not just mathematically a disaster, it's irresponsible. The financially independent investor cannot afford to be irresponsible.
- The equation itself can't change. There are only two variables, not three, and they are dependent on each other. If you change the total portfolio amount, it changes the amount you can spend, and vice versa. But you can't decide to change the 20 factor to make it easier to meet your goal. If you decide to live on 7 or 8 percent of your total portfolio each year, you give away your cushion against declines and inflation, and your plan will fall apart in the next really ugly market. You won't be able to adjust quickly enough, and you'll be in the same boat as the bond investor whose principal and yield are worth less and less each year. Most financial planners would say my plan

is already risky because it advocates a 100 percent investment position in stocks rather than bonds, although the hidden risks in bonds are equal to or riskier than stocks over a long period. So let's keep the safety factor built into the factor of 20 in place.

In Chapter 3 I will take a look at a sector of American business that already follows the principles I've outlined in *Money for Life* and then outline how those same principles can be applied to individuals facing a similar business model.

3

PRETEND YOU'RE THE FORD FOUNDATION

There is already a sector of the American economy that uses the planning strategies I'm outlining in *Money for Life:* charitable foundations or endowments. And the outlook these organizations have on planning, investing, and spending is very much the model that individual investors should be adopting for their own financial independence. Let's look briefly at how a charitable foundation might work, and then see how the same principles can (and should) apply to the rest of us.

Over the years, the Dream Charitable Trust (a hypothetical organization today, but someday . . .) has enjoyed growth of its assets to a level of $25 million. This money has come from a variety of sources. These include donations, bequests, and matching gifts—but much of it has come about as a result of solid investment strategies over a period of many years. The Dream Charitable Trust has a roster of some 25 organizations to which it contributes each year. Some of the charity recipients include college scholarship funds, literacy councils, youth academic and sports organizations, and the fine arts. Last year the trust was proud to announce its first annual budget of more than $1 million.

The trust's portfolio is managed strictly in large-company common stocks, with a strategy aimed at long-term growth. The board of directors has accepted the fact that the trust's portfolio won't always go up but understands that over the last 200 years, the stock market has been the only investment vehicle that has provided for consistent growth after accounting for inflation. So in bad years, the directors are prepared to cut their spending plans in order to remain consistent with their long-term goals.

This is precisely how the major foundations we've all heard of operate. The Pew Charitable Trusts, for example, currently have assets of $4.9 billion, and in 1999 they invested over $250 million in more than 200 nonprofit organizations. That represents 5.1 percent of their current assets.

The John D. and Catherine T. MacArthur Foundation has $4 billion in assets and annual grants of more than $170 million—4.25 percent of its total assets.

Finally, the Ford Foundation uses a slightly different formula for calculating its giving, but the same principles apply. The Ford Foundation sets its budget on a two-year cycle, using 5.8 percent of the average value of its portfolio over the previous 36 months. Assuming that the portfolio grows each year, this is right in line with the expenditure range of 5 percent per year.

A Permanent Plan

The reason the model of the charitable foundation or endowment is so applicable to us as individual investors who are becoming financially independent is that these organizations have no termination date. They work under the presumption that they'll exist forever—and then plan accordingly. The managers for the endowment at Harvard, for example, aren't trying to make their last dollar stretch until their deaths; they fully assume that the endowment will need to grow indefinitely. And while it's true, of course, that we'll all die (there I go being cheerful again), none of us knows precisely when that will happen, especially if we're planning while we're still young and healthy. So it only makes sense that we need to adopt the attitude that we, too, have no foreseeable termination date. In other words, we need to begin to think like we are our own private foundations. No longer are you simply Janet Franklin. You're now the Janet Franklin Private Foundation! Think like a foundation; plan like a foundation; invest for the very long term like a foundation; and limit your spending like a foundation.

While we are still members of the workforce, we actually have a huge advantage over most charitable trusts. Our annual spending needs aren't financed by our investments at this stage of our careers, but rather through our regular salaries. In fact, we're adding to our investments every year through regular savings without having to withdraw anything to meet our budgets. So our endowments (to use the industry terminology) continue to grow unabated for many years. But that advantage is reversed somewhat once we've reached a level of financial independence and decide to live on the growth of our portfolios. Charitable foundations, however—if they are at all viable entities—will continue to receive outside contributions over and above what their portfolio managers can earn for them. Once we leave the workforce, most of us will be limited exclusively to what we can generate from our investments.

Let's go back to the Dream Charitable Trust example and look at the way the trust's board of directors has to plan for each year's income and expenses. Each year the trust begins the year with a clear dollar amount for its annual budget. The dollar amount is, in fact, defined by the 20 Factor rules. (While charitable foundations undoubtedly don't call their

planning by this name, it's typical in the industry for an organization to limit its annual spending to 5 percent of the
endowment's value.) So with a January 1 portfolio value of
$25 million, the Dream Charitable Trust's 2000 budget would
be exactly $1.25 million. Having a clear dollar value to plan
with is so much easier than building a budget modeled on
economic forecasts or projected revenues like government
agencies do (that is, blind guesses, eternal optimism, and
throws at a dartboard).

As I've already discussed, no one can predict with any
degree of consistency or accuracy what the economy, the
stock market, or interest rates will do next year. You'll hear
endless predictions, to be sure, but rarely will you find any
two that agree. And whenever such a forecaster is called out
for a poor projection, you'll never hear the words "I was
wrong." Analysts are never wrong; they're just *early* with their
forecasts.

Preparing a Budget Couldn't Be Easier

So don't even bother playing the guessing game. The 20
Factor rules tell you what your budget will be—ahead of
time. It can't get much plainer. The Dream Charitable Trust,
then, can sit down on New Year's Day (oh alright, we'll give
them the day off to overdose on bowl games), and plan
exactly how they'll spend this year's budget of $1.25 million.

Some of it will go to administrative expenses: paying their
excellent portfolio managers; the cost of their advertising
campaigns, mailings, office staff salaries, office supplies, rent,
and utilities; all the things that keep the trust operating on a
day-to-day basis. Fortunately, the trust keeps a very stream-
lined staff and a tight rein on unnecessary spending so that
more of its budget each year can go directly to its charitable
projects. Let's assign $100,000 of the annual budget to admin-

istrative costs. In other words, of the $1.25 million allocated for the 2000 budget, 8 percent is chewed up in administrative costs. Ideally, the board of directors would like to see this segment of the budget shrink in percentage terms, even as the dollar amounts continue to grow because of inflation and additional staff members as the trust grows. (Remember that one of the best reasons to invest in common stocks is to remain ahead of inflation over the long run.) Fortunately, administrative costs won't rise much beyond the rate of inflation from year to year unless the size of the staff increases dramatically. So as a percentage of the overall annual budget, the administrative costs are likely to shrink as time passes.

The remaining 92 percent of the Dream Charitable Trust's 2000 budget (or $1.15 million) can be split up among the trust's current roster of 25 recipients. How that amount is divided isn't really important for our purposes. But the key point is that as the amount grows over time, the purpose of the trust (to contribute funds to charitable causes) is served more and more effectively.

What happens, however, in a year when the trust's investment portfolio loses ground? Just as with the example I laid out in Chapter 2, there will be years when any stock portfolio will lose money. And within the guidelines of the 20 Factor rules, there are two ways to look at this problem. In our example from the last chapter we started with a fixed dollar amount for the investor's annual income requirement and then increased that spending amount each year by the rate of inflation (the Consumer Price Index). That may not be the most logical method for a charitable trust, but it's certainly workable.

A Second Approach

An alternative approach is simply to ignore the fixed dollar amount idea and work from a straight percentage model.

Using 5 percent as our fixed spending amount, the dollar amount for each year's budget will fluctuate as the portfolio value fluctuates. The Dream Charitable Trust, for example, started 2000 with $25 million, and withdrew $1.25 million (5 percent) for its annual budget. Let's suppose that the remainder of the assets ($23.75 million) lost 6 percent in the stock market over the course of the year, ending 2000 with a total value of $22,325,000. Under the 20 Factor guidelines on percentage spending, the trust's budget for 2001 would be reduced from $1,250,000 the previous year to $1,116,250 in 2001 (5 percent of the new portfolio value after the year's losses).

This method lets the annual spending withdrawals fluctuate with the value of the portfolio. In years when the portfolio profits, the budget increases. In years when the portfolio loses money, the following year's budget shrinks in proportion. It's a simple manner of living within the organization's means. This method assures the trust will never go entirely broke (short of an entire economic collapse) because the annual spending amount is reduced after a weak year in the stock market in proportion to the losses. This is a very different scenario from the one we examined in Chapter Two, where the annual spending withdrawals were necessarily increased each year to keep pace with inflation. As such, this fluctuating withdrawal approach is more appropriate for an investor (organization or individual) whose fixed spending needs are a fairly small percentage of the overall portfolio value (even less than the 5 percent goal) and can afford to spend less in a year when his investments performed poorly. For an organization like the Dream Charitable Trust, for example, this model works very well because the actual fixed costs (administrative costs) are very small as a percentage of the overall portfolio (only 0.4 percent of the 2000 total portfolio value), and the rest of the annual budget can fluctuate if necessary.

Over the long haul, assuming the portfolio managers adopt a solid stock strategy, either of the two approaches to calculating the annual withdrawal amount will keep the portfolio ahead of inflation, and it is really a matter of the preference of the investor as to which method is more appropriate.

The Numbers Up Close

Let's examine a simple model using the fluctuating annual withdrawal method to see how the Dream Charitable Trust's budget will change over time. We'll begin the first year with a balance of $25 million. The annual budget will always be 5 percent of the year's starting portfolio value. As a charitable foundation, the portfolio is tax-free. Of the annual budget in the first year, we'll assume administrative costs are $100,000, and these costs will rise with inflation each year (measured by the Consumer Price Index). The rest of the annual budget accomplishes the trust's real objective—charitable contributions within the community. For the portfolio returns, I will once again use the actual returns recorded from 1960 through 1998 by the Dogs of the Dow strategy (see Table 3.1).

The first year begins with an endowment worth $25 million. Pulling 5 percent out for the annual budget (or $1.25 million) leaves the portfolio managers $23.75 million to invest. Of that $1.25 million budget, $100,000 goes towards administrative costs and the remaining $1.15 million gets distributed to the Trust's list of charities. The portfolio that year, however, lost 0.10 percent. So the final endowment value dropped to $23,726,250.

That means the budget for the second year will be smaller than the original budget, even though administrative costs will have risen because of inflation (albeit a very modest 1.48 percent). So the budget for the second year will be $1,186,313. Of that, $101,480 now goes to administrative costs and

TABLE 3.1   Dream Charitable Trust Using Percentage Annual Withdrawals

Year	Starting Value	5% Budget	Admin. Costs	Charitable Gifts	Return	Final Value	Inflation
1960	$25,000,000	$1,250,000	$100,000	$1,150,000	–.10%	$23,726,250	1.48%
1961	23,726,250	1,186,313	101,480	1,084,833	26.91	28,605,435	0.67
1962	28,605,435	1,430,272	102,160	1,328,112	0.15	27,215,926	1.22
1963	27,215,926	1,360,796	103,406	1,257,390	21.06	31,300,220	1.65
1964	31,300,220	1,565,011	105,112	1,459,899	20.28	35,765,509	1.19
1965	35,765,509	1,788,275	106,363	1,681,912	19.34	40,548,431	1.92
1966	40,548,431	2,027,422	108,405	1,919,016	–17.90	31,625,748	3.35
1967	31,625,748	1,581,287	112,037	1,469,250	25.68	37,759,879	3.04
1968	37,759,879	1,887,994	115,443	1,772,551	14.68	41,137,877	4.72
1969	41,137,877	2,056,894	120,892	1,936,002	–12.77	34,090,342	6.11
1970	34,090,342	1,704,517	128,278	1,576,239	4.73	33,917,674	5.49
1971	33,917,674	1,695,884	135,321	1,560,563	5.71	34,061,655	3.36
1972	34,061,655	1,703,083	139,868	1,563,215	23.79	40,056,676	3.41
1973	40,056,676	2,002,834	144,637	1,858,197	3.89	39,534,137	8.80
1974	39,534,137	1,976,707	157,365	1,819,342	1.04	37,948,027	12.20
1975	37,948,027	1,897,401	176,564	1,720,838	52.17	54,858,238	7.01
1976	54,858,238	2,742,912	188,941	2,553,971	33.24	69,438,460	4.81
1977	69,438,460	3,471,923	198,029	3,273,894	1.17	66,738,346	6.77
1978	66,738,346	3,336,917	211,436	3,125,482	2.44	64,948,423	9.03

1979	64,948,423	3,247,421	230,528	3,016,893	14.21	70,468,714	13.31
1980	70,468,714	3,523,436	261,211	3,262,224	27.95	85,656,484	12.40
1981	85,656,484	4,282,824	293,602	3,989,223	4.87	85,336,557	8.94
1982	85,336,557	4,266,828	319,850	3,946,978	20.87	97,988,982	3.87
1983	97,988,982	4,899,449	332,228	4,567,221	38.43	128,863,840	3.80
1984	128,863,840	6,443,192	344,852	6,098,340	7.45	131,540,986	3.95
1985	131,540,986	6,577,049	358,474	6,218,575	30.61	163,215,398	3.77
1986	163,215,398	8,160,770	371,989	7,788,781	29.43	200,687,205	1.13
1987	200,687,205	10,034,360	376,192	9,658,168	8.56	206,972,728	4.41
1988	206,972,728	10,348,636	392,782	9,955,854	17.96	231,937,779	4.42
1989	231,937,779	11,596,889	410,143	11,186,746	29.64	285,649,930	4.65
1990	285,649,930	14,282,496	429,215	13,853,282	-10.01	244,203,553	6.11
1991	244,203,553	12,210,178	455,440	11,754,738	35.24	313,747,841	3.06
1992	313,747,841	15,687,392	469,376	15,218,016	6.35	316,987,287	2.90
1993	316,987,287	15,849,364	482,988	15,366,376	23.54	372,025,790	2.75
1994	372,025,790	18,601,290	496,270	18,105,019	2.43	362,012,716	2.67
1995	362,012,716	18,100,636	509,521	17,591,115	37.10	471,503,462	2.54
1996	471,503,462	23,575,173	522,463	23,052,710	27.47	570,974,190	3.32
1997	570,974,190	28,548,709	539,808	28,008,901	20.39	653,026,036	1.70
1998	653,026,036	32,651,302	548,985	32,102,317	9.67	680,364,971	1.61

$1,084,833 goes to charities. The second year, fortunately, was a very good one for the endowment managers as the portfolio gained 26.91 percent. The total portfolio value at year's end was $28,605,435, which means a budget of over $1.4 million the following year. And so on.

Skip ahead a few years in the table (keeping in mind the data we're using are from the up-and-down 1960s and then the ugly bear market of 1973 and 1974). By the end of 1970, the endowment's total value had increased to nearly $34 million. That means a budget the next year of just under $1.7 million. Administrative costs have risen to more than $135,000, but charitable gifts have increased to $1.56 million per year.

Skip ahead again, through the bear market and several years of double-digit inflation. At the end of 1980, the endowment's portfolio value is up to $85.66 million. That generates a budget in 1981 of nearly $4.3 million. Of that, administrative costs have jumped to nearly $300,000, but charitable contributions have soared to just under $4 million.

Flip the calendar to the back page—the end of 1998. The portfolio has now reached the astronomical level of $680 million! That means the 1999 budget for the Dream Charitable Trust would be $34 million. Administrative costs have continued to rise because of inflation and now run $557,824, but that increase pales in comparison to the percentage increase in charitable giving. The trust is able to donate $33.46 million to its roster of projects in 1999.

First let's look at what inflation has done. Assuming the total administrative costs grew only as a result of inflation each year (rather than through changes in the trust's staff size), the 1960 cost of $100,000 became more than half a million dollars in 1999. That's an increase of 458 percent over nearly four decades. But now let's look at how the investment portfolio has outstripped that inflation rate and has grown considerably, even after the annual budget has been withdrawn each year. The first year's budget for charitable contributions was $1.15 million. In 1999 that figure would have been $33.46 million. Instead of the 458 percent increase in administrative costs resulting from inflation, the charitable giving increased over the same period by 2,530 percent! That's despite the fact that the portfolio suffered four years of actual losses and another eight years when the gains were smaller than the increases in the inflation rate.

What has made the plan so successful is the limit the board of directors placed on annual spending (the 20 Factor 5 percent rule) and their hard line on keeping administrative costs as low as possible. The percentage of the annual budget devoted to administrative costs dropped from 8 percent of the total in 1960 to just 1.6 percent of the budget in 1999. Because the administrative costs only rose to meet inflation while the portfolio had a considerably higher average annual gain, the balance available in each year's budget to give to charity increased by an average rate of 9 percent a year. That's a significant increase over and above the inflation rate year after year.

Taxes and the 5 Percent Rule

But that's not fair, I hear you cry. Charitable foundations don't have to pay taxes, and they can afford to let their budgets fluctuate. How can they be equated with the individual investor, whose expenses are more rigid and who has to pay capital gains taxes to Uncle Sam on each profit?

You're right; taxes do raise the hurdle somewhat, but as I demonstrated in Chapter Two, the tax haircut each year doesn't derail your financial independence express if you're using a solid strategy in the stock market. Your average annual gains should be high enough (over the long haul, not in every single year) that even after taxes and inflation, you will see consistent portfolio growth.

Also, as I suggested earlier, the fluctuating annual budget method is probably best reserved for investors whose annual income requirements have some built-in flexibility or are even lower than the 5 percent cap. For example, if your annual withdrawal includes a budgeted amount for a lavish trip overseas, that's something you can forego for one year if stocks fall into a significant bear market. Or you may decide to delay the purchase of that new Lexus another year. Look to your own plan to see if and where you've built in any flexibility. If you don't have much flexibility in your plan, you will probably want to calculate your annual spending increases, at least initially, based on inflation rates rather than on the floating model. The reason for this is that inflation has been averaging roughly 3 percent a year for decades. With typical portfolio growth considerably higher than that, limiting your spending increases to the rate of inflation means you'll start building in a cushion over time because your portfolio will be growing at a rate faster than your withdrawals.

But if you feel you have the flexibility built into your planning to sustain a drop in your annual withdrawals every now and then (whenever your portfolio loses money, or simply loses ground to the inflation rate), by all means consider the easy plan of withdrawing up to 5 percent of your portfolio each January. You might be pleasantly surprised after a few years when you realize that you don't really need to spend the entire 5 percent and you can afford to reduce your spending amount to 4 or even 3 percent of the portfolio's total and still maintain your comfortable lifestyle.

Let's look at a simplified example to show how this might work. In my previous examples, I've included historical return data and actual inflation data to show that even in ugly times, the right kind of approach to the stock market will see you through. But for the sake of this simple table (Table 3.2), let's make everything easy, fully understanding

TABLE 3.2 Individual Investor Using the 5 Percent Withdrawal Method

Year	Starting Value	Withdrawal (5%)	Gain (14%)	Taxes (20%)	Final Value
1	$1,000,000	$50,000	$133,000	$26,600	$1,056,400
2	1,056,400	52,820	140,501	28,100	1,115,981
3	1,115,981	55,799	148,425	29,685	1,178,922
4	1,178,922	58,946	156,797	31,359	1,245,414
5	1,245,414	62,271	165,640	33,128	1,315,655
6	1,315,655	65,783	174,982	34,996	1,389,858
7	1,389,858	69,493	184,851	36,970	1,468,246
8	1,468,246	73,412	195,277	39,055	1,551,055
9	1,551,055	77,553	206,290	41,258	1,638,534
10	1,638,534	81,927	217,925	43,585	1,730,948
11	1,730,948	86,547	230,216	46,043	1,828,573
12	1,828,573	91,429	243,200	48,640	1,931,705
13	1,931,705	96,585	256,917	51,383	2,040,653
14	2,040,653	102,033	271,407	54,281	2,155,746
15	2,155,746	107,787	286,714	57,343	2,277,330
16	2,277,330	113,866	302,885	60,577	2,405,771
17	2,405,771	120,289	319,968	63,994	2,541,456
18	2,541,456	127,073	338,014	67,603	2,684,795
19	2,684,795	134,240	357,078	71,416	2,836,217
20	2,836,217	141,811	377,217	75,443	2,996,180
21	2,996,180	149,809	398,492	79,698	3,165,164
22	3,165,164	158,258	420,967	84,193	3,343,679
23	3,343,679	167,184	444,709	88,942	3,532,263
24	3,532,263	176,613	469,791	93,958	3,731,483
25	3,731,483	186,574	496,287	99,257	3,941,938
26	3,941,938	197,097	524,278	104,856	4,164,264
27	4,164,264	208,213	553,847	110,769	4,399,128
28	4,399,128	219,956	585,084	117,017	4,647,239
29	4,647,239	232,362	618,083	123,617	4,909,343
30	4,909,343	245,467	652,943	130,589	5,186,230

the limitations of averages. (The market, which is very consistent in repeating performance over long periods of time, rarely repeats itself in shorter time horizons.)

Let's assume a financially independent investor—the Preston McManus Private Foundation—begins with $1 million. Preston's annual budget will be 5 percent of whatever the portfolio's final value is at the end of the previous year. His overall tax rate on the portfolio gains will be 20 percent (again, severely simplified). For the sake of simplicity and conservatism, we'll assume a 14 percent average annual stock return (slightly less than the average for the Dogs of the Dow since 1960).

The first year, then, the Preston McManus Private Foundation opens with $1 million. Preston withdraws 5 percent (or $50,000) to live on for the year and invests the remaining $950,000. Earning 14 percent, the portfolio enjoys profits of $133,000. Preston will pay a 20 percent tax on that amount ($26,600), which leaves his foundation a net value at the end of the year of $1,056,400. (I'll address inflation in a minute.)

In year 10, Preston McManus starts with $1,638,534, which gives him a spending budget of $81,927, the rest to be invested for the year. His 14 percent gain grosses $217,925 in profits, on which he pays $43,585 in taxes. The foundation ends the year worth $1,730,948.

In year 20, he begins with $2,836,217, pulls out $141,811 to live on for the year, earns $377,217 on the remaining portfolio, pays $75,443 in taxes, and finishes the year with $2,996,180.

And finally, in the 30th year, Preston's private foundation begins with $4,909,343. His annual spending allowance has increased to $245,467. His 14 percent profit brings in $652,943, on which he owes taxes of $130,589. And at the end of 30 years, the Preston McManus Private Foundation is worth a total of $5,186,230.

The Effects of Inflation and Growth

Now let's look at inflation. Preston wasn't adjusting his annual budget along with the changes in the Consumer Price Index. Instead he was simply sustaining his 5 percent withdrawals, assuming that his overall portfolio growth would keep him ahead of the inflation rate. Was he right? Let's look.

Starting with an annual withdrawal of $50,000 and increasing the amount by an average inflation rate of 3 percent per year, Preston's final withdrawal in year 30 would have been $117,828. Instead, using the constant 5 percent withdrawals, Preston actually increased his annual withdrawals to $245,467, more than double the amount generated by consistent boosts to stay even with the rate of inflation. In other words, by sticking to the 5 percent withdrawal each year, Preston doubled his standard of living in comparison to the inflation rate by the end of the 30 years.

I'm the first one who will argue that increasing our standard of living shouldn't necessarily be our goal. If we've started our planning with the ideal that financial independence is the level at which we would remain comfortable for the rest of our lives, then there's no realistic need to try to increase that level. Instead of allowing his spending to increase to equal the amount his portfolio said was available each year, the smart thing for Preston to do would be to gradually reduce the percentage he withdraws each year as he finds that he can live on less than the full 5 percent amount. Every time you can reduce the amount you need to pull out of your portfolio to live on, you increase your safety cushion against a market downturn and a resurgence in the inflation rate. It's the same old story: it's better to stay on the conservative side. The 5 percent withdrawal rule is the *maximum* withdrawal each year. If you can do nicely on less, so much the better. And if your portfolio is performing at all well, you'll find that you should be able to reduce that withdrawal percentage several times over the years.

Let's recalculate that same 30-year "average" progression for the Preston McManus Private Foundation, but instead of withdrawing 5 percent every year, let's reduce the withdrawal rate periodically as his portfolio grows and builds in a comfortable safety zone (see Table 3.3).

TABLE 3.3   Individual Investor Using a Graduated Withdrawal Method

Year	Starting Value	Withdrawal	Gain (14%)	Taxes (20%)	Final Value
1	$1,000,000	**$50,000**	$133,000	$26,600	$1,056,400
2	1,056,400	52,820	140,501	28,100	1,115,981
3	1,115,981	55,799	148,425	29,685	1,178,922
4	1,178,922	58,946	156,797	31,359	1,245,414
5	1,245,414	62,271	165,640	33,128	1,315,655
6	1,315,655	65,783	174,982	34,996	1,389,858
7	1,389,858	69,493	184,851	36,970	1,468,246
8	1,468,246	66,071	196,304	39,261	1,559,218
9	1,559,218	70,165	208,467	41,693	1,655,827
10	1,655,827	74,512	221,384	44,277	1,758,422
11	1,758,422	79,129	235,101	47,020	1,867,374
12	1,867,374	84,032	249,668	49,934	1,983,077
13	1,983,077	89,238	265,137	53,027	2,105,948
14	2,105,948	94,768	281,565	56,313	2,236,433
15	2,236,433	**89,457**	300,577	60,115	2,387,437
16	2,387,437	95,497	320,872	64,174	2,548,637
17	2,548,637	101,945	342,537	68,507	2,720,720
18	2,720,720	108,829	365,665	73,133	2,904,423
19	2,904,423	116,177	390,355	78,071	3,100,530
20	3,100,530	124,021	416,711	83,342	3,309,878
21	3,309,878	132,395	444,848	88,970	3,533,361
22	3,533,361	**123,668**	477,357	95,471	3,791,579
23	3,791,579	132,705	512,242	102,448	4,068,668
24	4,068,668	142,403	549,677	109,935	4,366,006
25	4,366,006	152,810	589,847	117,969	4,685,073
26	4,685,073	163,978	632,953	126,591	5,027,459
27	5,027,459	175,961	679,210	135,842	5,394,865
28	5,394,865	188,820	728,846	145,769	5,789,122
29	5,789,122	**173,674**	786,163	157,233	6,244,379
30	6,244,379	187,331	847,987	169,597	6,735,437

For the first seven years, let's say, the portfolio is treated exactly as it was in our previous example (Table 3.2). The starting amount in year one is $1 million. The annual withdrawal is 5 percent (or $50,000 to start). The yearly profit in the stock market on the investment portfolio is 14 percent (or

$133,000 in year one). And taxes on the profit will be paid at a rate of 20 percent ($26,600 the first year).

But instead of maintaining these percentages throughout the 30 years, in the eighth year Preston decides to trim his annual withdrawal because the portfolio growth is generating more than he really needs to spend each year. So instead of an annual draw of 5 percent in year eight, he trims the rate to 4.5 percent. That means instead of increasing his budget from just over $69,000 in year seven to more than $73,000 in year eight as in the original model, Preston takes a modest pay cut, withdrawing only $66,071 in year eight. (In Table 3.3, I've placed these transition points in Preston's budget in boldface.)

Everything else in the model progression remains the same: The annual portfolio profit rate and the tax rate both remain constant. Then in years 9 through 14, Preston continues to withdraw just 4.5 percent per year. In year 15, however, he cuts the withdrawal rate again, to 4 percent a year. Then in year 22 he slices another half percentage point a year off of his withdrawals, taking out only 3.5 percent a year. And then finally in year 29, he cuts the rate once more, down to just 3 percent per year.

In the thirtieth year, using this gradually reduced withdrawal scheme, Preston's annual withdrawal is $187,331. That's quite a bit less than the constant 5 percent model's final budget value of $245,467 in year 30. But the important key to remember is that the reduced withdrawal value is still considerably more than what Preston needs simply to keep up with a constant annual inflation increase of 3 percent a year. That would have required him to pull out only $117,828 in year 30. So not only has Preston's private foundation stayed markedly ahead of inflation; his total portfolio base has actually grown considerably faster because of his reduced withdrawal rates. Taking out less each year means there is more to grow. If you'll recall, with the constant 5 percent withdrawals, his portfolio's final value was $5,186,230 after the thirtieth year. Using the graduated withdrawal rates, the extra compounding power of the money he's been able to let grow in the portfolio has added more than $1.5 million in total value to his foundation. The total portfolio value after 30 years under this model is $6,735,437.

Remarkably, in just another 13 years (in year 43), the amount Preston would be taking out of his portfolio each year in the model where he reduces withdrawals gradually from 5 percent a year to 3 percent would actually surpass the dollar amount he would be pulling out using the constant 5 percent method. The portfolio with the reduced withdrawals would grow so much faster because it's not tapped as heavily each year that even though Preston's pulling out a smaller percentage from it, he is doing so on such a larger asset base that after 43 years his annual budget would still be greater. It's one of those odd mathematical marvels, where less turns out to be more after enough time passes.

Let me reiterate my caution, however, that the stock market never moves in "average" patterns. You may be fortunate to launch your private foundation right at the beginning of a bull market run and your safety cushion will be enhanced almost immediately. Don't count on it, though. If you're unfortunate enough to start living on your assets right as we tumble into a bear market, your planning has to have accounted for such a possibility, and your strategy had better include a safety zone right from the beginning. That's why the 5 percent rule is so crucial as a maximum withdrawal. When I was working as a daily columnist, I received countless e-mail messages from investors wanting to know why they couldn't pull out 6, 7, or even 8 percent or more per year to live on, since their portfolios were going up 15 percent, 20 percent, or even more in recent years. And the simple answer is another question: How long will the current bull market run remain intact? No one knows—and planning as if it will always be thus is shortsighted at best and catastrophic at worst.

Summary

Let's review, then, the principles we as individual investors have to borrow from the charitable foundation sector in setting up our own long-term plans:

- **Start today in thinking like a private foundation.** Long before you reach the stage at which you're financially independent, start planning as a foundation would. That means planning with no termination date in mind. You must have enough assets invested to generate the required income indefinitely (that is, forever).
- **Limit yourself to an absolute maximum withdrawal of 5 percent of your total portfolio value.** Even though your investment portfolio may be generating gains of 20 percent or more in recent years, don't use that as license to get sloppy in your planning. When the market has its next ugly period (and there will be more of them, rest assured), your plan has to be set up in a way that will allow you to ignore the short-term fluctuations and stick to your strategy.
- **As your portfolio grows, reduce your withdrawal percentage over time.** Assuming that you're investing wisely, your stock portfolio should increase at a rate faster than inflation, which means that you'll need to withdraw less than 5 percent of the total portfolio value over time. Whenever you can comfortably reduce that rate of withdrawal, do so. Your safety cushion increases; your portfolio grows faster; and paradoxically, over a long period of time, you may actually find that your annual income withdrawals get larger than if you had maintained the constant 5 percent withdrawal (because of the compound growth of a larger portfolio).
- **Invest using a sound common stock strategy.** You'll see me refer to this again and again through this book. If you aren't investing well, none of the rest of your planning will matter.

You'll still end up penniless. The entire 20 Factor strategy rests on what for many people is a huge assumption—that you can invest for growth and outperform the major market indices. But you can if you approach the problem correctly. The opportunity is there for anyone who wants to take it, but it requires some qualities and actions that too many Americans ignore: long-term planning, discipline, care, discipline, responsibility, discipline . . . (okay, you get the point, right?).

In the next chapter I'm going to survey a variety of subjects that each of us needs to address as we make our long-term financial plans. Unfortunately, financial planning has become such a diverse and complex industry (the more complicated it becomes, the more likely you are to turn it over to the "professionals," right?) that most people have no idea how to begin, and the task is generally so daunting that they don't bother. I'll examine the issues that are crucial for us to get under control first (the need for wills, insurance do's and don'ts, how and how much to save, and others) and then point you in the direction you can go if you want to pursue such topics in more detail.

4

THE BEST WAY TO GET THERE FROM HERE

The first three chapters of *Money for Life* are aimed at defining your ultimate goal—financial independence. It's time now to change direction and to begin looking at how you can get to that goal from where you are today. As you might suspect, I have some fairly strong (and perhaps unconventional) views about the best way to handle your financial life, and it will be the purpose of this chapter to discuss some of the issues you must address along the way. But equally important, I will also discuss some of the financial planning techniques and products you *should not* bother with.

First of all—a disclaimer (with a disclaimer of its own). The disclaimer: I am not a certified financial planner (CFP). In our advisory firm, we don't handle general financial planning issues except informally. We're strictly portfolio managers (registered investment advisors). Now the disclaimer's disclaimer: The foregoing is entirely by design. One thing my partner and I discovered quickly when planning our firm is that the world of finances is woefully too complicated, and we didn't want to get bogged down in the minutiae of the industry. Any single area within the industry (for example, insurance or estate planning or tax planning or asset allocation) is enough to engulf and demand one's entire working attention. Trying to do it all is insane, especially when so much of it is unnecessary. We decided to focus on the one sector that we were the most interested in and felt we could accomplish successfully—asset management, specifically within the common stock arena. Everything else we threw overboard from our tiny ship.

Fortunately, it's completely unnecessary to try to become an expert in all of these fields. The vast majority of financial products and services offered to the typical consumer are unnecessary. They're not in the consumer's best interests, but rather they profit the seller of the product at the consumer's expense and prey on his or her naiveté. And the more complicated the products become, the more true this is. In other words, a good solid financial plan doesn't have to be complicated, and in fact a simple plan is probably more appropriate for most people.

Call me a cynic, but I'm afraid the financial services industry loves the complexity of the offerings available. The more complicated everything becomes, the more the average consumer will be required to rely on the advice of a specialist who may or may not really share the consumer's goals. (At a later point, I'll discuss working with professional advisors and tell you what to look for and what to avoid.)

Just as with my philosophy on investing once you leave the workforce, I'm going to boil a number of the major financial planning issues down to their simplest forms so that you can stop wallowing in the Slough of Despond and can start setting up a plan that works for you because it's sound and because it's simple enough to be maintained easily.

Saving and Budgeting

As bizarre as this may sound, it's nevertheless true: most Americans haven't a clue about how to save their money. It's not that they are unable to save, mind you. They simply don't know how—and much of the problem stems from the way we have been conditioned to look at budgets.

The typical family looks at saving and budgeting this way. On the first of the month (or every week or two weeks), when they receive their paychecks, they sit down and plan out the month. (There are, of course, far too many people who do no planning at all; they may be beyond help. Instead, I'm referring to the conscientious types who still fail to get it right through lack of knowledge, not lack of effort.) This typical family pays the mortgage, the car payment, the utilities, the lawn care bill, the auto and life insurance premiums. They stock up on groceries. They pick up a couple of household items and garments the kids need for school. They haven't had any money for a month now, so they treat themselves to a night out or a weekend trip to the lake. And of their take-home pay of, let's say, $4,000 for the month, they should still have about $400 or so left over at the end of the month to put into savings. That's the plan anyway.

What happens? Well, if your family is like most, the end of the month arrives and there's not a penny left to put into savings. Someone's birthday rolled around and boom, $40 is gone. It's time to sign up for soccer league again and boom, $60 is gone for the league and $30 is gone for some new shin guards and a ball. That new pair of shoes you've been eyeing for weeks is on sale at the mall, and even though they're still $80 now, that's $50 cheaper than you thought they'd be. Another $80 gone. Your washer springs a leak and the repair bill eats another $75. You can't put off getting your suits dry-cleaned any longer (they're starting to walk to work without you). There's another $45 out the door. Another $50 simply disappears into the ether. (It's not in your couch, either. I looked.)

Now we're at the end of the month and how much is left to put into savings? Twenty measly bucks. You're so frustrated that you don't even bother to deposit it. Instead you order pizza and vow to do better next month. But will you? A better question to ask is *can you?* And as long as this is the way your budgeting goes each month, the answer is no.

I'm the first to admit that I hate budgets and trying to plan where every penny is going to go. It's not only that the whole enterprise seems so Puritan, but more important, it just doesn't work. Aside from the fixed regular expenditures we all have (mortgage, car payment, and the like), very little of our lives is easy to plan for precisely. If you go back through the last several years' worth of your check stubs, you will undoubtedly find at least one payment every month (of a somewhat substantial size) that you had no way to plan for ahead of time. As the G-rated bumper sticker would have it, Life Happens. And you can't plan for it in such detail ahead of time. So if you're planning your budget and savings based on what's expected, you're doomed from the outset by all those things that will happen that you can't foresee.

There's a little-known physical property of money that financial physicists call the Elastic Rule of Monetary Expansion, and its corollary, the Impossible Nature of Specific Budgeting. The Elastic Rule of Monetary Expansion applies whether you make $50,000 a year or $500,000. Simply stated, the rule is that no matter how much money you earn, your expenditures will automatically expand to meet that level. And the corollary, of course, means that no amount of earnings is ever adequate to provide you with any money "left over" if you try to plan your entire budget ahead of time. It's amazing how quickly a *want* becomes a *need* in our minds when we think there's an extra $50 or $100 floating around. We've all had the proverbial holes burned in our pockets when we've had money. And I don't want you to think for a minute that you shouldn't get enjoyment from the money you've earned. You simply need to learn a new way of looking at budgeting and savings so that you can enjoy your money completely guilt-free. But you're doomed to failure from the start if you're following a traditional budgeting/savings plan.

So don't bother. I can hear you now: "This lunatic is telling me that I have to become financially independent, which means having a large investment portfolio, but now he's telling me not to bother budgeting and saving? I want my money back for this book!"

That's not quite what I'm saying, however. When I said "Don't bother," I meant don't bother with a traditional budget and savings plan. They're too hard and they set you up for failure. You need to begin to see saving and budgeting in a different fashion to make it successful for you. And believe me, once you do you will find it's tremendously easy to save and you'll be reducing your monthly stress level as you watch your wealth increase.

Now if you're waiting for an earth-shattering revelation, you are going to be disappointed. What I'm about to say is not exciting (except for what it can generate), it's not even particularly new (the concept has been around for a long time, but few people seem to understand or use it), and the best news yet, it's not even hard. Alright, enough of the late-night infomercial hype . . . get on with it!

Pay yourself first! That's right; make yourself your most important creditor. Before you pay any bills, even before you write that check for the mortgage payment or for your car payment, deposit *10 percent* of your take-home paycheck into some kind of long-term savings account (in the stock market preferably). Don't worry about calculating the percentage from your gross salary amount. Make it easy. If your employer cuts you a check for $1,000, the first $100 of that check is automatically whisked away into your wealth account. If your check is $10,000, the first $1,000 is for savings—period. But you must write that check first or I promise you, 9 times out of 10, you'll never write it at all and you're back to where you were—frustrated and getting nowhere with your savings. In fact (and this is especially helpful if you get paid a regular salary), have that amount set up with your bank as an automatic payment directly from your checking account into your wealth account. That way you don't even have to bother writing the monthly (or weekly) check. The money's protected because you never see it.

Don't think for a minute that the amount you have to save is too small to bother with. Remember the power of compounded growth? Even small amounts can generate huge profits if they are put to work early enough. Time is your most precious ally. Let it work for you as much as possible.

Just to show you the incredible importance of starting early, let's compare two neighbors. Party Paul and Conscientious Carl graduated from college together, took identical jobs at the same company, and live in the same apartment building. Being young, Party Paul hasn't a care in the world. He isn't even thinking about saving money. He figures he's got all the time in the world to save for his future; now that he's finally got some walking-around money, he's going to enjoy it for a while. Conscientious Carl, however, remembers his finance class where an enlightened professor drummed into the students' heads the power of compounded growth. So Carl is anxious to start saving something right away, even if it's not a huge amount.

For the next 10 years, then, Carl will save $2,000 a year in a stock portfolio that will average, let's say, 15 percent growth a year. During this decade, Paul doesn't save anything but has a fabulous time. (Carl isn't exactly living like a pauper, either; he's just not blowing everything he makes.)

Ten years later, for some inexplicable reason, Carl decides to stop adding his annual $2,000 to his savings. (Maybe he discovers that he's the long-lost love child of Bill Gates and figures with Bill's billions, his measly two grand doesn't matter?) Who knows? But for whatever reason, Carl only invests new money for the first 10 years, a total of $20,000. And at the end of that decade, Carl's account has grown to $46,699 (see Table 4.1).

Now that Paul's in his thirties, though, he's starting to realize that wearing sweats, eating pizza, and drinking beer in a dormlike apartment isn't all that life should be about, and it's time to get to work on his future. So he, too, will begin putting $2,000 a year into the same 15 percent-a-year account Carl is using. But to make up for his late start, Paul decides that instead of 10 annual deposits, he'll make 20. Surely by doubling the amount of money he's investing, he'll end up with more than Carl after 30 years. Meanwhile, Carl's money continues to grow at 15 percent a year, even though he's not adding anything new to the pot.

After year 15, Carl's account has grown to $93,927 and Paul's has reached $15,507. But Paul's just getting started; he's only put in five deposits and still has 15 years of additional savings to come.

After year 20, Paul has reached the point Carl reached in year 10, of course. He's added 10 deposits, and each year the entire portfolio has grown by 15 percent. So Paul's account is now worth $46,699. But now his additional 10 years of deposits will start to kick in and close the gap, right? Carl's still living at the Gates compound near Seattle, but he's left his account to grow steadily. It's up to $188,922 now.

Jump ahead the final 10 years. Party Paul's extra 10 deposits have been included and the additional growth has

TABLE 4.1 *Conscientious Carl and Party Paul*

Year	Carl's Savings	15% Annual Gain	Paul's Savings	15% Annual Gain
1	$2,000	$2,300	–	–
2	2,000	4,945	–	–
3	2,000	7,987	–	–
4	2,000	11,485	–	–
5	2,000	15,507	–	–
6	2,000	20,134	–	–
7	2,000	25,454	–	–
8	2,000	31,572	–	–
9	2,000	38,607	–	–
10	2,000	46,699	–	–
11	–	53,703	$2,000	$2,300
12	–	61,759	2,000	4,945
13	–	71,023	2,000	7,987
14	–	81,676	2,000	11,485
15	–	93,927	2,000	15,507
16	–	108,017	2,000	20,134
17	–	124,219	2,000	25,454
18	–	142,852	2,000	31,572
19	–	164,280	2,000	38,607
20	–	188,922	2,000	46,699
21	–	217,260	2,000	56,003
22	–	249,849	2,000	66,704
23	–	287,326	2,000	79,009
24	–	330,425	2,000	93,161
25	–	379,989	2,000	109,435
26	–	436,987	2,000	128,150
27	–	502,535	2,000	149,673
28	–	577,916	2,000	174,424
29	–	664,603	2,000	202,887
30	–	764,294	2,000	235,620

increased his overall growth rate. In fact, he's turned his $40,000 worth of deposits into a pretty impressive $235,620 in just 20 years. But what about Conscientious Carl's account? Despite only depositing $20,000 to Paul's $40,000, Carl's total account value has soared to $764,294. That's three and a quarter times as much money as Paul amassed, despite actually depositing half as much capital. The big difference was time. By getting an early jump, and even though Carl blew it by stopping his deposits after 10 years, he still ended up with over three times as much as Paul, who deposited twice as much capital over the years.

In fact, getting the late start he did, Party Paul would have had to deposit $6,500 a year for the 20-year period (a total of $130,000) and achieve growth of 15 percent a year just to generate the same final value as Carl's account. Now if Carl had really been smart and continued his annual deposits of $2,000 for the entire 30 years, at the end his account would be just $100 shy of a million dollars ($999,914).

In case you've missed the point of my tale: **Start now!** And start with whatever you have. It's time that matters more than the amount. The easiest way to accomplish that is simply to have that first 10 percent of every single paycheck go directly into your savings plan. Once you get used to that money disappearing off the top you won't even notice it.

Then once you've paid yourself, you can write those checks for your regular bills and see what's left. And the beauty of this system is that whatever's left is completely guilt-free money. If you have a couple of hundred dollars left after you've paid yourself and all your bills, by all means go shopping, or take a trip, or have a night out on the town. You deserve it. And you can spend that money knowing full well you've already met your responsibilities both to your future and to your bills.

Can you see what's disappeared from this picture? That's right—the misery-making budget. It doesn't matter whether you blow every last penny of what's left over each month because you've already saved ahead of time. You'll enjoy your money a whole lot more this way; you won't have to agonize over every last penny; and best of all, 30 years down the road you'll have a whole lot more of it, too. But it takes discipline. You have to commit to saving first, then playing with what's left over rather than hoping something will be there at the end of each month's budget to save. You know where *that* road leads.

Throughout your working career, of course, your savings amounts increase automatically as your salary rises. Make sure that you immediately increase that savings withdrawal each month when your salary goes up. Don't cheat your own future for a quick fling at the mall with that first month's extra cash. You won't miss that 10 percent if you never get used to wasting . . . er . . . spending it.

Let's look at the progression of Faithful Felicia's savings over the span of an entire career (Table 4.2). Let's say at age 23, Felicia takes her first job, making $30,000 a year. We'll also assume that each year, between inflation and raises, her salary will increase by 7 percent. As each pay increase kicks in, her savings amount increases in proportion. And again, we'll assume she's investing this money in a stock portfolio of some kind, earning 15 percent per year. (Forget about taxes for now. We're going to assume that Felicia pays her income taxes from funds outside her investment portfolio so that she doesn't slow its growth.)

In her first year, then, Felicia takes home $30,000, the first $3,000 of which she invests in stocks, which earn an average of 15 percent. So by the end of the first year, Felicia's portfolio is worth $3,450.

In real life, of course, Felicia isn't likely to be paid in a lump sum at the beginning of each year. So her deposits into her stock portfolio would be spread out over a year, buying in at different times. But for the sake of simplicity in this example, let's stick with the illusion of a once-a-year paycheck.

The next year, her take-home pay rises to $32,100 (a 7 percent increase). Her 10 percent savings for the year, then,

TABLE 4.2   *Faithful Felicia's Career Automatic Savings*

Age	Salary	Savings	Portfolio
23	$30,000	$3,000	$ 3,450
24	32,100	3,210	7,659
25	34,347	3,435	12,758
26	36,751	3,675	18,898
27	39,324	3,932	26,255
28	42,077	4,208	35,032
29	45,022	4,502	45,464
30	48,173	4,817	57,824
31	51,546	5,155	72,425
32	55,154	5,515	89,631
33	59,015	5,901	109,863
34	63,146	6,315	133,604
35	67,566	6,757	161,414
36	72,295	7,230	193,941
37	77,356	7,736	231,928
38	82,771	8,277	276,235
39	88,565	8,856	327,856
40	94,764	9,476	387,932
41	101,398	10,140	457,782
42	108,496	10,850	538,927
43	116,091	11,609	633,116
44	124,217	12,422	742,369
45	132,912	13,291	869,009
46	142,216	14,222	1,015,715
47	152,171	15,217	1,185,572
48	162,823	16,282	1,382,132
49	174,221	17,422	1,609,487
50	186,416	18,642	1,872,348
51	199,465	19,947	2,176,139
52	213,428	21,343	2,527,104
53	228,368	22,837	2,932,432
54	244,353	24,435	3,400,398
55	261,458	26,146	3,940,525
56	279,760	27,976	4,563,776
57	299,343	29,934	5,282,767
58	320,297	32,030	6,112,016
59	342,718	34,272	7,068,231
60	366,709	36,671	8,170,637
61	392,378	39,238	9,441,356
62	419,845	41,984	10,905,842
63	449,234	44,923	12,593,380
64	480,680	48,068	14,537,665
65	514,328	51,433	16,777,463

would be $3,210. Add that to her portfolio total from last year of $3,450 and she's investing $6,660. And with another 15 percent gain for the year, the final value after two years is $7,659. Already, then, in just two years, you can start to see the power of compounded growth. Felicia's deposited a total of $6,210 into her stock account, yet her portfolio value is already worth better than $1,400 more than her deposits. Each year, the entire portfolio plus her new deposit grows again. And again and again.

By the time Felicia is 30 years old, her take-home pay has increased to $48,173 a year. Her savings have increased to $4,817 a year, and her total portfolio value has jumped to $57,824. She's nowhere near her long-term goal of financial independence after just eight years, but she's already saved more money than most Americans (sad to say). Now watch the real power of her simple savings plan get going.

When Felicia is 40 years old, her take-home salary has continued to climb at 7 percent a year, now up to $94,764. The first 10 percent of that ($9,476) still goes into her stock account. And at the end of the year, her portfolio value has increased to $387,932.

By the time she's 50, Felicia is taking home $186,416 a year, saving $18,642, and her portfolio has ballooned to $1.87 million. At age 60, she's making $366,709 a year, saving $36,671, and her portfolio is worth $8.17 million.

And finally, at age 65—the conventional "retirement" age—Felicia will be bringing home $514,328 a year. Of that she would save $51,433. And after that final year of growth, her portfolio would be worth $16,777,463.

Of course, by this time Felicia will have long since passed the level where she would still have to keep working out of financial necessity. In fact, her portfolio has grown to the point where the growth it achieves each year brings in significantly more than her salary does, so she could easily stop working and continue to give herself indefinite "pay increases" simply by using the 20 Factor rules. For example, if she limits herself to a 5 percent withdrawal from her final portfolio value at age 65, she would "pay" herself nearly $840,000 the next year. That's $290,000 more than she would be taking home from her job after the next year's 7 percent pay raise.

That's precisely how simple and effective the Pay Yourself plan is. A very simple 10 percent off the top out of every paycheck and a solid investment strategy and you will set yourself up to be wealthy. And we haven't even talked about Felicia's corporate retirement account yet. This is just what she has saved independently of Social Security, Individual Retirement Accounts, and 401(k) plans.

All it takes is time and discipline, both of which you've heard me blather on about before. You must start as soon as possible and you have to send in those deposits. No one can do it for you—but frankly, it shouldn't be that tough. If you've got enough discipline to pay your mortgage and car payments once a month, you've got the discipline to pay yourself. Just look back at the numbers for Felicia's career, or the comparison between Party Paul and Conscientious Carl, if you need motivation. Putting off saving, even for a little while, wipes out your best tool—time.

Types of Savings Accounts

Now that you're saving, where should you save? Let's look at several alternatives.

Emergency Savings

There are any number of reasons why you should save (e.g., financial independence, college for your children, glamorous trips you've always dreamed of, a vacation home), but the most depressing and mundane of all reasons is simply for emergencies. No one knows when the car will require an engine overhaul or a new transmission. If a family member or close friend becomes ill or dies, the cost of a quickly planned trip across country can be enormous. Or your washer or dryer might finally give up the ghost and you haven't saved ahead of time for a replacement. Whatever the reason, there are always unexpected and unfortunate events that require you to lay out some money that you haven't built into your typical monthly plan.

Most people, if they save at all, will simply skip their deposit into their savings account that month to use the money for the emergency. You can already tell what I'm going to say about that idea. Any time you postpone your savings plan, you're simply derailing your own journey to financial independence. One of the financial services companies is currently running a very clever television advertising campaign which shows someone contemplating buying a beautiful designer watch, or another such luxury item, and then right before the purchase is complete a calculator appears to show them how much that purchase would have earned them in portfolio growth over many years. The obvious problem is that most Americans never think this way. We tend to live in the moment and have no idea what the long-term consequences of our actions might be. I'm convinced that if Congress enacted new legislation requiring retailers to include a comparison showing what the value of each purchase would be in 30 years at 11 percent growth next to the item's actual price, most people would begin making better decisions. (Not much of a dreamer, am I?)

But I digress. The point is that you need to plan for the unexpected emergencies, even though it's impossible to anticipate what they'll be or when they'll strike. There are a couple of ways you can do this. The first is by having a very good credit rating and maintaining a credit card account on which you *owe nothing.* I hesitate even to suggest this option because the temptation for too many people is to run up the credit card balance on optional purchases, thereby defeating the entire purpose. If you're maintaining a credit card account for emergencies only, it should be a card you don't even carry in your wallet or purse on a regular basis, in order to remove the temptation of impulse purchases. Only use it when you simply must pay for something immediately and your regular cash-flow planning simply doesn't provide enough room to cover it.

For this to be an effective tool, however, the credit card account needs to have a credit limit large enough to cover any serious contingencies. Anywhere from $3,000 to $5,000 should be enough to accomplish your purposes here. Any major emergency larger than that is likely to be covered by your insurance policies if you're covered appropriately. (I'll discuss insurance later in this section.)

Even more important, if and when you are forced to use the credit card, you must pay off the entire balance as quickly as possible. Don't fall into the credit trap of paying the mini-mum balance due each month. That's how credit card compa-nies make their living. If your card is for emergencies, use it only in a genuine emergency and then clear the balance away rapidly to prepare for the next emergency.

Using a credit card as your emergency vehicle has one advantage over a more traditional method in that it doesn't require you to leave a lot of cash sitting idle in a bank account. (Face it, the interest rates banks pay on savings and money market accounts take them out of the realm of real investments. Money parked there barely keeps up with infla-tion. In some cases it may even lose to inflation. These days, "a penny saved" may well be a tenth of a penny lost.) So hav-ing an open credit line to cover short-term emergencies frees up the cash you would normally leave in such an account so that you can invest it elsewhere. Also, many credit cards today give bonus frequent-flyer miles as an incentive to use the cards more. If you can be disciplined and pay that balance off immediately, it's a good way to save money on future travel. But if you allow the balances on the credit card to grow and remain open, you'll pay more in interest to the credit card company than you'll ever save accumulating those bonus miles. Don't carry a balance a day longer than absolutely necessary—period.

The danger of using a card for emergencies, of course, is that it requires a tremendous amount of discipline. It's so easy to fall into the pattern of putting discretionary purchases (that is, stuff you don't really need right now but can't keep yourself from buying) on the card and worrying about paying the balance off later. Most people simply don't have the self-discipline required to manage a credit card this way. They'll run the balances up over time, and then when a genuine emergency hits, they have neither a cash emergency fund saved nor the room on their credit card limit to cover the emergency. Then they're *really* digging the hole deeper.

The other alternative for your emergency fund is the more traditional cash account. For 9 out of 10 people, I would recommend this alternative over relying on a line of credit. Set up a separate bank account (either a plain old passbook savings account or a money-market account) for your emergency fund. Don't mingle this money with any other type of savings. For example, if you're saving for a vacation or for holiday gifts or for a new car, keep these savings out of your emergency fund. The whole point of the emergency fund is to have a safety net available in times of quick need. If you mix the money with other kinds of savings, you may be tempted to spend it on that new car—and then you're at risk again if a genuine emergency crops up. It doesn't cost you anything to maintain several different accounts for different purposes, and it will be much easier to keep track of your different savings plans this way.

It's also important that your emergency money be in a type of account that's completely safe (that is, not in stocks, which can fluctuate in value), and one that's completely liquid. That is, it needs to be in an account that you can gain access to immediately. So a certificate of deposit, for example, would not be a good choice for an emergency fund, because you would be required to pay penalties to withdraw the money before the CD matures. So accept the fact that this money is not really an investment at all; take whatever lousy return is offered by your bank or credit union; and forget the money's even there (until you really need it).

How much money should be in your emergency fund account? Here, perhaps, my views are a bit unorthodox. Most financial planners will tell you to have six month's expenses in cash reserves. I frankly think this is a ridiculous excess. I have struggled to find an emergency that can't be dealt with for $5,000 or less, and I simply haven't been able to. If something major occurs, a disaster to your home, your health, or perhaps your automobile, all of which can be extremely costly, that's when the right kinds of insurance coverage will kick in. But you're not going to have to pay those bills directly. For the kinds of emergencies you're likely to have to pay for in cash, a $5,000 safety net seems perfectly adequate. If it makes you more comfortable to have a larger emergency fund, by all means do so. But keep in mind that every thousand dollars you leave idle in such an account is more than $65,000 you could be generating in a stock portfolio over 30 years. So be careful about leaving too much cash sitting idle. You don't want to cheat your own future unnecessarily.

Of all the saving you will do over your career, get your emergency fund in place first, even at the expense of other savings temporarily. Once it's been built up to $5,000, or whatever level you decide upon, then you can forget about it until you have to draw on it. When and if that happens, of course, build it back up immediately.

The next several types of accounts that I'll discuss are all geared toward your long-term wealth creation, either toward the day you become financially independent, or for such big future expenses as a child's college tuition. These are the accounts where time and consistent saving can make you wealthy.

401 (k) and 403 (b) Retirement Plans

In past generations, there was a closer tie between company and employee than exists today. It was typical for employees to spend their entire working lives with a single company, starting in their late teens after high school and retiring in their 60s, after 40 or 50 years with the same employer. It's not surprising that the companies felt some responsibility to provide for a decent pension plan after their long-term employees stopped working.

Today, however, where the typical American changes professions—not just jobs—five or six times over the span of a career, that loyal bond between company and employee has obviously disappeared. So instead of getting the gold watch and a lifetime pension income, today the employee is much more responsible for providing for his or her own income after leaving the workforce. Employers still often provide some assistance along the way, however, even if it comes in the form of less permanent attachments.

The typical company today offers some kind of retirement plan, usually a 401(k) plan. If your employer is a nonprofit organization like a hospital or university, you have a 403(b) instead. The way these plans work is that the employer works with an investment firm—typically one of the many large mutual fund families—and sets up an account for each employee. The employee is allowed to (or in some cases, required to) contribute a certain percentage of his or her salary, before income taxes are withheld, into the retirement account. In many cases, the company will also match a portion of the employee's deposit. And then the employee has the responsibility of managing the money by choosing from among the investment options (mutual funds) made available in that particular plan.

For example, when my wife was teaching at the University of Kentucky, the first 5 percent of her salary was deposited in her 403(b) account automatically. This was required in her case. Then the university matched that contribution two-for-one. That is, for every dollar my wife deposited, the university deposited two more. (This percentage, by the way, is very unusual. Most employers match contributions with less than a one-to-one ratio. That is, for every dollar you put in, they might put in fifty cents. I suppose universities feel somewhat guilty for what they pay their faculty and try to make up for it slightly in other ways.)

Usually such matching contributions only extend to a limited percentage of what the employee contributes. In my wife's case, after that first 5 percent mandatory deposit and the university's matching contribution, she was allowed to contribute more if she wished (up to the IRS limit), but the university would not match additional deposits.

The big advantage for these kinds of retirement accounts is that the money deposited into them grows on a tax-deferred basis. In other words, it is income you're not paying income taxes on at the time it is earned. The money goes into your retirement account "pre-tax," and then continues to grow without tax consequences until you withdraw the money at retirement age (59½ currently). Another advantage is that these accounts are portable. Once your account is fully vested (some employers require you to remain with the company a certain period before their contributions to your account become legally yours), you can take your account with you to your new employer, or you may roll the money over into your personal IRA (Individual Retirement Account). I always suggest rolling the money over into your own IRA. Why limit your investment alternatives to your new employer's plan when you can manage your IRA any way you wish?

There are, however, two big disadvantages to these kinds of retirement accounts. (And this is where the financial planning community will brand me a heretic.) The first disadvantage is that the plans are almost always invested through mutual funds. As I've explained earlier, industry wide, mutual funds have a deplorable track record against the mechanical market indices. And given that a retirement account is by definition long-term investment money, this is the kind of investment that should be aimed at top-quality growth. Yet the best option available to most retirement plans is a simple S&P 500 Index fund.

There are a few enlightened 401(k) plans that allow employees to manage their portfolios in individual stocks, but they represent a very small minority. It's more expensive to administer such a plan and most plan administrators simply don't know better, believing that mutual funds are their best alternative. So, check your plan's investment alternatives and demand they at least provide you with an Index fund choice. (That's a 500-stock basket so you could certainly put your entire account there and have all the diversity you'll need. Forget the models that tell you to put a little bit in every alternative. That's a recipe for guaranteed long-term underperformance.) And then lobby your plan administrator to provide the option for you to choose individual stocks for your account. Her money's in the plan, too, so teach her why it's in her best interests to do so.

Now because mutual funds are typically the only alternative in a 401(k) plan, I usually tell investors **not** to contribute to their accounts beyond the point where their employers stop matching their contributions. Let's face it, if your employer is giving you fifty cents on the dollar, that's free money and a guaranteed 50 percent return up front; you have to take advantage of that. But beyond that point the question becomes whether your next dollar (the first one that isn't matched by your employer) is better off in a tax-deferred account that doesn't perform particularly well over time or in a taxable account you can manage in individual stocks. In some cases it's a close call to make, but let's look at one comparison.

Nannette Number Cruncher has $2,000 to invest each year, over and above what she's already investing in her 401(k) plan at work (and beyond what her employer is matching). The employer won't match this additional $2,000. Nannette's two options are to contribute the extra $2,000 to her retirement plan at work on a pretax basis, which means, if she's lucky, putting it in her S&P 500 Index fund. Many 401(k) plans, as I've mentioned, offer a very poor-performing range of alternatives. Or she can take the $2,000, pay the income tax on it now (she's in the 28 percent tax bracket) and invest it in her taxable stock portfolio. That means she'll also pay an additional 20 percent tax on the capital gains each year (provided the stocks are held a full year and a day). If her index fund returns 11 percent a year and her stock portfolio (before taxes) returns 15 percent a year, which option is really the best one? (See Table 4.3.)

Let's look at the taxable stock portfolio alternative first. To invest the money here, Nannette first must pay the income tax on the $2,000. That leaves her just $1,440 of the total that she can actually put to work in her portfolio. In the first year, then, at a 15 percent return, that $1,440 earns her $216. The tax

TABLE 4.3 Taxable Stock Portfolio versus Tax-Deferred Index Fund

Year	Open	Deposit	Invested	Return	Gain	20% Taxes	Final	Open	Deposit	Invested	Return	Gain	Final
1	$ 0	$1,440	$1,440	15%	$ 216	$ 43	$ 1,613	$ 0	$2,000	$ 2,000	11%	$ 220	$ 2,220
2	1,613	1,440	3,053	15	458	92	3,419	2,220	2,000	4,220	11	464	4,684
3	3,419	1,440	4,859	15	729	146	5,442	4,684	2,000	6,684	11	735	7,419
4	5,442	1,440	6,882	15	1,032	206	7,708	7,419	2,000	9,419	11	1,036	10,456
5	7,708	1,440	9,148	15	1,372	274	10,246	10,456	2,000	12,456	11	1,370	13,826
6	10,246	1,440	11,686	15	1,753	351	13,088	13,826	2,000	15,826	11	1,741	17,567
7	13,088	1,440	14,528	15	2,179	436	16,272	17,567	2,000	19,567	11	2,152	21,719
8	16,272	1,440	17,712	15	2,657	531	19,837	21,719	2,000	23,719	11	2,609	26,328
9	19,837	1,440	21,277	15	3,192	638	23,830	26,328	2,000	28,328	11	3,116	31,444
10	23,830	1,440	25,270	15	3,791	758	28,303	31,444	2,000	33,444	11	3,679	37,123
11	28,303	1,440	29,743	15	4,461	892	33,312	37,123	2,000	39,123	11	4,304	43,426
12	33,312	1,440	34,752	15	5,213	1,043	38,922	43,426	2,000	45,426	11	4,997	50,423
13	38,922	1,440	40,362	15	6,054	1,211	45,205	50,423	2,000	52,423	11	5,767	58,190
14	45,205	1,440	46,645	15	6,997	1,399	52,243	58,190	2,000	60,190	11	6,621	66,811
15	52,243	1,440	53,683	15	8,052	1,610	60,125	66,811	2,000	68,811	11	7,569	76,380
16	60,125	1,440	61,565	15	9,235	1,847	68,952	76,380	2,000	78,380	11	8,622	87,002
17	68,952	1,440	70,392	15	10,559	2,112	78,840	87,002	2,000	89,002	11	9,790	98,792
18	78,840	1,440	80,280	15	12,042	2,408	89,913	98,792	2,000	100,792	11	11,087	111,879
19	89,913	1,440	91,353	15	13,703	2,741	102,316	111,879	2,000	113,879	11	12,527	126,406

20	102,316	1,440	103,756	15	15,563	3,113	116,206	126,406	2,000	128,406	11	14,125	142,530
21	116,206	1,440	117,646	15	17,647	3,529	131,764	142,530	2,000	144,530	11	15,898	160,429
22	131,764	1,440	133,204	15	19,981	3,996	149,188	160,429	2,000	162,429	11	17,867	180,296
23	149,188	1,440	150,628	15	22,594	4,519	168,704	180,296	2,000	182,296	11	20,053	202,348
24	168,704	1,440	170,144	15	25,522	5,104	190,561	202,348	2,000	204,348	11	22,478	226,827
25	190,561	1,440	192,001	15	28,800	5,760	215,041	226,827	2,000	228,827	11	25,171	253,998
26	215,041	1,440	216,481	15	32,472	6,494	242,459	253,998	2,000	255,998	11	28,160	284,157
27	242,459	1,440	243,899	15	36,585	7,317	273,166	284,157	2,000	286,157	11	31,477	317,635
28	273,166	1,440	274,606	15	41,191	8,238	307,559	317,635	2,000	319,635	11	35,160	354,794
29	307,559	1,440	308,999	15	46,350	9,270	346,079	354,794	2,000	356,794	11	39,247	396,042
30	346,079	1,440	347,519	15	52,128	10,426	389,221	396,042	2,000	398,042	11	43,785	441,826
31	389,221	1,440	390,661	15	58,599	11,720	437,541	441,826	2,000	443,826	11	48,821	492,647
32	437,541	1,440	438,981	15	65,847	13,169	491,658	492,647	2,000	494,647	11	54,411	549,058
33	491,658	1,440	493,098	15	73,965	14,793	552,270	549,058	2,000	551,058	11	60,616	611,675
34	552,270	1,440	553,710	15	83,057	16,611	620,155	611,675	2,000	613,675	11	67,504	681,179
35	620,155	1,440	621,595	15	93,239	18,648	696,187	681,179	2,000	683,179	11	75,150	758,329
36	696,187	1,440	697,627	15	104,644	20,929	781,342	758,329	2,000	760,329	11	83,636	843,965
37	781,342	1,440	782,782	15	117,417	23,483	876,716	843,965	2,000	845,965	11	93,056	939,021
38	876,716	1,440	878,156	15	131,723	26,345	983,535	939,021	2,000	941,021	11	103,512	1,044,533
39	983,535	1,440	984,975	15	147,746	29,549	1,103,172	1,044,533	2,000	1,046,533	11	115,119	1,161,652
40	1,103,172	1,440	1,104,612	15	165,692	33,138	**$1,237,165**	1,161,652	2,000	1,163,652	11	128,002	1,291,654

28% Taxes **$361,663**

Total **$929,991**

due on that gain (at the 20 percent long-term capital gains tax rate) is $43. That leaves Nannette a final value after the first year of $1,613. That's lower than the original $2,000 in income. This can't possibly be the smart way to go, can it? After all, she can put the entire $2,000 to work in her 401(k) plan and earn 11 percent a year!

Even though it sounds like a bad plan (and all the financial planners will tell you it is), humor me and follow the comparison all the way to the end. Each year Nannette continues to take the $2,000, pay the income taxes up front, and then invest the remaining $1,440 in her taxable stock portfolio, earning 15 percent a year. And on the gains each year, she pays an additional 20 percent in capital gains taxes.

By the end of year 20, Nannette's taxable stock portfolio will have grown to $116,206. After 30 years, it will reach a level of $389,221. And after 40 years, Nannette's portfolio value will be $1,237,165. Keep in mind that this value is after all taxes have been paid.

Now let's look at Nannette's other alternative. If she decides to contribute this money to her 401(k) plan, the entire $2,000 goes into her S&P 500 Index fund (as pretax money), so the entire amount goes to work right away. In addition, Nannette would get another advantage in that the 401(k) account continues to grow tax-deferred, so she's not paying that 20 percent tax on the profits each year she had to shell out from her taxable portfolio.

In year one, then, she adds her first $2,000, it grows by 11 percent, and she ends the year with $2,220. (If you recall, her taxable portfolio ended the first year with only $1,613.) Each year she adds another $2,000 in pretax money, and the entire portfolio grows tax-deferred at another 11 percent. After 20 years in this plan, Nannette has $142,530 instead of $116,206 in the taxable portfolio. After 30 years, the total has grown to $441,826 instead of $389,221. And after the full 40 years,

Nannette's 401(k) contributions will have grown to $1,291,654, compared to $1,237,165 in the taxable stock portfolio.

Even accepting a lower rate of return, then (11 percent in the index fund, as opposed to 15 percent in her own stock portfolio), Nannette has come out better in the long run by choosing the tax-deferred 401(k) plan, right? That's what too many financial planners believe, anyway. But what have we failed to account for in the 401(k) plan as of yet? That's right—taxes. These retirement plans are not tax free; they're simply tax-deferred. At the end of the game, when you pull your money out, *the entire amount* in the account is taxable income. You never paid any income taxes on this money when you began investing it so not only the original income in now taxable but the entire growth is taxable as well. And what's more, it is taxable as *ordinary income* rather than capital gains income, which is taxed less heavily. So in fact, the tax-deferred option takes back the supposed tax break it gives you in the beginning by taxing the growth at a higher level on the back end. Nice, huh?

So while Nannette's position in the index fund is now worth $1,291,654, she still owes 28 percent of that entire amount to Uncle Sam. Her real net worth in the index fund is only $929,991. That's actually over $300,000 **less** than she would have accumulated by paying the double taxes each year (income taxes up front and capital gains taxes on each profit) and getting the money into a better-performing investment vehicle (a stock portfolio that she can manage herself).

The point of all this is that, like a mutual fund, the theory behind a 401(k) plan is better than its actual worth. When more than four out of five actively managed stock mutual funds lose to the totally mechanical S&P 500 Index, and as long as mutual funds are your only option in a 401(k) or 403(b) plan, you know there's got to be a better alternative out there somewhere. That's why I only recommend contributing to such a retirement plan up to the point where your employer ceases to match your contributions. Don't pass up that kind of free money, but don't invest a penny more than that into a weak investment alternative just on the promise that it's a better tax situation. Americans will too often cut off their noses to spite their faces. That is, they'll turn down a better after-tax return just because they think the other alternative will save them some taxes. And it will; but what's more important to you—how much you pay in total taxes or how much you have left after paying all of your taxes? If it's the latter, a good taxable stock portfolio will typically outperform a tax-deferred mutual fund account, even though it means you're paying far more in total taxes (much to the financial community's chagrin).

Now that I've crawled out on a limb in suggesting that 401(k) plans are not all they're cracked up to be, let me build a slight support under my precarious perch. In other words, there is one very good exception to my suggested rule. Because 401(k) and 403(b) plans are portable, if you change jobs fairly frequently, you may well be better off plowing as much as you are allowed into your 401(k) plan, even beyond the point where your employer stops matching your contributions. The reason for this is that when you do leave your employer, you can then roll over that entire 401(k) plan into your own Individual Retirement Account (IRA) and manage the money directly in individual stocks. That way you get the best of both worlds—tax-deferred growth and the power of an individual stock strategy. In the short run while in the 401(k) plan, you'll at least keep pace with the index in the index mutual fund even though you could get better returns on your own, but then once you leave that company and roll the money into your own IRA you will enjoy better returns and long-term tax-deferred growth. For executives who change companies frequently, this is one way to amass a large individual portfolio fairly quickly.

I stand by my original contention, though: if you expect to be with the same company a long time and are participating in its 401(k) or 403(b) plan, your additional investment dollars are better served in your own taxable portfolio rather than in its tax-deferred mutual funds.

Individual Retirement Accounts

I was a little unfair in stacking the deck a few moments ago. Nannette actually has a third alternative for that extra $2,000 in addition to her 401(k) plan or her taxable portfolio, and in fact, it's the alternative I think she should choose. I omitted it until now to demonstrate the weaknesses of 401(k) plans in certain circumstances. But the alternative Nannette can and should also take advantage of is an Individual Retirement Account (IRA). Technically, these plans are called Individual Retirement *Arrangements,* but since no one calls them that, I won't bother either.

The range of IRA possibilities has expanded in recent years, but let's start with the traditional IRA. Like a 401(k) plan, an IRA allows you to save money you've earned before you pay income taxes on it (pretax money). Each year you may save up to a maximum of $2,000 of your earned income. The actual amount you're able to take a tax deduction for depends on your income level and whether you also participate in a retirement plan at work. (This is one issue where you are best served meeting with an accountant who understand all of the latest tax laws. A CPA will be able to tell you how much you're entitled to contribute and whether you're allowed to take a tax deduction for it.)

Also like a 401(k), the traditional IRA account remains tax-deferred until you begin to pull money out after you reach age 59½. One big advantage of an IRA over a 401(k) plan, however, is that you may manage the money any way you see fit. You aren't stuck with whatever alternatives your employer chooses for you. You can stick it in the bank in a certificate of deposit (*don't* do it); you can invest it in mutual funds (again, *don't* do it); or you can even set up your own self-directed IRA at your favorite broker and manage a stock portfolio (ding, ding, ding, we have a winner!). Because the IRA is a tax-deferred vehicle, your portfolio grows unchecked for decades, and using a powerful stock strategy, this can lead to tremendous gains over the years.

That said, there are two drawbacks to the traditional IRA. Just as with the 401(k) plan, when you begin withdrawing money from your account, the entire balance is taxable as ordinary income, which is always taxed at a higher rate than are long-term capital gains. So even though you've deferred taxes, they're still waiting to bite you in the end. Also, Congress has seriously dropped the ball in not increasing over the years the amount one can invest in an IRA. That $2,000 wedge gets smaller and smaller in importance each year after inflation nibbles away at it. If our government was genuinely interested in seeing Americans saving more for their own financial independence, they'd start rewarding saving rather than penalizing it. (I know; you didn't show up for a sermon. Back to IRAs.)

A second type of "traditional" IRA is simply the Rollover IRA you set up when you leave an employer and move your 401(k) plan into an account you're then responsible for managing. As I mentioned earlier, this is a great way to gain control of a larger asset pool. Every time you change jobs, don't move that 401(k) account to your new employer's plan; roll it into your own IRA account and manage the money yourself. Like the traditional IRA, this is pretax money, so you'll pay ordinary income tax rates on the withdrawals you may begin making at age 59½.

The newest incarnation of the IRA is the only one I genuinely find exciting. The Roth IRA is different from traditional IRAs in that the money you invest each year (still a maximum of $2,000 of earned income) does not go into the account as pretax money. You will pay the income taxes on that money up front, just as with any other income. How can that be an advantage? The kicker is that from the moment you invest in your Roth IRA, the investment is completely tax free. No, not tax-deferred like the other IRAs, but tax *free*. So when you start pulling money out after age 59½, there's no tax bite waiting for you. You've already paid the income tax on the money you've deposited, and the growth is a bonus. By far, this is the best IRA deal in town.

In fact, most people are discovering that they will be better off converting their traditional IRAs over into Roth IRAs, even though it means paying the built-up tax liability all at once right now. This is especially true if your traditional IRA is relatively small or if you're still relatively far away from the age where you'll begin making withdrawals. The beauty of the Roth IRA is that the growth is also tax free, which really allows the power of compounding to work unchecked.

Do you remember Conscientious Carl and Party Paul (see Table 4.1.)? If they started their $2,000 annual deposits into a Roth IRA account at age 23 and continued making similar deposits for 37 years, imagine what they could have amassed. Alright, you don't even have to imagine it; here are the details (see Table 4.4). At a growth rate of 15 percent a year, their Roth IRAs would have accumulated $2,685,244 in *completely tax-free wealth!* Now it's true that inflation will reduce the actual buying power of that $2.7 million, but we're only talking about a single aspect of their savings plans. We haven't touched their 401(k) plans or their regular taxable savings. This is just from the growth of $166.67 a month over many years in a tax-free Roth IRA.

For those of you who are self-employed, the best vehicle is a SEP-IRA. Like traditional IRAs, SEP-IRAs work on a pretax

TABLE 4.4   *Roth IRA Savings*

Year	IRA Deposit	15% Gain
1	$2,000	$ 2,300
2	2,000	4,945
3	2,000	7,987
4	2,000	11,485
5	2,000	15,507
6	2,000	20,134
7	2,000	25,454
8	2,000	31,572
9	2,000	38,607
10	2,000	46,699
11	2,000	56,003
12	2,000	66,704
13	2,000	79,009
14	2,000	93,161
15	2,000	109,435
16	2,000	128,150
17	2,000	149,673
18	2,000	174,424
19	2,000	202,887
20	2,000	235,620
21	2,000	273,263
22	2,000	316,553
23	2,000	366,336
24	2,000	423,586
25	2,000	489,424
26	2,000	565,138
27	2,000	652,208
28	2,000	752,339
29	2,000	867,490
30	2,000	999,914
31	2,000	1,152,201
32	2,000	1,327,331
33	2,000	1,528,731
34	2,000	1,760,340
35	2,000	2,026,691
36	2,000	2,332,995
37	2,000	2,685,244

deposit system, allowing the self-employed to deposit money before paying income taxes on it and then allowing it to grow tax-deferred until withdrawal after age 59½. But since the self-employed aren't involved in employer-sponsored 401(k) plans, they're not subject to the $2,000 annual limitation on deposits. Rather, a participant in a SEP-IRA can deposit up to 13.04 percent of his or her self-employment earnings, less half of his or her self-employment tax (Social Security tax). There is a maximum dollar limit (currently in the neighborhood of $25,000), which rises each year with inflation. For the self-employed, it's crucial to take advantage of the full extent of the SEP-IRA contributions. When you leave the company, you won't have the same 401(k) account sitting there that a traditional employee will have. You've taken the responsibility of building your own career, but that carries an added responsibility (more an opportunity really) of building your own retirement plan as well.

And finally, let's talk about the new Education IRA. Under the rules of this plan, you can save up to $500 a year for your child's tuition. While you don't get a tax deduction for this investment, it does grow tax free. Unfortunately, $500 a year isn't an awful lot. Still, as a tax-free investment, it's not a bad start. If you invest $500 the day your child is born and another $500 each birthday (earning 15 percent a year in growth), your child would have over $43,000 with which to begin college. That's not going to pay for an Ivy League degree, but it'll cover a year or two or even most of a state college plan—not a shabby beginning. Anything not used by your child can be transferred to another child's account, or when your child reaches age 30, a distribution of any remaining money will be made (and some taxes will be due).

There you have the major individual retirement accounts available to you. In any long-term plan toward financial independence, you have to look at these alternatives as part of your strategy. While there are limitations to the plans (limits on the amount you can deposit, age restrictions on withdrawals, back-end taxes on tax-deferred plans), they are nevertheless a very good way of building your assets for your own private foundation. Don't ignore them.

What's Left?

That covers everything, doesn't it? Well, actually no. A large part of your overall savings plan will ultimately end up in plain old taxable accounts. When you're first starting out, most of your savings will undoubtedly go toward tax-advantaged accounts. But as you begin earning more and more in your career, you will quickly reach the limits of what you're allowed to deposit in these tax-advantaged accounts—but by no means does that mean you should stop saving there.

The rest (and in many cases, the bulk) of your savings will go into a stock brokerage account that you manage directly. True, you will already have paid income taxes on this money. True, you will pay additional income taxes on any dividends or capital gains you earn (can you say double and triple taxation?), but there's no way around it. If you plan to become financially independent, you'll have to save quite a large portfolio. And if you plan on becoming independent before you can begin withdrawing funds from your government-regulated retirement accounts (at age 59½), you'll have to pay for your annual spending, at least for some time, from a taxable portfolio.

The Savings Lineup

By way of review, let's look at how a typical married couple might set up their savings plan. Jeremy and Cheryl earn a combined pretax salary of $140,000. How should they go about planning their savings?

- **401(k) plans.** The first line of their savings plan should be their company-sponsored 401(k) plans. In their cases, the company requires them to invest 5 percent of their salaries and then matches that amount with an additional 50 cents on the dollar. So Jeremy and Cheryl are saving $7,000 a year in an S&P 500 Index fund through work, and their employers are kicking in an additional $3,500. But at the point where their employer stops contributing, so do Jeremy and Cheryl.

- **Roth IRAs.** Since Jeremy and Cheryl make a combined salary of less than $150,000 ($95,000 if you are single), they qualify for a full contribution to a Roth IRA. So the first $2,000 of each of their take-home checks should go into a Roth IRA account. Remember that the 401(k) money comes out of your salary before you or the tax man ever see it. The Roth IRA deposits are after-tax money you must deposit out of your paychecks.

- **Taxable Portfolios.** Everything else Jeremy and Cheryl save for their financial independence should go directly into their taxable stock portfolio. If you remember the primary rule of savings (Pay Yourself First), they should be putting at least 10 percent of their take-home pay into their private foundation savings. This doesn't include the 401(k) money that comes out before they see it. So if they make $140,000, and $7,000 of that goes into their 401(k) plan, they'll pay income taxes on the remaining $133,000. Let's estimate that one-third of that total is withheld for taxes and Social Security. That would leave them a take-home amount of approximately $89,000 per year. Their total savings into their private foundation accounts, then, should be just under $9,000 a year. With $4,000 already spoken for in their two Roth IRA accounts, that means another $5,000 a year should get deposited into their taxable stock portfolio.

Are you ready for something amazing? Even if Jeremy and Cheryl never get a raise (and how likely is that?), look how their current savings plan would provide for their financial independence. (See Table 4.5.) In the first part of their

TABLE 4.5 Jeremy and Cheryl's Three-Part Savings Plan

Year	401(k) Savings			Roth IRA Savings			Taxable Stock Portfolio Savings				
	Open	401(k)	11% Gain	Open	Roth IRA	15% Gain	Open	Taxable	15% Gain	20% Tax	Final
1	$ 0	$10,500	$11,655	$ 0	$4,000	$ 4,600	$ 0	$5,000	$ 750	($150)	$ 5,600
2	11,655	10,500	24,592	4,600	4,000	9,890	5,600	5,000	1,590	(318)	11,872
3	24,592	10,500	38,952	9,890	4,000	15,974	11,872	5,000	2,531	(506)	18,897
4	38,952	10,500	54,892	15,974	4,000	22,970	18,897	5,000	3,584	(717)	26,764
5	54,892	10,500	72,585	22,970	4,000	31,015	26,764	5,000	4,765	(953)	35,576
6	72,585	10,500	92,224	31,015	4,000	40,267	35,576	5,000	6,086	(1,217)	45,445
7	92,224	10,500	114,024	40,267	4,000	50,907	45,445	5,000	7,567	(1,513)	56,498
8	114,024	10,500	138,222	50,907	4,000	63,143	56,498	5,000	9,225	(1,845)	68,878
9	138,222	10,500	165,081	63,143	4,000	77,215	68,878	5,000	11,082	(2,216)	82,744
10	165,081	10,500	194,895	77,215	4,000	93,397	82,744	5,000	13,162	(2,632)	98,273
11	194,895	10,500	227,988	93,397	4,000	112,007	98,273	5,000	15,491	(3,098)	115,666
12	227,988	10,500	264,722	112,007	4,000	133,408	115,666	5,000	18,100	(3,620)	135,146
13	264,722	10,500	305,497	133,408	4,000	158,019	135,146	5,000	21,022	(4,204)	156,963
14	305,497	10,500	350,756	158,019	4,000	186,322	156,963	5,000	24,294	(4,859)	181,399
15	350,756	10,500	400,994	186,322	4,000	218,870	181,399	5,000	27,960	(5,592)	208,766
16	400,994	10,500	456,759	218,870	4,000	256,300	208,766	5,000	32,065	(6,413)	239,418
17	456,759	10,500	518,657	256,300	4,000	299,345	239,418	5,000	36,663	(7,333)	273,749
18	518,657	10,500	587,365	299,345	4,000	348,847	273,749	5,000	41,812	(8,362)	312,198

Year	401(k) plan			Roth IRA Accounts			Taxable Stock Portfolio				
19	587,365	10,500	663,630	348,847	4,000	405,774	312,198	5,000	47,580	(9,516)	355,262
20	663,630	10,500	748,284	405,774	4,000	471,240	355,262	5,000	54,039	(10,808)	403,494
21	748,284	10,500	842,250	471,240	4,000	546,527	403,494	5,000	61,274	(12,255)	457,513
22	842,250	10,500	946,553	546,527	4,000	633,106	457,513	5,000	69,377	(13,875)	518,014
23	946,553	10,500	1,062,329	633,106	4,000	732,671	518,014	5,000	78,452	(15,690)	585,776
24	1,062,329	10,500	1,190,840	732,671	4,000	847,172	585,776	5,000	88,616	(17,723)	661,669
25	1,190,840	10,500	1,333,487	847,172	4,000	978,848	661,669	5,000	100,000	(20,000)	746,670
26	1,333,487	10,500	1,491,826	978,848	4,000	1,130,275	746,670	5,000	112,750	(22,550)	841,870
27	1,491,826	10,500	1,667,582	1,130,275	4,000	1,304,416	841,870	5,000	127,031	(25,406)	948,494
28	1,667,582	10,500	1,862,670	1,304,416	4,000	1,504,679	948,494	5,000	143,024	(28,605)	1,067,914
29	1,862,670	10,500	2,079,219	1,504,679	4,000	1,734,981	1,067,914	5,000	160,937	(32,187)	1,201,663
30	2,079,219	10,500	2,319,588	1,734,981	4,000	1,999,828	1,201,663	5,000	181,000	(36,200)	1,351,463
Tax due		28%	$649,485		0%	$0				0%	$0
Net Total			$1,670,104			$1,999,828					$1,351,463

Combined Total After Taxes

401(k) plan	$1,670,104
Roth IRA Accounts	$1,999,828
Taxable Stock Portfolio	$1,351,463
Grand Total	$5,021,394

three-part savings strategy, they're depositing $7,000 a year into their 401(k) plan and their employer deposits another $3,500. So $10,500 goes into an S&P 500 Index fund every year. If we assume an 11 percent annual return (the average return for large-company stocks over the past seven decades), that schedule of deposits will grow to $2,319,588 after 30 years. They still owe income taxes on the whole account since this is all pretax money, however, so let's reduce that total amount by 28 percent and their 401(k) plan's actual net worth is $1,670,104.

In the second part of their plan, Jeremy and Cheryl deposit another $4,000 a year into their Roth IRAs. Assuming their privately managed stock portfolio averages 15 percent a year growth, this annual savings amount will grow to $1,999,828 after 30 years. Keep in mind that this account grows completely tax free, since the $2,000 they invest every year is after-tax money, and thus the whole $2 million is theirs.

And their excess savings from their 10 percent Pay Yourself First withdrawal ($5,000 a year) goes into a taxable portfolio. If this privately managed stock portfolio also grows at 15 percent a year, and then Jeremy and Cheryl pay 20 percent long-term capital gains taxes on each year's profit, the account will grow to $1,351,463 over 30 years. Again, because it's a taxable account and they pay that bite each year, there's no big tax liability waiting for them at the end.

Altogether then, after 30 years, Jeremy and Cheryl have an after-tax private foundation worth $5,021,394! That's a portfolio large enough to generate a quarter of a million in annual income for them, using the 5 percent guide from the Money for Life plan. That's an income 79 percent larger than what their employer was paying them. And this whole scenario is assuming that their salaries never increase. Imagine how much stronger their portfolio would be with a more realistic picture of regular salary increases, which naturally would increase the amount they would be able to save as well!

It really is that simple. Max out the useful portions of your tax-advantaged accounts first, and then everything else goes into your taxable portfolio. In your 401(k) plan, opt for an S&P 500 Index fund if none of the other options affords you a history of market-beating returns. In your IRAs and taxable accounts, manage your own portfolios of common stocks. Forget about all the other savings vehicles out there competing for your money. These are the most efficient and the easiest for you to control.

In the next chapter, I'll continue my discussion of several other basic financial planning topics you should understand as you're building the strategies for your own private foundation. As exciting as the prospect of watching one's savings accounts bloom can be, some of the more mundane aspects of personal finance are extremely important. Let's get all the basics covered once and for all, and then you can get on to the real fun—wealth creation.

5

THE NEW SCHOOL OF FINANCIAL PLANNING

In Chapter Four I covered what I consider the fun stuff. I've always been a compounding junkie and when I wrote for The Motley Fool, that was undoubtedly my favorite column topic. It never ceases to amaze me how time can transform fairly small amounts of money into incredible wealth. I hope the examples in the past few chapters have turned your head, too. But now, you'll be saddened to learn, we have to spend time on the gloomier side of financial planning. It's time to talk about responsibility, protection, and preparation for our deaths. Cheery, huh? Not unless you're a mortician, I suppose, but nevertheless this is one area of financial planning too many people put off because they simply don't want to think about it. Don't put it off any longer. Get it done correctly now, while you're still motivated to straighten out your financial life, and then put this part on cruise control and enjoy watching the growth of your private foundation accounts.

Wills

Whether we like to discuss personal topics or not, we have to, at least for a while. Face the facts; we will all die, and too many of us, perhaps, will die sooner than we expect to. If you have family or friends that you wish to receive your assets when you die, or if you have minor children, you better get a will drawn up. It's that simple. Every adult with anything to his or her name and with responsibilities to his or her family should have a will. Otherwise you're giving over control of your assets, and perhaps even the custody of your children, to someone else who doesn't even know you or care about your personal wishes—namely your state government. And if that happens, it's no one's fault but your own. Don't let it happen to your family.

What happens to your assets if you die *intestate*, that is, without a valid will? It varies from state to state, which is one reason the process seems so confusing to most people, but the first thing that happens is that your wishes, even if they're very well known to those people closest to you, become immaterial. Each state has very rigid laws determining how estates will get distributed in the absence of a will. You might assume that all of your assets will automatically go to your spouse, but that may not be the case in your state. In fact, it may turn out that first the assets are frozen while the government wheels begin to grind very slowly, and then a large portion of your estate may ultimately be split among your children. If you intended for your spouse to have control over your entire pool of assets for the remainder of his or her life, the state won't care. If you don't have a will, the money goes where the state says it must.

Do you need a will if you're single? Absolutely. You may want to leave whatever assets you have to siblings or to charities, yet if you don't have a will the state's guidelines might grant your entire estate to your parents whether they need the money or not. Any number of unintended consequences can result if you leave your affairs up to the state to settle, and that's precisely what you're doing if you fail to have a will prepared.

We like to think we'll all live to some cheerful old age and that we can put off thinking about our estates and custodial care for our children until some future date, but that's exactly the wrong attitude. Part of this procrastination is probably because it's natural to feel uncomfortable talking about ourselves in the past tense, but I'm convinced it's equally a result of the average citizen's lack of understanding of the laws and of any process requiring an attorney. And as bad a reputation as attorneys have acquired in recent decades (deserved or not), some things are best handled by them. In many cases, this is true for your will.

Let's look at some of the topics your will can and should cover. The most obvious item is how you wish your assets distributed (once your debts have been paid off). You may have an extensive list of charities to which you wish to leave bequests. You may have some unusual splits among your spouse and children. Each such bequest must be itemized specifically in your will. It doesn't matter that everyone in your home has heard you say for years that you're going to leave the cotton farm to your grandson Jimmy. If it's not in your will, there's going to be a legal squabble about it when you die. It doesn't matter that you've disowned your good-for-nothing fifth son; if you don't leave a will specifically accounting for your assets, he will receive whatever share of your assets the state determines should go to each child. So be specific in your will. Verbal plans don't mean a thing once you're gone.

Another vital element to include in your will is the name of your minor children's legal guardian. This is a dreadfully

tough decision for many people because the thought of someone else rearing our children sends shivers up our spines.
(For most of us the shivers are because we don't want to miss
our children's lives, but in some cases they may be the result
of imagining certain people as guardians. Choose wisely.) It's
also difficult to talk about because you have to discuss your
own death and wishes with the potential guardian before you
write it into your will. Don't surprise someone if you die prematurely and he's finding out at your funeral that you've
named him the guardian and you've never even discussed it
with him! Have the tough conversation now and then hope
it's never an issue, but don't just hope it's never an issue and
not bother to prepare for it. This whole chapter is about
responsibility, remember?

It's not unusual to name a relative as your children's potential guardian, but one factor you should consider is that it's
often a good idea only to name one person as the actual
guardian, not a couple. For example, let's say that in the event
of your death you would want your brother and his wife to
become the guardians of your children. What happens if two
or three years later they divorce? Do you want your children to
be subject to a custody hearing on top of all the other traumas
they would have to experience? Of course not. So bypass
that particular eventuality and name just one person as the
guardian, even if your choice is happily married. That way it's
clear where your children go should something happen to
your brother's marriage down the road. If nothing so dramatic
occurs, no harm's been done. Again, you're not going to play
the odds here and assume nothing will go wrong; you have to
plan for the worst-case scenario in the unlikely event it really
happens. It's all about thinking through the options carefully
and covering every possible outcome you can imagine.

It's also generally not a good idea to name your own parents as your children's guardians unless they are the only rea-

sonable choice. Whether we (or they) like it or not, age is a factor, and as most grandparents will tell you, a weekend with the grandkids is enough to wear them out. While the grandparents can obviously be a great resource for experience and unbridled devotion, they may not be the best choice for full-time parental responsibility, especially for very young children. Better to name someone who is your contemporary if possible, and let the grandparents be the heroic saviors who sweep in occasionally to help out.

At this point, then, you've specified everyone you're leaving assets to, and you've named your children's guardian. Now it is time to consider financial arrangements for your children. It's a good idea in most cases not to name the same person as guardian and financial custodian for your child. It's not that you don't trust the person you've named to care for your children with their money as well, but as a safeguard, naming a different financial custodian removes all temptation. So name someone else—an attorney, a financial advisor, a banker, a godparent, whomever you trust financially—as the custodian of your children's finances and make known to them your wishes about issues like college, how you would like their money invested, and so on. If you were well insured and died without a great deal of debt, your children may have a large amount of money coming to them for their support over the years. It's important that the money is really used in their best interests. And we've all read the Harry Potter books where poor Harry is relegated to the cupboard under the stairs by his aunt and uncle when Harry is thrust into their lives upon his parents' deaths. You can't control what people will do once you're gone, but by putting in some safeguards now, you can try to protect your wishes for your children.

Your will may also include a document called a living will, which declares your wishes about being kept alive on life-support systems. As with your actual will, laws will vary from state to state, and if you don't have the right documents, your hospital may not abide by your known wishes. Draw up all the details long ahead of time and review them periodically if your wishes change. It's also a good idea to include a letter with your will, outlining your wishes about things like memorial services, burial or cremation, and cemetery choice. While such a letter doesn't legally bind anyone to follow your wishes, it is a very tangible reminder of what you would have chosen for yourself. Funeral arrangements are often bungled because the people closest to you are asked to make very difficult decisions quickly at a time of great emotional stress. You can eliminate a lot of that stress, future regret, and wasted money for your family and friends if you make your specific wishes known.

A few final words about wills, and then we'll go onto another cheery subject: insurance. There exist today a number of companies who prepackage legal forms (including wills and living wills) for you to complete without the assistance of an attorney. And while I'm a firm believer in doing what you can to make your own decisions and control your own life, the do-it-yourself forms have a very limited use. Only the most straightforward, uncomplicated situations can be handled adequately by these templates. If there's anything at all out of the ordinary in your situation, or if your estate is of even average complexity, it's worth the couple of hundred dollars that's required to have an attorney draw up your will. Having done it countless times in the past, your attorney can foresee situations that would never occur to you and will know how to couch the language in the document to represent your actual wishes. So have a lawyer do your will and then leave a copy of it on file with the attorney's office; a will is no good to your heirs if no one can find it when you die.

I'd like to say that once you draw up your will, you're done with it forever—but alas, it's a document you'll undoubtedly need or want to change over the years. Your wishes about bequests will change as your estate changes. You'll need to update it when you have additional children or divorce, or remarry, or when your children are no longer minors. It's wise to review your will once a year or so, and have your attorney make any necessary changes.

I am certainly not an estate attorney, and the laws regarding the taxation of estates seem to change every month. So right up front, let me advise you to consult an estate attorney and your CPA if you have a fairly large and/or complex estate, so that they can help you set up your affairs in the way that's most beneficial to you and your heirs upon your death. I will, however, mention one such estate planning vehicle that's growing in popularity in recent years—the *revocable living trust.* This type of trust is often set up in conjunction with a will, but in some cases it can even take the place of a will. It allows you to retain control of your assets while alive, but you can designate to whom and when the assets will pass to someone else (even before you die). Such trusts are very flexible, and they allow you to bypass the probate process, which is typically very slow and sometimes very costly. The downside is that these trusts can be expensive to set up and incur ongoing maintenance costs. For complicated or large estates, however, a revocable living trust may be a good alternative. Again, spend time with your attorney and set up your estate planning right.

Insurance

I've undoubtedly tweaked a few noses in my time with my complaints about the mutual fund industry and about the financial planners who preach diversity and ignore performance. So it's time to change targets and tweak a few more noses, this time in the insurance industry.

Like the investment industry (and insurance companies love to cross over into investments), the insurance industry makes itself more and more complex every year. And the more complex it becomes, the more likely it is that the customer is going to end up spending a lot of money on a product he or she doesn't really want or need. Let's look at the kinds of insurance you should have—and equally important, let's also examine the insurance products you should avoid.

Health Insurance

If you're breathing today, you need health insurance. Period. The cost of medical care in America is astronomical. We've all heard tales of overnight hospital stays costing thousands of dollars, with five-dollar Tylenols and airline food at five-star prices. Even a short stay in the hospital and a modest surgical procedure can wipe out a fair chunk of your private foundation if you have to foot those bills yourself.

Health insurance comes in so many varieties these days that an entire book can be written (and has been, several times) about its complexities. So I'm not going to attempt even a superficial treatment of the possibilities here. All I will say is make sure you and your family members stay covered at all times, and don't let those premiums lapse. If you're without coverage for as much as a day, beside the obvious risk that that day will be the one when you get hurt or fall ill, there's also a risk that you can wipe out much of your coverage for the next year or so as well. For example, many insurance companies will not cover any preexisting conditions for one full year after you begin a policy with them unless you've had continuous coverage with another insurer for the previous entire year.

I ran into that very barrier when I moved recently from Kentucky to North Carolina. As a diabetic, I require prescriptions costing several hundred dollars per month, and I have to visit an endocrinologist every few months for laboratory tests and an ophthalmologist at least once a year to check for diabetes-related eye damage. If I had fallen out of coverage with my Kentucky carrier for even a single day before Blue Cross and Blue Shield of North Carolina began my coverage, I would not have been covered for any of my diabetes-related physician visits or prescriptions for a full year. Fortunately, I maintained my coverage in Kentucky until my policy in North Carolina picked me up and the standard waiting period was waived. Otherwise it would have cost me thousands of dollars over the next year.

What type of plan you choose is partially up to you. Many people are covered through employer-sponsored plans and often cover their family members in the same plan as well. Since your employer is likely to pay part or all of your coverage costs, that's not a bad idea. But you'll probably end up picking up the tab for your dependants. If you're self-employed, however, you'll need to shop around for your own policy. Assuming you're reasonably healthy, you shouldn't have any trouble becoming covered. What you'll have to decide, however, is the kind of deductible plan you want to work with. Most policies will offer you a range of deductibles that you pay each year as you require care before the insurance company starts picking up the excess charges. The larger the deductible you opt for, the lower your regular insurance premiums will be.

Deciding what's right for you is a bit of a guessing game, of course. But in general, if you're healthy, choosing a higher deductible will save you money because your premiums are lower. If you have a year, however, where you require more medical care than is typical for you, paying that higher deductible eats up whatever you saved in premiums and then some. I generally opt for the higher deductible and assume I'm going to be paying some out-of-pocket expenses throughout the year. The major thing you want to protect against is a catastrophic illness that can run up bills in the hundreds of thousands of dollars. No one can budget for that kind of contingency, and insurance is an absolute necessity to survive such an illness financially. Don't skimp on this type of insurance; you need it.

Auto and Homeowner's Insurance

This is another area where insurance is mandatory. If you have a mortgage on your home, your lender is going to require that you carry adequate homeowner's insurance. That doesn't mean, however, that you carry enough insurance to buy your home all over again. Included in any home's purchase price is an amount for the land, which your policy doesn't insure. But you'll need sufficient coverage to have your home rebuilt in case of a devastating fire or other natural disaster. These policies differ in every region of the country because of the different risks associated with hurricanes, flooding, tornados, earthquakes, and the like. In most cases, you'll want to consider a policy where the value increases with inflation so that your home will be replaced even though the value is now higher than when you purchased or built it. So-called replacement-cost policies are fairly standard today. The same applies, of course, to your home's contents. Get a policy that will replace the items at today's values, not what you paid for them 5, 10, or 20 years ago. Homeowner's insurance is remarkably inexpensive, especially when you set it next to the cost of health insurance, so cover yourself carefully and fully. Another issue to ask your insurer about is basic liability insurance, which can often be tied right into your home-owner's policy. If you are sued and lose a large judgment, a fairly inexpensive umbrella liability policy will rescue you.

If you don't own your home, obviously you're not responsible for replacing the building after a catastrophe, but you still need renter's insurance to cover your possessions. Too many young people in apartments go without such coverage and suffer losses they can't afford to replace simply to save on the small renter's insurance premiums each month. It's not worth that gamble. You're actually at greater risk for a loss in an apartment than someone in a single-family home because of the number of people living in a single building. Your neighbors can do something stupid and burn down the whole building and you still lose.

Auto insurance is also fairly basic. You need to cover yourself in case you cause an accident and wreck not only your car but someone else's. You need to cover yourself in case someone else with inadequate insurance wrecks your car. And you need to have coverage for medical and legal costs that might arise from an accident. Again, state laws will dictate your minimum coverage. And you'll be able to choose from a range of deductibles. One small way you can save on car insurance in addition to choosing a higher deductible is to reduce the amount of coverage on your own vehicle as the car ages. You don't want to lower your liability coverage since you don't know whether your accident will be with a 1979 Gremlin or a 1999 Porsche, but if you're driving a 10-year-old beater that's only worth $800, there's no sense covering it against your own mishaps as if it were a $25,000 beauty. My rule on all kinds of insurance is: Cover yourself adequately, but don't waste a penny on excessive insurance. Too many Americans have more insurance than they really need in some areas, and nowhere near enough in others.

Life Insurance

Life insurance is one of the big trouble areas in the insurance industry. It's the area where many people have too much of the wrong kind of insurance and not enough of the right kind. And each year, it seems, the industry comes out with yet another twist on the coverage to make the picture even murkier.

First of all, life insurance is not really life insurance at all; it's income insurance. A lot of "lives" simply do not need to be insured. Now don't take this personally. It has nothing to do with the intrinsic worth of any individual. It only has to do with one's financial needs. Let me explain.

The person who needs life insurance is one whose unexpected death would create a financial burden for others. For example, in a family of four with one working parent, if that parent dies prematurely, the financial security of the other three people is suddenly put in jeopardy. Life insurance is necessary to replace that individual's lost income until such time as the remaining parent can get an adequate job to take over the breadwinner's role. Life insurance shouldn't be intended to make your family wealthy for the rest of their lives. But it has to be sufficient to sustain your financial dependents until they can make up for that lost income on their own.

But let's look at some people for whom life insurance is unnecessary. Anyone who is financially independent already probably has no legitimate need for basic life insurance. (There are some exceptions to this rule in the case where life insurance is built into an elaborate estate-planning game where one is trying to avoid estate taxes and still pass along assets to heirs efficiently. But I'm talking about life insurance in its usual sense here.) If you're no longer working and are financially independent, what income do you need to replace through life insurance? Your assets presumably will go to the people you would want to protect anyway, and their continued growth protects that income. You don't need life insurance. You're self-insured through the power of your own assets. I'm amazed at how many elderly people who owe nothing, have no financial dependents, and no income to replace still send money to a life insurance company every month. It's wasted. If no one will suffer financially from your death, you don't need life insurance.

Single people who have no dependents typically don't need life insurance, either. While your family and friends will naturally be heartbroken should you die prematurely, they're not depending on your income for their own support, so no one is burdened financially by your loss of income. You don't need insurance.

And despite what most insurance salespeople will try to tell you, children typically do not need life insurance. Yes, we love our children dearly, but look at it strictly from a financial perspective. Children are not financial assets to us; they're financial burdens. Should we tragically lose a child, our financial positions are not going to be jeopardized, so there's no need for life insurance on a child who isn't contributing financially to the family. I realize that sounds cold and callous, but when it comes to insurance, you need to have a defense against a salesperson's best tool—their ability to play on your emotions. Don't get sucked into that game when planning insurance needs.

What about burial costs? Don't you need at least enough insurance to cover those costs? For a financially independent adult, absolutely not. His or her assets can easily pay the costs. If you feel it's absolutely necessary to insure your children for the cost of a potential burial, however, then go ahead. At least do it, though, by buying a very basic, low-cost term life insurance policy. (More on term versus whole-life policies later.) I would argue that for most people, a burial is the kind of expense your emergency fund can cover. And before I get flooded with e-mails, I'm aware that burial and funeral costs can easily run $10,000 or more, twice as much as I've said you need in the typical emergency fund. I don't want to go into a sermon on the funeral director industry, but I think what most people pay for these costs is outrageous. Whether you bury or cremate a loved one very simply or very lavishly, the amount of money you spend is not going to affect your memories of the lost family member or friend in the least. Spending thousands of extra dollars in a time of intense grief is a mistake many commit, but it's an understandable one. One other issue to remember about preparing for the possible loss of a child. You've undoubtedly been saving for your child's higher education over the years. That's another source of funds to cover the emergency of a burial rather than buying unnecessary insurance.

And second of all (I know, it's been a while since I said "first of all"), life insurance is **not** an investment. Forget all that you've heard from the multimillion-dollar marketing campaigns put forth by the big insurance companies; insurance is simply not a good investment. As I mentioned before, life insurance should be viewed as protection against the loss of income should you die prematurely, but it's not a vehicle for saving towards your financial independence.

There are two basic types of life insurance (with an unfortunate number of variations): *whole life* and *term life*. A whole-life policy combines basic life insurance (which pays out a prescribed amount of money at the insured's death) with an investment component. A portion of each premium is invested by the insurance company and builds up a cash value in the policy. The cash value continues to grow as the insurance company pays out regular dividends. Sounds great, doesn't it? Kills two birds with one stone ... sorry ... combines two useful issues in one regular payment.

The problem is that it's a lousy option. Insurance companies are notorious for the terrible-performing mutual fund investments that get tied to their policies. So as a real investment, insurance policies couldn't perform much worse. Even the tax-deferred annuities that planners push so frequently now, which again combine tax-deferred investments and insurance into a single product, are terrible options. First, they're invested through the same mutual funds that typically underperform the major market indices. Second, the insurance companies typically charge very high fees (in addition to the fees charged by the mutual funds) for managing the money, and third, you don't get nearly as much income insurance (life insurance) as you can by turning in a different direction. Even the tax-deferred status of the annuities doesn't help. As I showed in previous chapters, a tax-deferred index fund will often underperform a taxable stock portfolio that you can manage yourself. Now throw in a mutual fund that performs even worse than the index funds and that has high annuity fees as well, and you've got a horrible "investment."

What's the alternative? The only life insurance product that's really in the consumer's best interests is a simple renewable term life insurance policy. This is the basic, no-investment, no-cash-value, just-plain-insurance-on-your-actual-life policy. Term insurance is very inexpensive because nothing else gets rolled up into it. If you have a $500,000 term life policy, it only pays when you die. So it's the basic gamble on whether you'll die during the duration of your policy. The insurance company charges more for people who are older or in poor health and less on the young and healthy. There's no cash value building up in the policy. If you cancel it, you don't get a check from the insurance company for any dividends. But at the same time, you will pay very little for this policy. In terms of actual protection for your family against the loss of your income, a term policy is the only sensible alternative. Since I argue that only those people who are still working towards financial independence need life insurance anyway, the costs are minimal. By the time you're older and infirm, if you're following the plan laid out in *Money for Life,* insurance won't even be necessary for you.

Most insurance agents will try to convince you that they're helping you with a whole-life policy or a variable annuity, that they're forcing you to save by sending in your premium checks. One of my previous insurance agents actually told me he didn't think people had the discipline to save on their own so the insurance company was doing them a big favor. Believe me, the combination insurance/investment products are doing the *insurance companies* a big favor, not you.

The cost for term insurance is extremely affordable. For example, a 34-year-old male can buy a $500,000 policy with fixed premiums for the next 10 years for only $200 per year. If you want to guarantee your premiums remain the same for 15 years, the annual cost is only $230. (You can get a sample quotation from several insurers on the Internet at www.selectquote.com.)

If you are looking at insurance strictly as protection against the loss of income, term insurance makes perfect sense. If you were to try to cover your income adequately using a whole-life policy, you wouldn't be able to afford enough coverage because of the investment component the insurance companies throw in.

The ideal balance between insurance and investment is to buy a term policy for whatever amount of insurance you really need and then take the difference between what you're actually paying the insurance company and what you would have had to pay in a whole-life policy or in a variable annuity and invest that money in your own stock portfolio. Your insurance policy will be simpler and more adequate, your investments will be better, and once again, you'll be in control of your finances. Another advantage to term insurance is that you can change policies relatively easily. If you find a company offering a better deal for you (and right now term rates are extremely competitive), it's easy to cancel your old policy. Once your new policy is active, just drop a note to the old company and stop paying the premiums. Just make sure your new policy is in force before you cancel the old policy. Don't tempt fate.

And as you become financially independent, you simply cancel the unneeded policy. At some point, you won't have any debts, your children will be grown, and your own assets will provide adequate protection of income for your spouse against your death. You don't need life insurance then, so simply cancel the policy and spend that annual premium on something else. Insurance has been made way too complicated over the years, and consumers are just now learning enough about their own financial needs so that term insurance is becoming popular again. Buy term to cover your real need and invest the rest of your money the insurance company won't be getting from you.

How much life insurance do you need? The insurance industry wants you to buy anywhere from 5 to 10 times your annual salary. That may be plenty or not nearly enough, depending upon your situation. It's better to sit down with pencil and paper and figure out exactly what you want the insurance money to do rather than to follow such a guideline blindly. Let's look at an example. Suppose Ron and Darla are in their forties, have two teenage children, a $100,000 mortgage, and college tuition staring them in the face in a few years. Ron makes $80,000 a year, and Darla works part-time, earning $10,000. They have a private foundation account worth $200,000, Ron's 401(k) account worth $75,000, and college savings accounts for each child of $25,000. Let's look at how much coverage Ron and Darla should have.

If Ron were to die prematurely, that would cause the biggest financial burden since his salary makes up the vast majority of the household's income. So he's obviously going to need to carry a larger policy than will Darla. But in addition to replacing his income, a policy should also clear the couple's debts. Not having to worry about things like a mortgage can greatly reduce the stress for the family as they go through the traumatic transition after Ron dies. So up front, his policy should be at least $100,000 to pay off their mortgage. Next, it should include enough to get the children through college. Ron and Darla would have saved another $10,000 or so before the children began school, so with portfolio growth, figure another $15,000 each. Now we're up to $130,000. Figure in $10,000 or so for funeral expenses. The total's now $140,000.

With the house paid off, it won't be necessary to replace every penny of Ron's income, but Darla will probably still need the bulk of it for several years until the children are in college and she can catch up on some job training to reenter the workforce full time (if she chooses to). So let's assume she'll need $50,000 a year to replace Ron's lost income. To generate that kind of annual income, she would have to invest the proceeds and pull out an annual withdrawal, just as if she were financially independent and living on her private foundation growth. Since this withdrawal on insurance is only intended to be a temporary one (perhaps 3 to 5 years instead of 30 or 40), it's reasonable to assume Darla can pull 8 percent a year out of the insurance fund. So we need to calculate how much insurance money she'd need to invest to generate $50,000 at 8 percent a year. ($50,000 ÷ .08 = $625,000.)

That means Ron needs $625,000 in term insurance to replace the part of his income necessary for Darla and the kids to maintain their lifestyles for at least three to five years. Together with the $140,000 they need to bury Ron, pay off the mortgage, and fully fund the children's college accounts, that's a total of $765,000. Ron's employer, however, covers him with a $100,000 term policy, so the actual need for Ron is $665,000.

That sounds like an enormous amount of insurance and an impossible amount to afford, but it's actually not. The premiums will run a few hundred dollars a year, and then down the road if Ron remains healthy, when the mortgage is paid off and the kids are all on their own, he won't need the policy at all. But should he die prematurely, this amount of insurance will guarantee that Darla and the children will get to stay in the house and continue with the lifestyle they had been building already. In addition, Darla will be able to continue saving and investing towards financial independence as she and Ron always had.

What about Darla? How much life insurance should she carry? While it's true that her $10,000 annual income isn't vital to the household's financial stability, keep in mind that a lot of what Darla does without pay will have to be done by someone Ron will need to hire should she pass away. Also, as we discussed in Ron's calculations, it would be a good idea to cover the mortgage and the children's college fund expenses with her insurance policy as well. That means a minimum of $140,000 in coverage: $100,000 for the mortgage, $30,000 toward the two college funds, and $10,000 in funeral expenses.

Let's say that Ron feels he'd need to generate Darla's $10,000 in income plus another $15,000 a year to hire the help he'd need around the house. To generate $25,000 a year at an 8 percent return, Darla would need an additional $312,500 in insurance coverage which Ron could invest. Altogether, then, Darla should have a policy of roughly $450,000. That may seem like a lot of coverage for someone who's generating only a small part of the tangible take-home pay of the family, but the cost of hiring someone to do many of the unpaid tasks Darla does is crucial in the transition the family would undergo. For considerably less than $1,000 a year, then, both Ron and Darla can buy all the life insurance they'll ever need, and they can lock in the premiums for 10, 15, even 20 years. After that, they're not likely to need any life insurance at all and can cancel the policies any time during that period when they decide they are adequately self-insured by their own assets.

When you begin calculating how much insurance you really need, don't base it on the salesperson's formula. Look at what you want the insurance to replace and make your calculations accordingly. Make sure that your insurance pays off all of your debts, finishes the process you started for accounts like college tuition, and then generates the income that you'll need to replace in the event of a premature death. (It's reasonable to assume roughly 8 percent returns on this investment for the purposes of calculating the insurance amount.) But that's all the insurance is good for. It's not an investment, and it's not a get-rich-quick scheme. In fact, the odds are still in the insurance company's favor that you'll never cash in a term policy. In most cases the insured will live long enough that the policy will get canceled rather than paid out as the insured discovers he no longer needs the coverage. All those annual premiums go to the company's bottom line. But in the unfortunate case where that's not true and you or your spouse do die prematurely, a sound policy of adequate term life insurance is extremely important to your surviving family.

Disability Insurance

The final kind of insurance I'll discuss is, unfortunately, the one most Americans overlook. You've got health insurance, homeowner's insurance, auto insurance, and life insurance, so if you have a calamity that wipes out your home or your car or even kills you, you have a policy to protect you or your surviving family. But what happens if you're stricken with a debilitating disease or are seriously injured in an accident and can't work? Your health care is covered, of course, but what about your lost income?

Roughly 25 percent of all adults will become disabled at some point for as much as an entire year. And if you're unable to work, especially when you're young, you've lost your most important asset—your earning ability.

You have to protect yourself against such a possibility, or you might see your entire well-laid financial plan go to ruin in a very short time.

How much disability coverage do you need? Just as when you were calculating how much you would need to live on in perpetuity once you reach financial dependence, sit down and calculate how much per month it would take for you to get by right now if you couldn't work for six months or a year. Policies are typically based on a monthly payout, so once you arrive at a reasonable figure, contract for a policy that provides that much coverage.

You may well have some disability insurance through your employer, but read through the policy regulations carefully. Some of these employer-sponsored plans are not adequate, and you may need to supplement yours with a private plan as well. Just as with term insurance, disability insurance is generally less expensive for the young and healthy. Fortunately, if your career is advancing well, the higher premi-

ums you'll pay when you are older are more affordable as
your salary rises too. And at some point, your financial independence will make disability insurance—just like life insurance—unnecessary. Until that date, though, make sure you're
covered. Don't assume that it can't happen to you just
because you work in a low-risk occupation. My wife, for
example, just six weeks before our wedding, was in an automobile accident that broke her back, leaving her unable to
teach for several months. We were lucky; her injury could
have been much worse and left her disabled for a lot longer.
Because of a generous and understanding department head,
we were able to scrape by financially. If we had been savvy
about disability insurance back then, though, we'd have been
a lot better off. Don't overlook this insurance because you
can't afford it; you can't afford *not* to have it. So skip that
extra new suit or delay that new set of irons if you must, but
get all of your insurance coverage in place.

Home Mortgages

Enough of this gloom-and-doom planning. As necessary as it
is, it's nonetheless morbid. Let's switch topics now to the
American dream: home ownership. I'll admit up front that I
have mixed feelings about home ownership. The idea of owning your home, and molding it into a residence that reflects
your own tastes, personality, and lifestyle is naturally appealing. It's genuinely nice to be able to "go home." But it's also a
real pain at times. Something's always breaking or in need of
replacement. The need for new furniture and furnishings
seems unending. And for someone like me (the antithesis of
Mr. Fix-It), renting a home seems a very sensible alternative
at times. Nevertheless, we're in the pool of home owners,
treading water furiously with our mortgage, our home
improvements, our "American dreams."

But there are some big financial issues associated with home ownership I'd like to address because I see so much advice about mortgages that's simply misleading. A mortgage is a simple concept, of course. A bank lends you money to purchase a home, allowing you to put the home up for collateral against the loan in case you default, and you pay the bank a regular monthly payment, part of which goes toward interest on the loan while the rest pays off a portion of the loan balance (or principal) itself. While loans come in all sorts of configurations today, the most basic mortgage is a 30-year fixed-rate loan. That is, you borrow a set amount (let's pick a round number like $100,000) at a fixed rate of interest (let's say 8 percent per year), and you will pay that loan off over a 30-year period, one payment coming due every month. (Incidentally, your payment for the principal and interest on that loan would run $733.76 a month, plus your property taxes and homeowner's insurance if they're included in your payments.)

Countless financial planning articles in recent years, however, have extolled the virtues of paying off one's mortgage as quickly as possible by making extra payments. The result, of course, is that you pay the principal down much more quickly and save quite a bit of money in interest charges. But that's only half of the picture. What else might you do with the extra money you're using to paying off your mortgage ahead of schedule? What about investing it in your portfolio instead?

Let's look at a very simple and extreme example to show how the alternatives stack up. Imagine a couple in their early thirties, Sidney and Sydney, who have just taken out a 30-year fixed-rate mortgage at 8 percent per year. Their mortgage balance is $100,000, and their payments are $733.76 per month. Completely unknown to them, Sidney has an uncle who has died and left them exactly $100,000 in his will. They could pay off their brand-new mortgage entirely and own their house outright. No mortgage whatsoever! What a break for a young couple. But *should* they choose that option?

If they pay the mortgage off on its planned schedule, the total of their payments over the 30 years will be $264,153.60. So by paying off the mortgage early, Sidney and Sydney will save $164,153.60 in interest payments—quite an amount, you'll agree. And they know they could invest the money instead of paying off their mortgage with it, so let's assume they decide to continue "paying" that $733.76 mortgage payment to themselves each month rather than the bank, depositing it into their stock portfolio (which earns 15 percent a year). Over the course of 30 years, they will have deposited that total amount of $264,153.60, and it will have grown to the incredible amount of $4,132,348. (I have not withdrawn anything for taxes on these gains along the way, just to show the maximum growth this method can achieve.) That's a wonderful plan, it seems, and Sidney's uncle's bequest has set them on a path to financial independence much sooner than they ever could have hoped.

But . . . and you knew the "but" was coming . . . what would happen if Sidney and Sydney decided *not* to pay off their mortgage early? After all, their budget is already working around the monthly payment of $733.76, and since the interest rate is fixed for the entire 30 years, they know that their monthly payment can never go up. Even if it stays the same, because of inflation each year they're actually paying off the loan with cheaper and cheaper dollars. In fact, the rate may even go down if rates drop significantly and they choose to refinance their mortgage. So instead of using the $100,000 to pay off their mortgage, they can invest the entire lump sum in their stock portfolio for the 30 years and let compounding perform its magic. Want to guess what the result would be?

After 30 years of growth in their stock portfolio at 15 percent a year, their initial $100,000 investment would grow to $6,621,177! (Again, I've made no allowance for income taxes on the capital gains along the way in either scenario. While taxes would change the final numbers, they would not alter the relationship between the two alternatives.)

In either case, then, after 30 years Sidney and Sydney will own the identical house, worth whatever the real estate values have taken it to over the three decades. They will also have made the identical 360 monthly payments of $733.76 in both scenarios. The only difference is that under the first option the payments went into their own stock portfolio, and in the second the payments went to their bank. But despite having paid over $164,000 in interest to their bank in the second scenario, by deciding **not** to pay off their mortgage early and opting instead to invest the long-lost uncle's entire bequest, Sidney and Sydney end up with a portfolio worth $2.5 million **more.**

That's what the financial planners are failing to tell their readers. There's a potentially massive lost opportunity cost that you pay in choosing to pay off a fixed-rate mortgage early just to save the interest. It's precisely the same misguided logic that tells you to avoid income taxes that occur when you sell an appreciated stock, even if doing so means you ultimately achieve a lower after-tax return. It just doesn't make financial sense. Who cares if you pay more interest to your bank or more taxes to the government—if by doing so you also end up with more money in your pocket?

If your stock portfolio earns a higher return (on average) over the long run than you are paying to your bank in interest on your mortgage, then you're better off leaving the mortgage alone to run its natural course, and investing that additional money in the stock market instead. And I've also saved a final trump card to play for my hand. I haven't even figured in the tax savings you garner through the home-mortgage deduction if you're paying the interest to your banker every year for 30 years. Because that interest is tax deductible, you're actually paying an even lower rate of effective interest on your mortgage than the stated 8 percent per year (or whatever rate you currently pay). That makes the discrepancy between our two scenarios even greater.

In other words, there are some *good* kinds of debt, provided that they are managed well. Mortgage debt is one of them. If you can earn more on the money you would otherwise use to pay off a mortgage than you have to pay the banker for borrowing it, financially you'll be better off at the end of the natural mortgage by not paying it off early. Now in no way am I talking about the obvious psychological advantage you will enjoy by not owing a penny on your home. I'm strictly comparing the financial difference between the two choices. But if I asked you which you'd rather have, the house and $4.1 million in 30 years on one hand, or the identical house and $6.6 million in 30 years on the other hand, which would you choose?

I know I take a somewhat unusual stance on home ownership, but perhaps it's because I don't see my home as an investment. You've undoubtedly heard that your home is the biggest investment you'll make in your life. But that's dead wrong, or at least it should be. Over 30 years—the life of your mortgage—you should make considerably more in your stock portfolio than you will ever make in the appreciation in value of your home. Real estate just doesn't stack up for long-term returns against the stock market. (It's also very costly and time consuming when you buy or sell. The stock market is much more liquid, which lends itself toward investing.)

But that doesn't mean we shouldn't buy a home, of course. It only means that we should begin to look at home ownership differently from the models of past generations. The value of my house isn't listed in the newspaper every day as if it were a common stock. I don't consider selling it just because it's either depreciated or appreciated in value over a certain span of time. It's my home, period, and while I fully expect it to appreciate in value over the years, I'm under no illusions that it will outpace the growth of the stock market over the same period. Financially I'd undoubtedly be much better off if I rented modestly and invested every penny into the stock market. But since I don't view my home primarily as an investment, I still see an intrinsic value in home ownership. It just has nothing to do with the financial worth of the physical piece of property. Changing your view toward your home may also break the unnecessary pattern many Americans fall into of trading up to a bigger and better home every few years under the illusion that these moves are investment-oriented.

Buy your house and turn it into a home. Your investments, though, should be in stocks.

Other Types of Debt

If home mortgages are to be considered good debt, the opposite pole has to be credit card debt. Sure, credit cards are convenient because you don't have to keep running to your bank for more cash periodically or lug your check register around with you. But unless you're one of the rare individuals who actually pays your entire credit card balance every month, the credit trap can spring on you in a painful way. According to the folks who track these things, most people aren't paying those bills off automatically. In fact, the average American carries a credit card balance of nearly $5,000 from month to month.

Let's see what this kind of credit card debt can do to ruin your financial well-being. Interest rates on credit cards range from fairly low (in the range of 10 percent a year) for those individuals with the best credit ratings, to absurd levels (18 or 19 percent) for most consumers. Of course, the consumers with the best credit also tend to be those who can pay off their bills each month and don't even need a break on the interest rates. It's the consumers carrying the large balances that often get stuck with the worst rates.

Each month the credit card company will require you to pay somewhere around 1.5 to 2.5 percent of the outstanding balance, or $10, whichever is greater. And believe me, the credit card companies love those people who pay only the minimum due each month. Those consumers who pay their bills in full each month cheat the card companies out of the opportunity to make a bundle in interest. But if you're conscientious, paying the minimum amount due every month on time, you're the card company's consumer-debt circus pony. They make a living riding you from month to month.

Let's look at an example. Our neighbor Sucker Saul owes the Bank of Bad Credit approximately $5,000 on his Plutonium-Gastrointestinal-Astronomic-Millennium Card. Saul's getting stuck with an 18 percent annual interest rate (or 1.5 percent per month) and he is required to make a minimum payment each month of 2 percent of the outstanding balance (or $10, whichever is greater). If Saul's the model customer, paying the minimum every month right on time, how long do you think it will take him to pay off his entire balance?

In the first month, for example, the interest on Saul's balance of $5,000 is $75.00. If Saul pays the minimum required payment of 2 percent, he'll send a check to the bank for $101.50. In other words, 74 percent of Saul's payment to the bank is just going toward interest. He's really only paying off $26.50 of his debt with this monthly payment. And the same holds true month after month. After an entire year of paying his minimums, Saul has only brought the total debt level down to $4,691.11. After five years of minimum payments, Sucker Saul still owes the bank $3,634.94. After 10 years, his debt is only reduced to $2,642.56. Can you tell this is going to take a while? You're not kidding!

Believe it or not, assuming Saul never even charges another penny to his card (and how likely is that?), it will take him nearly 44 years to pay off the total debt! And in the process of doing so (if he lives that long), Saul will end up paying the Bank of Bad Credit more than $13,000 in interest for his original $5,000 balance. It puts that new boat in a little different light, now, doesn't it, Sal?

To make matters worse, none of this interest expense is tax-deductible, either. Unlike your mortgage debt, where the rate is relatively low in most cases and the interest is tax-deductible, credit card debt is the worst kind. The interest rates on cards are typically more than you can reasonably expect to earn in the stock market, so you're not gaining anything by carrying this kind of debt; you're losing every single month. And none of the interest helps you on your taxes. The best thing you can do to get out of the credit card trap is to cut up your cards so that you don't add to your outstanding balances, and then pay them off as quickly as you can. If your bank is charging you 18 percent a year in interest on your card balance, paying that debt off is a guaranteed 18 percent a year return. (You're keeping that 18 percent instead of sending it to the bank.) As much as I love the stock market as a savings vehicle, I'm not silly enough to guarantee you an 18 percent return every year. Paying off your high-interest debts is guaranteed. Do it first!

As I mentioned before, this chapter is all about responsibility. Only use a credit card when you know you can pay off the entire balance every month. If you're that disciplined, then a credit card can be a very useful tool. With all of the affinity programs available to cardholders, you can actually acquire some worthwhile benefits using certain cards. Many offer frequent-flyer miles; some offer discounts on automobile purchases; some are tied to long-distance savings.

By all means, search for the best bargains on freebies and interest rates. If you have a good credit rating, you may be able to transfer your balance to a different card carrier and reduce your interest rate, but be careful that the new card rate isn't just one of those three- to six-month teaser rates you get in your mailbox daily. Those rates look wonderful until you read the fine print and realize that they soar to an ugly rate in a few months. Try to find the card with the lowest permanent rate until you can pay off the entire balance. And then make sure you're using a card that doesn't charge an annual fee. If you're paying off the balance every single month from that point on, the interest rate doesn't matter as much because you won't be paying any.

But the minute you find yourself paying a monthly payment that doesn't clear away your entire balance, it's time to put the cards away before you fall into the credit card trap again. Be responsible, and if you're finding it impossible to clear away your credit card debts, switch to an all-cash system until you get your finances under control. America was built upon the notion of self-reliance—and yet we're the worst credit abusers in the world. Let's start changing that direction for the next generation's benefit.

There's actually a black pit more harrowing than the credit card trap, but it's hard to call it a legitimate debt at all. In fact, in my opinion, it ought to be criminal. I'm referring to so-called cash advance centers. These outlets prey on the most desperate people in society and make it virtually impossible for them to recover their financial footing. Their scheme is set up so that if you don't have enough money to make ends meet today, you write them a check (a hot one, of course) for what you need. They will advance you the money and hold your check for a brief period (for a fee, of course).

That's not so awful, but here's the catch. What typically happens, naturally, is that the people taking the cash advance don't have the money in two weeks when they're to pay off the advance (if they had a decent cash flow they wouldn't have turned to such a business in the first place), so the center gladly renews the contract, usually requiring a payment of nearly the original amount advanced. The companies don't call this payment interest on a loan because they'd certainly run afoul of the usury laws if they did. So instead of calling it interest, it's labeled a contract renewal fee or some such euphemism. But let's call it what it is. It's loan sharking and I'll call here and now for the government to make the practice illegal. Borrowing a couple hundred dollars this way can cost you thousands in a very brief time. If you're desperate enough to turn to these centers, it's time to call the bankruptcy lawyers, because that's where you're headed.

In the next chapters, I'll turn away from the basics of financial planning and begin to talk about strategies you can use to manage your stock portfolios toward financial independence and then, once you're there, to remain independent.

6

PORTFOLIO MANAGEMENT 101

In the first five chapters, I've defined what your goal should be (financial independence rather than retirement); why you should look toward the stock market rather than the bond market (overall growth to keep you ahead of inflation and taxes); why you should set yourself up as a private foundation and use the *20 Factor* guidelines in your planning (assuming no terminal endpoint and limiting annual spending to 5 percent of your portfolio's total value); and how to get your personal financial planning in order (wills, insurance, credit cards, and savings plans).

Now that you have all of those topics under control, it's time to talk about the actual nuts and bolts of managing your stock portfolio (or choosing the right kind of portfolio manager to do it for you). Most of my arguments in the first five chapters assume that over the long run, your stock portfolio can achieve a return in the neighborhood of 15 percent a year before taxes. If you can't achieve that return, of course, a lot of your plan begins to crumble. So it's vital that your portfolio does two things: (1) it has to employ a consistent and disciplined strategy that you will follow through both good times and bad, and (2) it has to perform consistently better than the overall stock market over extended time periods. Fortunately, those two requirements have proven possible, even for the most inexperienced investors, if they'll follow an appropriate strategy.

In addition to talking about strategies, I'll cover a variety of associated topics in this chapter: How to pick an advisor if you don't manage your own portfolio, how many stocks you should hold in your portfolio, how to implement margin leverage, why you should rebalance your portfolio periodically.

How to Choose an Advisor

I write this section knowing full well that critics will see it as self-serving and a marketing ploy for my own firm. I accept that risk because my partner and I have set up our firm precisely upon the principles I believe are in the interests of individual investors in the first place. For many years I believed vehemently that every individual should manage his or her own portfolio directly. Deep-discount brokers make the cost of managing a portfolio very minimal, so that even someone with a modest portfolio can buy stocks without getting hammered in trading commissions.

But I've since tempered my do-it-yourself zeal as I've begun working with more and more individuals on a face-to-face level. For a number of reasons, some people, even though they are perfectly capable of managing their own portfolios, may be better off hiring a professional manager to do it for them. I liken it to a lawn care company in some regards. I'm perfectly capable of learning what's required to maintain my own lawn the way I want it to appear, buying the equipment, the fertilizers, the mulch and pine straw for the ornamental beds. And I can make the time required to do it myself. But I simply don't take any pleasure in doing it myself. For some people, it's a therapeutic joy. For me, it's a chore I'll put off, to the detriment of my landscaping. So I hire someone who will maintain the lawn regularly based on my expressed plans and wishes.

The same is obviously true for many people when it comes to managing their investments. First, everyone is too busy these days. And while some stock strategies require a bare minimum of time, if even the prospect of that seems like a chore rather than an opportunity to you, hiring a good manager may be worthwhile. Choosing stocks doesn't have to be the 100-hour-a-week activity some managers make it, but it does require some ongoing maintenance that shouldn't be allowed to slide because you're too busy to attend to your investments when it's time.

Second, many people simply turn off when it comes to investments. They know investing is important and they know intellectually that they can do it themselves, but it simply doesn't interest them at all. I know that for those of us who are market watchers, that seems unfathomable, but believe me, they're out there. If you've ever started discussing the latest earnings report for the technology industry and you've seen someone's eyes roll back in his head like he's been felled by a sledgehammer, it's a safe bet he's not a candidate for managing his own portfolio. Unless you're really interested in following it regularly, human nature is to let inertia take over and you'll end up ignoring your investments instead of managing them.

Third (and this is probably the most crucial reason), far too many investors can't get out of their own way. My first book was called *The Unemotional Investor* because the biggest hurdle for each of us to clear is our own natural inclination to do exactly the wrong thing in the market. When stocks are plunging, what is your first reaction? Probably that you should get out of stocks and wait until things settle down.

When stocks have been soaring for months, that's when everyone wants to back up the truck and dump every spare penny into stocks. And of course, this is exactly the opposite of what you should do. Think of it this way, when would you rather buy that new set of graphite-shafted multimetal irons you've been convinced will drop you from a 25 handicap to a scratch golfer: on the day they're first released at top price, or when they've been cut in price four or five times and you can pick them up for a fraction of the original price? You didn't hesitate to answer that one, did you? Yet when it comes to stocks, the typical investor sells when his stocks are low and buys them back when they're higher. It's no wonder people are intimidated by the stock market if they're trying to make money by doing it backwards. Human nature and emotion work against you in the market unless you find a way to short-circuit those natural tendencies.

Since our firm opened in June 1998, the major market indices have gone through a number of quick and dramatic gyrations. And inevitably, every time the market hits another air pocket, my partner or I will receive a handful of e-mails and phone calls from nervous clients who wonder whether we shouldn't sell all of their stocks and wait for better times. And in every case, doing so would have cost them substantial profits, as the market recovered shortly thereafter. It's uncanny that we'll get at least one very nervous call or e-mail on the day we hit a bottom.

The point is that many investors simply can't stick to a disciplined stock strategy if they're managing their own portfolios, even when they're convinced by the long-term record of the approach. The day-to-day fluctuations drive them to make big mistakes. They become nervous when times are bad and they fall in love with certain stocks when times are good and they can't make themselves follow their own strategy. In the long run, they hurt their portfolio's performance significantly by constantly second-guessing their original intentions. Those kinds of investors are better off in many cases turning their portfolios over to a manager who uses a strategy they are comfortable with, knowing that the manager will stick to the strategy even when the market turns against them.

Let's say, then, that you've decided to hire a manager to handle your stock portfolio. How do you go about it? While there are thousands of money management firms available, finding the right one for you can be a daunting task. One way to select some possible candidates is to ask for recommendations from friends and colleagues. Word-of-mouth is powerful in the money management industry, but be aware that most people don't really know how their money manager is really performing. Too often Wall Street sounds like Lake Wobegon, where all the managers are "above average."

Wall Street has a habit of presenting information in the most attractive light, just like those soft-focus filters celebrities use in their publicity photos to cover up the signs of ageing. You'd be amazed at the periodic statements you'll receive as a client of many firms. Your quarterly statement might be 7 to 10 pages long and filled with charts, graphs, tables, everything so jumbled it's hard for you to find what you really need. It's no wonder most investors can't tell you precisely how their managers are doing, yet almost every one of them wants to believe his manager is thrashing the market.

For a stock portfolio, it's very easy to measure a portfolio's progress. You should be able to compare your returns quickly against a major stock index like the S&P 500 Index. If the manager you are considering has a track record of beating the S&P 500 (net of all commissions and management fees), consider him strongly. That's your goal—to beat the S&P 500 over long time periods. If the manager is losing to the S&P 500 consistently, don't be swayed by his justifications that he's taking on less risk or lowering your volatility. That's just blather to explain away a bad performance. You are invested in stocks to beat the index, period. Otherwise you might as well just plow all your money into an Index fund and at least keep pace with the market. So rule number one for using an advisor is to make sure he's accounting for his real returns compared to the appropriate benchmark and that over time he is beating it.

Rule number two is to examine how your manager's fee is calculated. The traditional full-service stock broker who handles your account may be compensated based on how much he generates in commissions. If that's the case, his motivation isn't the same as yours. He gets paid more when he gets you to trade more frequently, regardless of how well or poorly his recommendations perform. That's going to run up your costs and probably your short-term taxes as well, and ultimately will probably ruin your returns. Avoid a commission-based manager.

Ultimately, a fee based solely on performance would be the fairest for the investor, but the Securities and Exchange Commission has prohibited such fees in all but some very restricted cases. The reason behind the prohibition is that a performance-based fee can lead some unscrupulous managers to take unwarranted risks in the attempt to boost their own fees. For example, let's say the money manager is to be paid a percentage of the portfolio's profits quarterly. If the portfolio doesn't make any money, of course, the manager goes hungry that quarter. In the first quarter, then, let's assume he had a terrific run, racking up a gain of some 50 percent for your portfolio. He's earned a hefty fee. But then in quarter two, because he's already made a big fee and can afford to take some chances on a home run, he loses all of that gain plus a little bit more in a risky set of investments. In six months, then, you've racked up some short-term taxes, paid out a hefty management fee after the first quarter, and you've actually lost money for the first half of the year. Yet the manager collected a sweet fee after the first quarter, even though he didn't make anything after the second quarter. That's what the SEC is trying to avoid in banning performance-based fees.

The more typical fee arrangement is the one adopted by mutual funds, where the fee is based upon the value of the portfolio. The average stock mutual fund charges a fee of roughly 1.5 percent per year. This money is withdrawn right from the fund and is accounted for in the fund's performance returns. The advantage of this model for the investor is that it aligns the interests of both client and manager. The way a manager makes a bigger fee is by increasing the value of the client's account through good management techniques. It doesn't encourage reckless trading and gambling for big home runs at the risk of losing it all. It doesn't encourage churning the account to generate more commissions. An asset-based fee is the most reasonable one for both client and manager, then, and it's the arrangement you should insist upon when selecting your own manager.

How much should the fee be? Believe it or not, I'll argue that the exact amount of the fee isn't really important. Fees in the money-management industry can run as low as 0.5 percent per year to as high as 3 percent. The average stock mutual fund, for example, charges 1.5 percent per year. My own firm uses that mutual fund benchmark of 1.5 percent a year for its base rate, too. In our case, however, our fee is reduced as accounts cross certain size thresholds.

But it doesn't really matter whether you're paying 0.5 percent a year or 3.0 percent a year. What matters is your money manager's returns *after* all the fees have been deducted. If your manager has generated a 20 percent return for you, net of all fees, while the S&P 500 Index has risen 15 percent, you shouldn't feel cheated that he's charged you a 3 percent management fee along the way. But if your manager only charges you 0.5 percent, yet your net return is only 10 percent while the S&P 500 Index is returning 15 percent, you're not getting a bargain. Compare the net performance to the benchmark index return and you will see a much more accurate measure of the manager's worth.

Just as with taxes, everyone wants to think he's getting a bargain on fees. No one wants to pay more in taxes and no one wants to pay a higher advisory fee. But you can't lose sight of what's really important—the after-tax return and the after-fee return. If you're paying more in total taxes or more in total fees than the next guy, yet your actual net return is higher because of your portfolio manager's successful investments, you have cause to celebrate, not to moan.

When picking a manager, then, don't automatically assume that a low fee equates to stellar performance; it doesn't. Check out the net performance records of the managers you're considering and forget about the fee in isolation.

How Many Stocks?

As you're setting up your stock portfolio for your IRA account or your private foundation account, one issue you'll need to address is the number of stocks you should try to hold at one time. You'll want to strike a comfortable balance between the risk you're going to allow any one stock in your portfolio to carry and the costs and potential lost performance associated with holding each additional position.

In most mechanical stock-market strategies, like the ones I advocated in *The Unemotional Investor* and my essays while a columnist, the fewer positions you hold the better the long-term performance of the portfolio is likely to be. By concentrating on your strategy's very best ideas, you can often boost the performance over a portfolio sporting many more positions. One of the main reasons mutual fund performance is systematically weak is that the managers have to buy so many stocks to meet their own and the SEC's diversity requirement that they greatly water down their best ideas. Let's face it; when you buy everything, it's impossible to beat the market because you *become* the market.

On the other hand, if you concentrate too much of your portfolio in one stock, hoping thereby to maximize the performance of your strategy, you run a much greater risk that a single event can wipe out a large percentage of your portfolio quickly. Let's say, for example, that in 1998 you were trying to run a very concentrated five-stock portfolio strategy and one of your holdings was Cendant Corporation (NYSE: CD). Cendant was a large-company Wall Street growth favorite in late 1997 and early 1998, its stock price rising as the company maneuvered through successful acquisition after successful acquisition. By the middle of April 1998, the stock price peaked at $40 per share. And on April 15, the stock closed at $36 per share.

Then catastrophe struck. After the market closed on the 15th, the company announced an "irregularity" in its accounting methods and allowed that its past financial results would have to be restated. Wall Street reacted in typical unsympathetic fashion to the negative news and the following morning, the stock opened at nearly half its previous day's closing price. Cendant's stock hit a low of $17 a share on the 16th before closing at $19¹⁄₁₆. That's a 47 percent loss overnight! And there wasn't a thing a Cendant shareholder could have done. The stock closed at $36 and opened the next morning in the teens. There weren't any trades in between where an investor watching it extremely closely could have sold out to minimize his losses. If you owned Cendant, you took a bath—period. And it wasn't simply a case of Wall Street overreacting, so that all the shareholder had to do was hold on and he'd recover his investment. A year and a half later, Cendant stock still trades at less than $17 a share.

If you were holding only five stocks at the time, that is, with 20 percent of your portfolio in each position, the overnight loss in Cendant alone cost your entire stock portfolio a loss of 10 percent. Can you sleep with that kind of risk attached to each individual stock? Most people can't, and frankly, they shouldn't try. A very concentrated portfolio, then, will force many investors to adopt a short-term orientation because they will become anxious to dump any stock that's not immediately performing up to expectations. That leads to a lot of excess trading and associated commission costs, and also to higher taxes, and does not necessarily lead to higher long-term returns. The studies showing that 80 to 90 percent of all day traders lose money over time are eye-opening. Frenetic activity and quick thinking don't necessarily translate into solid long-term growth. If you need to gamble for excitement, go to Las Vegas once a year and blow some money there. But treat it as entertainment. Don't gamble with your private foundation funds. You'll never become financially independent that way.

The opposite extreme, however, is just as wrong. If you try to hold too many stocks, you'll go the way of the mutual funds. Each stock you add can potentially weaken your strategy because you're sinking further and further down your list of really good candidates. At some point you'll begin holding so many positions that it becomes virtually impossible to outperform the major market indices because your portfolio is mimicking them. Add in the much higher trading costs of managing a portfolio with 50, 75, even 100 stocks or more and the returns are jeopardized even further. If your goal is to hold that many stocks, you'd be better off buying into an index mutual fund where at least the costs are very low and you're relieved of having to perform the day-to-day maintenance.

A stance that falls somewhere between the two extremes makes the most sense. Working exclusively with relatively stable large-cap stocks as I do, I favor a portfolio of 20 positions. With 20 market-leading companies in your portfolio you haven't watered down your best strategic choices to the point that your returns can't outperform those of the market indices. Your trading costs are relatively low if you hold these positions for a full year. Let's assume all 20 turn over once a year. That's a maximum of 40 trades per year. At a deep discount broker today, that will cost you somewhere between $200 and $400 a year in total trading costs. You can easily spend that much on a single trade at a full-service brokerage. In addition, if you're holding these positions a minimum of a full year, you also get long-term capital gains tax treatment on the profits when you do sell. Today that means a maximum tax of 20 percent on the profits. So a 20-stock portfolio is very efficient in terms of trading costs and taxes.

But most important, 20 positions spreads your total portfolio value across enough stocks so that no single company-specific event can rock your entire portfolio like we saw in the Cendant Corporation example for a five-stock strategy. If only 5 percent of your portfolio is invested in each stock, a 50 percent disastrous loss like Cendant experienced overnight only costs your overall portfolio 2.5 percent. That still hurts, of course, but it's not the kind of enormous overall loss that will push you to abandon a sound ship in the wake of one unsettling wave.

By limiting your per-stock losses to 5 percent of your overall portfolio, you don't have to micromanage each stock choice. You have to assume that in every year, a couple of your 20 stocks will be disappointments—even ugly disappointments.

But if your strategy is sound, your good choices will more than offset those weak performers. What you should care about isn't how each individual stock performs in isolation; rather, your focus should be the entire basket of stocks as one unit. If at the end of the year, your portfolio has gained 18 percent while the S&P 500 Index gained 13 percent, you've won that contest. It doesn't matter if you had a couple of players step up to the plate and look foolish swinging at balls in the dirt. As a team, your lineup got the job done. That kind of more global viewpoint will help you avoid the second-guessing and undisciplined trading that most investors fall victim to. By limiting the risk per stock, you can stick with your strategy more easily and let the overall portfolio do its work.

Regardless of how many stocks you own, nothing can protect you completely against the overall stock market going down. It's reasonably safe to assume that if the market drops on more global issues (inflation and interest rates rising, for example), your portfolio is going to suffer some losses as well. But that's equally true whether you're holding 5 stocks or 500. There's no foolproof protection against total market risk. What the 20-stock portfolio does, however, is afford you a balanced measure of individual stock risk (only 5 percent of your total value in each position) with a reasonably concentrated selection of your best ideas. When the overall market goes down, you just have to rely on your strategy for picking stocks that will survive better than the average stock. When a specific stock collapses, though, that's when you need to be holding enough positions to minimize the damage, because no matter how good a stock picker you are, sooner or later you're going to hold a stock that releases bad news and you'll watch a substantial portion of your investment in that company disappear within hours. Limit your losses by holding 20 positions and then don't bother second-guessing your choices.

Periodic Rebalancing

Over the span of a year, of course, your 20 positions will perform differently from each other and the weightings for each individual position will become skewed, sometimes markedly. Let's say you're using a strategy that requires you to evaluate 10 of your stocks in January and the other 10 in July (holding every stock at least one year). When your next evaluation date rolls around, several of your stocks are likely to comprise more than 5 percent of your overall portfolio value, while others may be significantly less than that average. It's a good idea to pull those positions back into alignment with your 5 percent target each time you evaluate your holdings.

For example, let's assume that in January you've been holding the following 10 stocks for one year and they're now worth these dollar amounts.

International Business Machines	$5,700
Merck & Co.	$4,200
Wal-Mart Stores	$5,300
America Online	$8,000
Philip Morris	$2,900
Hewlett-Packard	$4,700
General Electric	$5,100
Microsoft	$6,200
Home Depot	$5,500
Cisco Systems	$7,300
Total	$54,900

Furthermore, the other 10 stocks that you're holding (and which you'll update again in July) are worth a total of $46,500; thus your total portfolio value is $101,400.

There are two ways you can go about this process of periodic rebalancing. One is easier, while the second is a little more effective. Either one is acceptable, however. Let's begin with the easy one. Of those 10 stocks being reevaluated in January, let's say our stock-picking strategy tells us we should continue to hold three of them for another year: America Online, Cisco Systems, and Microsoft. The other seven are to be replaced by new selections for the next year.

In the easy rebalancing model, you'd simply sell those seven stocks you're replacing, which generates $33,400 in cash. And since you want all 10 positions to start the new year equally weighted, you'll need to sell some of your positions in America Online, Cisco Systems, and Microsoft as well, since they are much heavier than the average position weighting in this group. If you divide the entire sum of $54,900 by the 10 positions, each stock should begin the new year with an investment of $5,490. That means we'd need to sell $2,510 worth of the position in America Online, $1,810 worth of the position in Cisco Systems, and $710 worth of the Microsoft holding. Those three sales generate an additional cash amount of $5,030. Add that to the $33,400 raised from the sale of the seven other stocks and there is $38,430 to spread across the seven new purchases you must make, or exactly $5,490 each.

Each of the 10 stocks in your January group is now equally weighted to begin the new year. They're not, however, weighted equally across the entire portfolio of 20 stocks. With a total portfolio value of $101,400, each of the 20 stocks would ideally be weighted with $5,070. But, since you're not scheduled to evaluate and adjust your other 10 holdings for six more months, you don't want to adjust them in January or you'll incur additional trading costs as well as short-term tax complications. For this easy method of rebalancing then, you simply live with a slight discrepancy between the two groups of 10 stocks. At least the 10 individual positions are weighted the same and you've spread your risk evenly across them. The second method for rebalancing, which I'll address in a moment, takes care of this discrepancy between groups.

Some investors swear by the principle that one should never take money out of a winning position. And perhaps for traders with a short-term horizon that's a reasonable philosophy. But for longer-term investors who are committing to each stock for a minimum of one year, I disagree with that approach. I don't want any single stock to grow to such a large percentage of my portfolio that it can dominate the returns of the whole. As we all know, stocks that soar can also plunge again, and having too much of your portfolio in a single stock can cause tremendous pain for you when and if that stock begins a rapid descent. So if I have a star performer that is going to remain in my portfolio for a second year (or a third, or fourth), I will trim it back to an equal weighting with the other positions. That accomplishes two things. First, it protects against the stock blowing up and dragging the entire portfolio down more than is necessary. And second, it funnels some of the terrific gains into new stock choices that may themselves be the next big star. Granted, if the original big winner goes on to another fantastic year, I will have hamstrung its growth somewhat, but that's the risk I'm willing to accept to protect against a worse mistake.

In *The Unemotional Investor* I cited Micron Technology (NYSE: MU) as an example of this kind of explosive stock crashing back to earth. In a little over a year (in 1994–1995), Micron Technology soared from $16 a share to $95. But then in equally dramatic fashion it plunged back to earth, settling in the $30 range. Another example of this pattern can be seen in a stock closely identified with The Motley Fool at the time I was writing for them. Iomega (NYSE: IOM) became a legendary Fool stock as it rose from a split-adjusted 50 cents a share or so in January 1995 to a high of more than $27 a share in May 1996. But in just three months from that peak, the stock was slammed down and landed in a trading range of between $6 and $7 a share. In the following 15 months the stock reclaimed some ground, rising again into the $16 to $17 range, only to plunge once more. Since the beginning of 1998, the stock has declined rapidly to its current price of approximately $3 a share.

If you're an investor who commits to each stock for a full year, that's quite a dramatic ride. And unless you're the best timer in the world (and I won't bet my lunch money that you are), you didn't buy Iomega at 50 cents, sell it at $27, buy it back at $6 and sell it again at $16. If you were using a periodic rebalancing system, however, you might still have enjoyed a great deal of the stock's gains without giving everything back in the ensuing plunges.

If your timing was fortunate with a stock like Iomega, you would still have made a wonderful profit from holding the stock, despite its wild ride. After all, from 50 cents to $7 a share in a year and seven months is still a profit of 1,300 percent, even though you didn't get out when the stock was in the mid-twenties (which would have been a profit of better than 5,000 percent). The problem, however, is that most investors don't have great fortune with timing. Undoubtedly thousands of people lost fortunes in Iomega, buying it in the $20s and selling it during the ensuing plunge to $6, and then trying it again on its climb back to $16, only to end up selling it around $4 or $5 a share a short time later.

My point is that a wildly successful stock can be very volatile on the downside as well, and none of us is brilliant enough to call the tops and bottoms of stock movements. That's why in my mechanical investment strategies I don't even attempt to try. I identify stocks that are likely to outperform the overall stock market indices over the following year—and that's the extent of it. I can't tell you a target price for an individual stock, or a date by which it will get there. So when my strategies are accurate enough to pick a huge winner, like an America Online or a Dell Computer, I have no idea how long that ride will last. To protect myself against a huge gain being swallowed up in a rapid plunge, I rebalance all of the portfolio's holdings when I make the periodic adjustments.

Rebalancing Your Portfolio Using Margin

I've already explained the easy method for rebalancing part or all of your portfolio. When it's time to reevaluate your holdings, you sell all of the positions you won't be holding another year; you calculate how much money should be invested in each of the positions for the new year; you adjust the weightings of any stocks you're carrying over from the previous year; and then you buy the new additions to your portfolio. If you're adjusting your entire portfolio at one time, or you're adjusting an IRA portfolio where you're restricted to a cash account only, this is the most logical way to go.

But there are some advantages in splitting your holdings up into miniportfolios, staggered throughout the year. If you're trying to hold 20 stocks, for example, you water down your best ideas if you buy all 20 at the same time each year. It's unlikely that stocks 15 through 20 will perform as well as numbers 1 through 5, but for diversification protection you really need those 20 positions. One way to get the best of both worlds is to split your 20 positions up into a couple of groups (either two groups of 10 separated by six months or four groups of five separated by quarters). That way you're adjusting part of your portfolio throughout the year to pick up on changes in your strategy's rankings more frequently, but every stock is still held a full year, so that you aren't sacrificing long-term capital gains tax treatment.

But splitting your portfolio into miniportfolios that are adjusted at different times throughout the year makes rebalancing all 20 positions virtually impossible. A fine way to minimize the inevitable discrepancies in the miniportfolio weightings is to use a modest amount of *margin leverage* as a slush fund. Let me explain how this works. Margin leverage is money that one borrows directly from a stockbroker in order to invest more than the actual value of one's portfolio. For example, if your portfolio is worth $150,000, you're entitled under current SEC margin rules to borrow up to another $150,000 from your broker in order to buy stocks. That ratio is considered 50 percent on margin. In other words, you're buying $300,000 worth of stocks, and 50 percent of it is your money and 50 percent of it is margin borrowing.

Anything near the maximum 50 percent on margin, of course, is extremely speculative. In fact, I advise investors to cut off any margin borrowing they do at somewhere around 20 percent (that is, 80 percent of whatever you're buying is with your own money and only 20 percent is borrowed on margin). At the much more modest 20 percent margin limit, you will be able to stick to your strategy during normal market pullbacks. If you're on very heavy margin and the market slides, you will get a margin call from your broker, requiring you either to add additional money to your account or to sell stocks and repay a portion of the loan. Neither of those moves is in your interest when the market has just sold off, so avoid a margin call by limiting the amount of leverage you use.

The typical broker requires that 30 to 35 percent of your total investment be your own capital. Let's say that you have $80,000 and borrow another $20,000 on margin. If your $100,000 investment gets sliced in half over the next few months, of the remaining $50,000, your ownership is $30,000. (You still owe your broker $20,000.) At that level, your equity is 60 percent of the total value, still far above the broker's requirement of 30 or 35 percent. In fact, when limiting yourself to 20 percent on margin, your entire portfolio value would have to drop almost 70 percent before you would trigger a margin call. Assuming you're investing in quality companies rather than gambling on wildly speculative stocks, it's unlikely you're going to run into any margin call difficulties by limiting yourself to 20 percent leverage.

Now let's look at that second method for rebalancing your portfolio and see how margin leverage can help you with split miniportfolios. For a simple example, let's assume your portfolio is split into two groups, with a six-month separation between their adjustment dates. In January, when one of the groups comes due, it's worth a total of $60,000. The July group is worth $73,000. Instead of simply accepting this discrepancy and continuing with each stock in the January group worth $6,000 for the next year while the other group's stocks are worth more than $7,000 apiece, you can borrow a bit on margin and even things out.

Let's adopt a 15 percent margin target for this example. Take the total portfolio value of $133,000 and divide by 0.85 (that is, 1 minus 15 percent), which gives you a value of $156,471. That represents the total dollar amount of stock you can buy using 15 percent margin leverage. If you go fully on 15 percent margin leverage and buy $156,471 in stocks, each of your 20 positions should be worth approximately $7,824. So instead of simply buying $6,000 worth of each of the January's group of 10 stocks as you would in an all-cash system, you would buy $7,824 of each. By doing so, you've borrowed $18,240 from your broker on margin. That and your actual portfolio value of $133,000 equal only $151,240, so you're actually still below your 15 percent margin target. But that's fine. Your goal was not to hit the target exactly, but to use your margin leverage to help you rebalance the positions across the two groups of stocks.

Six months later when you need to update and rebalance the July group of stocks, go through the same routine.

- **Calculate your portfolio's net value.** That is, figure out how much your ownership position is for your entire portfolio after you clear away your current margin balance. If all your stocks together are worth $158,000 and you owe your broker $18,000, your actual net value is $140,000.
- **Calculate your target investment amount.** Divide that net worth figure by one minus your margin target. If your margin target is 10 percent, you would divide the $140,000 by 0.90 (that is 1.00 − 0.10.) The result in this example is $155,556.
- **Calculate the average position value.** Take the result from the previous step ($155,556), which is the total target amount for your investments including margin borrowing, and divide by the number of stocks in your whole portfolio. If you're holding 20 positions overall, the average position value should be $7,778.
- **Use the average position value to adjust this group's holdings.** Take that figure of $7,778 and make the adjustments to this group's miniportfolio.

Obviously, this will not bring all 20 positions back into exact balance, since you're only adjusting part of the portfolio right now. But by following this process for each of your partial adjustments throughout the year, whether they come quarterly or semiannually, you will be rebalancing every stock in your overall portfolio once a year. That's a perfectly acceptable way to keep every position roughly in balance at the outset of each new investment period. What happens to the weightings between adjustments is largely a matter of chance, and a mechanical strategy won't interfere with that. Your actual margin leverage percentage will fluctuate within a reasonable range as you make your adjustments. If the group you're adjusting has been weaker than other groups in your portfolio over the past year, you will end up borrowing a little more to bring it up to the average level. On the other hand, if you're adjusting a winning group, you may end up paying off a little of your margin debt by trimming those positions back. So your margin borrowing is a simple mechanism for keeping each stock balanced once a year, even though your positions are being updated at different dates.

Margin's Other Benefits

Using a bit of margin leverage affords you two additional benefits. First of all, margin leverage can actually increase your returns substantially over long periods of time. Just as with mortgage debt and the debate over whether you should pay your home loan off ahead of schedule, margin debt can be seen as "good" debt because the sheer act of borrowing and investing on margin can increase your net worth over the long haul. Let's look at how this might work.

Let's say that Mary Margin's portfolio is worth $100,000 and that she has decided, for a handful of reasons (increased leverage, ease of rebalancing her positions) that she's going to use 20 percent margin each year. Most deep-discount brokers charge interest on margin loans in the neighborhood of 7.0 to 7.50 percent per year. Let's say Mary's investments are earning 15 percent a year. How much will that fairly modest amount of margin increase her total value after 30 years?

In an unleveraged portfolio, Mary's original investment will compound at 15 percent per year—a very nice gain, to be sure. After 10 years (see Table 6.1) her $100,000 will have grown to $404,556. After 20 years, it's grown to $1,636,654. And after 30 years of 15 percent growth each year, her $100,000 original investment will have grown to a very impressive $6,621,177.

But let's look now at Mary's portfolio, invested in an identical mix of stocks, but using 20 percent margin each year. In the first year, Mary begins with the same $100,000 we used in

TABLE 6.1 The Power of Margin Leverage

	Without Margin			With 20% Margin					
Year	Open	Gain (15%)	Total	Open	Borrow 20%	Invest	Return (15%)	Interest (7.5%)	Total
1	$100,000	$ 15,000	$115,000	$100,000	$25,000	$125,000	$18,750	$(1,875)	$ 116,875
2	115,000	17,250	132,250	116,875	29,219	146,094	21,914	(2,191)	136,598
3	132,250	19,838	152,088	136,598	34,149	170,747	25,612	(2,561)	159,649
4	152,088	22,813	174,901	159,649	39,912	199,561	29,934	(2,993)	186,589
5	174,901	26,235	201,136	186,589	46,647	233,236	34,985	(3,499)	218,076
6	201,136	30,170	231,306	218,076	54,519	272,595	40,889	(4,089)	254,876
7	231,306	34,696	266,002	254,876	63,719	318,596	47,789	(4,779)	297,887
8	266,002	39,900	305,902	297,887	74,472	372,359	55,854	(5,585)	348,155
9	305,902	45,885	351,788	348,155	87,039	435,194	65,279	(6,528)	406,906
10	351,788	52,768	404,556	406,906	101,727	508,633	76,295	(7,629)	475,572
11	404,556	60,683	465,239	475,572	118,893	594,465	89,170	(8,917)	555,825
12	465,239	69,786	535,025	555,825	138,956	694,781	104,217	(10,422)	649,620
13	535,025	80,254	615,279	649,620	162,405	812,025	121,804	(12,180)	759,244
14	615,279	92,292	707,571	759,244	189,811	949,054	142,358	(14,236)	887,366
15	707,571	106,136	813,706	887,366	221,841	1,109,207	166,381	(16,638)	1,037,109

16	813,706	122,056	935,762	259,277	1,037,109	1,296,386	194,458	(19,446)	1,212,121
17	935,762	140,364	1,076,126	303,030	1,212,121	1,515,151	227,273	(22,727)	1,416,666
18	1,076,126	161,419	1,237,545	354,167	1,416,666	1,770,833	265,625	(26,562)	1,655,729
19	1,237,545	185,632	1,423,177	413,932	1,655,729	2,069,661	310,449	(31,045)	1,935,133
20	1,423,177	213,477	1,636,654	483,783	1,935,133	2,418,916	362,837	(36,284)	2,261,687
21	1,636,654	245,498	1,882,152	565,422	2,261,687	2,827,109	424,066	(42,407)	2,643,347
22	1,882,152	282,323	2,164,475	660,837	2,643,347	3,304,183	495,627	(49,563)	3,089,411
23	2,164,475	324,671	2,489,146	772,353	3,089,411	3,861,764	579,265	(57,926)	3,610,749
24	2,489,146	373,372	2,862,518	902,687	3,610,749	4,513,437	677,016	(67,702)	4,220,063
25	2,862,518	429,378	3,291,895	1,055,016	4,220,063	5,275,079	791,262	(79,126)	4,932,199
26	3,291,895	493,784	3,785,680	1,233,050	4,932,199	6,165,249	924,787	(92,479)	5,764,508
27	3,785,680	567,852	4,353,531	1,441,127	5,764,508	7,205,635	1,080,845	(108,085)	6,737,268
28	4,353,531	653,030	5,006,561	1,684,317	6,737,268	8,421,585	1,263,238	(126,324)	7,874,182
29	5,006,561	750,984	5,757,545	1,968,546	7,874,182	9,842,728	1,476,409	(147,641)	9,202,951
30	5,757,545	863,632	6,621,177	2,300,738	9,202,951	11,503,688	1,725,553	(172,555)	10,755,949

the unleveraged example. To go on 20 percent margin, Mary has to divide her portfolio value ($100,000) by 0.8. This gives her a total of $125,000 that she should be investing. Obviously, $25,000 of that will be borrowed on margin from her broker, who charges her 7.5 percent a year in interest. If the whole amount invested ($125,000) earns the same 15 percent return we used in the cash-only example, Mary will see a profit of $18,750 at the end of year one. But because she's borrowed $25,000 from her broker, she's also incurred an interest liability of $1,875 (7.5 percent of the borrowed $25,000). So after paying back the interest on the margin balance and deducting the $25,000 loan she still owes her broker, Mary's actual portfolio value at the end of the first year is $116,875. That's $1,875 more than Mary ended up the first year with in her cash-only portfolio. In other words, Mary boosted her real returns by 12.5 percent (in precisely the same investments, mind you) over what she was able to achieve without using margin.

In year two, then, Mary starts with $116,875. To go to 20 percent margin, she'll increase her margin loan with her broker to $29,219. That means she's investing a total of $146,094, which earns a return of $21,914. After paying the interest of $2,191 and deducting the portion of her portfolio she owes to her broker, Mary's total portfolio value is $136,598. That is $4,348 more than in the cash-only example.

Of course, the power of compounding will make that discrepancy larger and larger as each year passes. After 10 years, instead of the $404,556 she had in the cash-only example, with 20 percent margin Mary has built her portfolio to $475,572. After 20 years, she would build it to $2,261,687 instead of $1,636,654. And after a full 30 years, Mary's leveraged portfolio would swell to $10,755,949. That's more than $4 million larger than the cash-only portfolio invested in identical stocks for the 30-year test. That little bit of leverage each year—not enough to invite a margin call in normal market corrections—turned a 15 percent annual gain into a 16.88 percent gain. A mere difference of 1.88 percent, you say? But over 30 years, that seemingly minor difference generated an additional $4 million in wealth for Mary.

Keep in mind that margin exaggerates returns on the downside as well. I don't want you to imagine for a minute that it's a foolproof way to generate easy returns. The real issue at stake is this: If your portfolio strategy returns more on average than the cost you pay to your broker to borrow money on margin, then using some leverage is a good idea. That doesn't justify going nuts, however. If a little margin is this good, why not use the full load of 50 percent margin? All it will take is one big correction and the pain of a margin call to teach you the importance of moderation. There's a difference between being calculatedly aggressive and being greedy. If you're aggressive with a savvy strategy, you will do well over the years. If you get greedy and stupid, you'll end up squashed.

We've seen two very good reasons, then, to use a modest level of margin leverage. Not only will it make your periodic portfolio rebalancing more effective, but it can boost your returns over the long run. But there's a third benefit of using margin that's especially helpful while you're still saving regularly and adding to your private foundation portfolios.

The cost of a number of small stock purchases (or sales) can eat away at your long-term portfolio returns. And if you're following the 10 percent savings rule I discussed earlier in this book (and you should be, of course), you will be adding small regular amounts to your portfolios. If you have to buy small amounts of stock each month, not only do you waste a lot of money in commissions, but you end up greatly increasing the time you spend maintaining your portfolio, and you introduce short-term tax consequences back into the

picture. Each month when you add a couple of hundred dollars, you have to decide which of your 20 stocks gets the new
money, and to some degree your mechanical strategy starts
becoming less automatic and more intuitive. And we already
know what human nature and intuition will do to your
returns.

If you're using a margin strategy, however, this problem is
completely eliminated. Whenever you send a check in to your
brokerage account, the cash amount is automatically applied
toward your outstanding margin balance. In essence, the
money you are sending in April has already been invested in
your portfolio since January (or whenever your last update
occurred). That way, each month's new deposit doesn't have
to be invested in new purchases, with all of their attendant
costs and additional maintenance. Your check pays off a portion of your margin balance and at your next regular update, you can reestablish whatever target margin percentage
you've been using. There's no extra trading even though
you're adding new money to your portfolio regularly. It's
another best-of-both-worlds solution.

For example, Richard Regular wants to send $400 every
month into his portfolio, which is worth $75,000 and is sepa-
rated into two semiannual groups of 10 stocks each. If
Richard is using 20 percent margin, he would have a margin
balance of $18,750 (that is, $75,000 / 0.80 = $93,750). Over the
course of six months, Richard's monthly deposits of $400
would pay that margin loan down by $2,400 without his hav-
ing to make any additional stock transactions along the way.
Let's say that his entire portfolio has grown by roughly 7 percent in the first six months. His net worth of $75,000 is now
$80,000, and he's added $2,400 in new cash. So going into his
semiannual update, his total portfolio value (without margin)
is $82,400. At the time of his update, then, he'd be increasing
his margin amount to get back to a target of 20 percent, so he

would be investing a total of $103,000 (that is, $82,400 ÷ 0.80 = $103,000). Of that total $20,600 is now his outstanding margin balance.

And so on. Each month Richard will continue to add $400 (or more as his salary increases) and will use his margin balance to absorb those deposits without requiring him to make any additional transactions in his portfolio. Each time he adjusts his holdings, he resets the margin amount to his desired target and he's back on track. It's the easiest way of saving regularly I know of without generating any additional trades, taxes, and hassles. And the cherry on top is that margin interest is a useful deduction as an investment expense come tax time.

Dollar-Cost Averaging

Speaking of saving regularly, one of the financial planning community's favorite saws (along with mutual funds and asset allocation) is the practice of *dollar-cost averaging*. When you save a fixed amount of money each month (as I've suggested you should as part of your 10 percent Pay-Yourself-First plan) and invest it in the same mutual fund, you will buy varying numbers of shares with each purchase as the *Net Asset Value* (the price, in other words) of the mutual fund fluctuates. The theory is that when the mutual fund price is low, you'll get to buy more shares. On the other hand, when the price is high, you're buying fewer shares. Overall, then, your average cost per share is reduced.

Let's look at an example. Andrew Average invests $500 each month into the Diversified Technically Fundamental Asset Allocation Balanced Fund. If the fund's net asset value is $30.00 per share in January, Andrew will purchase exactly 16.667 shares. (You can purchase fractional shares of mutual funds, but you must purchase common stocks in whole numbers.) In February, the price of the fund has risen to $31.25, so Andrew is only able to afford 16.000 shares with his $500 deposit. In March the price has risen to $31.70, and Andrew can afford 15.773 shares. April's price of $32.25 means he can afford 15.504 shares. May's price of $33.00 means he buys 15.152 shares. And in June, he can buy 14.641 shares at $34.15 a share.

Table 6.2 shows each of these monthly transactions. After the six monthly purchases, Andrew owns a total of 93.737 shares, for which he has paid $3,000. That means his average price per share is $32.00. As you can see from the prices he paid in April, May, and June, this is lower than the more recent actual prices for the mutual fund. By purchasing more shares at the earlier lower prices and fewer shares at the more recent share prices, his overall average cost per share is minimized. If at the end of June, the net asset value of the fund continues to rise to $34.50, let's say, the total value of his 93.737 shares is $3,233.93. Obviously, in a situation where the fund value was declining instead of rising, the process would work in reverse; Andrew would be able to buy more shares each month at lower and lower prices.

TABLE 6.2   Dollar-Cost Averaging

Month	Deposit	Fund N.A.V.	Shares
January	$ 500.00	$30.00	16.667
February	500.00	31.25	16.000
March	500.00	31.70	15.773
April	500.00	32.25	15.504
May	500.00	33.00	15.152
June	500.00	34.15	14.641
July		34.50	
Total Shares	93.737		
Total Invested	$ 3,000.00		
Avg. Price/Share	32.00		
Total Value Now	$63,233.93		

The financial planning industry makes a lot of noise about this concept, but I have to say, "Big deal!" This is simply plain old savings. It's not as if Andrew is making a strategic choice to invest the same amount each month to lower his overall cost per share. It simply works out that way because he's adding the money as he acquires it. Naturally, I'm all in favor of this kind of regular savings plan, not because of the dollar-cost averaging theory, but because the power of compounded growth is enhanced when you add money regularly. Look at this simple comparison. If Nancy invests $1,000 today (at 15 percent a year growth) and doesn't touch it for 30 years, it will grow to $66,212. If her best friend Connie invests the same $1,000 the first year and then adds the paltry sum of $100 every year after that, at the end of the 30 years, Connie's portfolio would be worth $109,586. *That's* the power of regular savings, and it has precious little to do with dollar-cost averaging. So by all means take advantage of whatever supposed advantage dollar-cost averaging gives you by saving regularly. What you're really enjoying is the advantage of speeding up your compounded growth rate.

Where I really take exception with the cult of dollar-cost averaging, however, is when we stop talking about regular monthly savings as you earn more money and start to talk about investing a lump sum of money. Suppose you just cashed out your pension plan at work. Or perhaps you've been given a large sum of money as a gift or as an inheritance. Or maybe, against all odds, you won your state lottery or had a big payout in Las Vegas. Should you invest the money all at once or "dollar-cost average" it into the market over a period of months or a year?

Nine out of 10 financial planners (in my completely unscientific poll) will tell you that in order to reduce your risk of investing right into the teeth of a market correction, you should invest it in segments over the course of many months.

That way if the market drops you don't have all of the lump sum at risk yet. Sounds good, doesn't it?

Well, it's advice that flies in the face of historical reality. Once again, the conventional response is "let's not lose anything" even when that means "let's not make much." And by focusing on one risk (real or imagined?), the dollar-cost averaging approach takes on an unseen risk (or opportunity cost) of not being invested in the market.

A number of studies have actually modeled the lump-sum investment question, and the consensus of the researchers who looked at the details themselves rather than at the conventional assumptions is that on average the stock market rises from 70 to 75 percent of the time. If that's the case, where should your money be—in the market to take advantage of the probability that the market will rise, or on the sidelines worrying about that 25 to 30 percent chance that the market will go down?

The whole point of being in the stock market in the first place is that over the long run it goes up and outperforms every other asset class. By sitting on the sidelines worrying about a short-term correction in the next year (which no one can predict anyway), you will cheat yourself out of a year's potential growth. And as you know from my many examples of compounded growth, every year you cheat yourself on the front end means a huge amount of potential wealth lost on the back end.

When I first began writing regular columns for The Motley Fool, the Dow Jones Industrial Average was making new record highs and investors were nervous. Almost daily in e-mail or on the forum's message boards I was asked whether it wouldn't make sense for investors to wait for the inevitable correction and then jump back in at lower prices. My answer was always the same: Sure, I said, do that if you can tell me when the correction will begin and when it will end. Otherwise, you belong in the market if you're a long-term investor.

That was in early 1995, when the Dow was just approaching 4,000! At the end of 1995, the Dow was over 5,100. The Dow ended 1996 at nearly 6,500. It was just under 8,000 at the end of 1997. It crossed 9,100 in 1998. And today it sits at roughly 11,000. Presumably the bears are still waiting for the "inevitable" correction. Now I'm not laying this history out to gloat on behalf of the bulls. No one knew this was going to be such a fabulous five-year run for stocks, and that's exactly my point. *No one knows!* So it makes more sense to me to play the averages than buck them on a hunch.

Let's look at Andrew Average's example in a little different light. Let's assume his $3,000 investment over the six months wasn't coming out of his paycheck at all but was a lump sum he received as a gift, and on the advice of his financial planner, he invested in dribs and drabs over six months. What if Andrew had instead deposited the entire $3,000 in January? At $30.00 per share, he would have been able to purchase 100.000 shares, which at the end of June would have been worth $3,415.00. Now I realize a difference of $181.07 between the lump-sum investment and the dollar-cost averaged approach doesn't sound like much, but imagine the discrepancy for a much larger amount of money over an even longer time period.

Of course it's true that by investing a lump sum all at once, you might do worse than with dollar-cost averaging, but on average only three times out of 10. If I have to make a rational investment choice based on what's likely to happen, I'll take seven out of 10 every time—and wouldn't you? After all, who's to say that the correction won't come two days after your last dollar-cost averaged deposit? So my rule about when to invest is simple: If your money is true long-term investment money, the best day to put it in the market was yesterday; the second-best day is today; the next-best day after that will be tomorrow. Get invested and stay invested. Anything else is fighting against historical odds and not worth your effort.

In the next two chapters I'll discuss some of the potential stock-picking strategies available to you as well as some of the situations peculiar to the investor who has become financially independent and has begun living on the growth of his portfolio.

7

MANAGING YOUR MONEY FOR LIFE PORTFOLIO

If I haven't been blunt so far, now's the time. Nothing you read in this book is going to make any difference to your financial independence if you don't become (or hire) a good investor. You have to generate returns somewhere in the neighborhood of 15 percent a year (for decades and decades, not just over the last five years of spectacular bull market gains) in order for this kind of financial plan to work for you.

For some 200 pages now, I've been telling you how you can save, invest, and live in financial independence by investing in the stock market and developing your own private foundation portfolio system. But if you are like I was when I began investing for myself, you're frustrated right now and saying, "Yeah, this all makes perfect sense, but what **stocks** do I buy to get this 15 percent return you keep talking about?"

Unlike *The Unemotional Investor,* this book's main purpose isn't to provide you with a series of in-depth stock-selection models you can implement on your own. But I do think it's a good idea for you to have a sense of the possible range of alternatives available for your own private foundation accounts. While this section will be by no means a complete survey of the best models available, it's at least enough to get you started while you learn more about stock-selection strategies. (In the final chapter, I'll also provide a list of some excellent books on stock-selection strategies that will help you develop a style all your own.) But for here and now, let's look at a series of basic steps you can take to get started.

S&P 500 Index Mutual Funds

The easiest of all strategies is to pile everything into an S&P 500 Index mutual fund. The fund simply buys the 500 stocks in the index, and the returns for the fund will mirror very closely the returns of the unmanaged index (less management fees charged by the fund). If you opt for this strategy, you never have to do any analysis or even give it a second thought. Month after month as you're saving you simply write a single check to the mutual fund and never look back. You'll outperform 8 or 9 out of every 10 professional stock portfolio managers over time, which isn't a bad standard to shoot for. In addition, the costs associated with the fund are very low because the mutual fund companies don't have to spend a lot on research departments and high-salaried managers. Turnover of the holdings in the portfolio is also very low, since the holdings will only change when Standard & Poor's changes the composition of the 500 stocks in the index, so it's a very tax-efficient investment as well.

Almost every major family of mutual funds offers an S&P 500 Index fund, so your choices are varied. The benchmark for these funds, perhaps, is the one offered by the Vanguard fund family. Vanguard has been championing the cause of indexing for years now and has been in the forefront of the movement to keep mutual fund cost ratios very low. But let's face it: to a large degree an index fund is an index fund (with some minor exceptions). Some quasi-index funds have begun showing up in recent years. These "index funds" use derivative instruments within the S&P 500 universe in the attempt to enhance their returns over the basic index. Some of these enhanced index funds have been more successful than others, so I suggest sticking with the plain vanilla variety of index fund. Shop around to find one with a comparatively low expense ratio and no hidden annual fees.

If this strategy—and the S&P 500 Index is, after all, a strategy that focuses exclusively on large-company stocks—is so wonderfully easy and outperforms the vast majority of professional money managers, why would anyone turn away from it for a long-term investment approach? Well, to put it simply, you can do better. Let's look at some of the drawbacks of a pure indexing strategy.

It's true, the S&P 500 Index has averaged an annual gain of 28.77 percent for the last decade (through 1998). The extraordinary bull market of recent years is something to be marveled at and thoroughly taken advantage of, but not a phenomenon which should be counted on to continue indefinitely. If we extend that S&P 500 Index history back one more decade, the average annual returns over the past 20 years drop more than 10 percentage points, to 17.75 percent a year. That's still a quite comfortable return, but no one knows how sustainable that pace is either. The last 30 years have only seen an annual rate of return of 11.51 percent. The even longer history, dating back more than seven decades, has generated an average return of approximately 11 percent per year. And for several stretches within that history, there have been losing periods when most investors would be hard-pressed to stand by while the market treats them so roughly.

For example, I've already discussed the disastrous collapse in 1973 and 1974 when the S&P 500 lost a cumulative 40 percent of its total value. But as painful as that was, it was recovered fairly quickly (at least quickly in the eyes of a long-term investor). But what about the investor who threw his hat in with the S&P 500 Index at the end of 1965? By the time the bear market was over in 1974, this poor soul had experienced a nine-year drought which brought him an annual average gain of just 0.06 percent! Even the most unemotional investor would have a difficult time waiting patiently through a decade of miserable returns for the reward that inevitably comes his way, especially when inflation was so high and eating away at his portfolio's buying power.

Don't suffer under the illusion that the market always goes up. One of the knocks professional investors put on the current movement of individuals managing their own portfolios is that most of them have never experienced a genuine bear market, and as soon as they do they'll panic and do themselves in. It's a valid concern, but the fact that one has never seen a war doesn't mean one can't prepare for one and recognize it for what it is when it occurs. If you have a sound strategy in place and aren't just managing your money based on intuition, you'll survive the bear markets as well as anyone else does. I find it curious, though, that in each of the last several abrupt but modest corrections we've seen over the last five years, invariably the cable news channels report that it's the institutional money manager and not the individual investor who sold in panic and then came crawling back to repurchase the same stocks just a few weeks later. Don't let the institutions patronize you that way.

Face it, sooner or later the overall stock market will experience weak periods. And your strategy may very well suffer along with the market. The drawback to the S&P 500 strategy, of course, is that you *are* the market to a large degree. You're invested in 500 of the largest stocks in America, those which comprise the lion's share of the trading volume on the New York Stock Exchange and the Nasdaq. When the overall market slides into a tough period, your index fund is going down with it. You have no way to distinguish your investments from those of the overall index, and you're simply along for whatever ride the overall benchmark takes. Not a bad plan most of the time, but not ideal either.

That doesn't mean you shouldn't consider the S&P 500 Index strategy, of course; it only means you must be prepared for periods of weakness, sometimes even very extended periods. If you can ride them out and don't panic yourself into a market-timing mode, this is a decent base-level investment option.

Other Indices

The S&P 500 isn't the only index you might want to consider, however. We've already discussed the Dow Jones Industrial Average. Over the past several years, the S&P 500 Index had surpassed the Dow Industrials as a more relevant benchmark of the American economy because it had a much stronger technology component than did the Dow Industrials. But that's changed just recently with the addition of Microsoft (Nasdaq: MSFT) and Intel (Nasdaq:INTC) to the Dow. Arguably the two most influential technology behemoths in the land, these additions, along with Hewlett-Packard (NYSE:HWP) and International Business Machines (NYSE: IBM) give the Dow a tremendous technology presence.

Another major index to consider in your planning is the Nasdaq 100, a group of the largest companies trading on the Nasdaq computer "exchange." Over the last decade, the Nasdaq 100 has proven a much more aggressive and growth-oriented index than has either the S&P 500 or the Dow Industrials.

Fortunately for individual investors, it has become easier over the past few years for us to use these indices in our basic portfolio management. Vehicles called *Unit Investment Trusts* have become available that allow individual investors to buy shares of these indices directly through their stockbrokers. These unit trusts are different from the traditional index mutual funds in that you may buy and sell your shares of the trusts directly on the open market at any time. All three indices are available on the American Exchange. The trust for the S&P 500 is available under the ticker symbol SPY. Because of that symbol, it's usually referred to as a *Spyder*. The trust for the Dow Jones Industrial Average is also available on the American Stock Exchange, under the ticker symbol DIA. This trust is generally called a *Diamond*. And finally, the Nasdaq 100 trades on the American Exchange with the symbol QQQ.

These trusts mirror the indices themselves, holding all the stocks in the index in the proportion required to mirror the index's returns as closely as possible. If you're interested in using an indexing strategy, then, but would like more options than the S&P 500 alone, you may want to consider these unit trusts. With the large technology component in the Nasdaq, you may want to split your funds between the three indices to take advantage of the more aggressive companies in the Nasdaq 100. Unless you believe this Internet thing is just a fad, you should give serious consideration to the kinds of stocks represented in the Nasdaq 100. (If you really do believe it's a fad, read Harry Dent's *The Roaring 2000s*.)

Be aware, though, that investing in these three indices means you will be duplicating many of your holdings. The largest technology stocks, for example, are in all three indices. And because of the way the S&P 500 and the Nasdaq 100 are computed using a market-capitalization weighting system, the largest companies influence the indices most heavily. As Microsoft and Intel go, so often goes the Nasdaq 100 and to some degree, the S&P 500. You will have a great deal of redundancy in a pure indexing portfolio if you're splitting your portfolio up among the three unit trust alternatives.

Investing in Individual Stocks

As you undoubtedly realize by now, it's my belief that while indexing is a decent starting point, I'd rather take my returns into my own hands rather than throw my lot in with the whole field of large-company stocks. Even in weak markets there are always some companies that are performing well. Your mission as an investor is to find the good stocks in a bad market when not much is rising and to find the superstars in a good market when almost everything is rising. That's the only way to outperform the market itself and while it sounds a daunting task, it's not. With a minimal investment of time and energy it *is* possible to perform better than the overall market indices.

I know, I know, many market professionals and especially academics in finance will tell you that the investor's life is a "random walk down Wall Street," and the best one can ever hope for is to stay even with the market. Fortunately, you can look for yourself at plenty of real-world evidence that disproves the theories coming from the ivory tower. Plenty of investors—private and professional—have outpaced the overall stock market for very long periods of time. The most famous, perhaps, are Warren Buffett and Peter Lynch. But trust me, you don't have to be the next Warren Buffett or Peter Lynch to manage a stock portfolio that will consistently beat the stock market for decades and decades. What you do need is a sound strategy and the discipline to follow it. Tens of thousands of people are doing it, and there's no reason you can't as well.

Earlier in this book I alluded to one such individual stock strategy that has outpaced the overall stock market for the past 75 years. And it's not just a theoretical exercise, either. Real investors using real money have been following the Dogs of the Dow strategy (or some variation of it) for decades and have been recording real profits. To me, seven decades of real performance from a model so simple our children can use it has put to rest the academics' notion that it's a vain effort to try to beat the market. But there you have it; theory and practice rarely bump into each other.

Let's look at the performance closely for the Dogs of the Dow, and then I'll discuss exactly how to follow the approach for yourself. For the last decade (through the end of 1998), the basic 10-stock Dogs of the Dow model has returned an average gain of 17.22 percent per year. That pales in comparison with the S&P 500's return over the same period (28.77 percent). But that 10-year span also includes the worst annual performance for the Dow Dogs in nearly three decades—a 10.01 percent loss during the 1990 recession. In fact, looking back further, 1990 was the only losing year for the approach since 1969. Not bad for stability, huh? But that sizeable loss in one of 10 years knocked the decade's average down fairly low.

If we extend that history to include a second decade, however, the relative picture looks a little better. The Dogs of the Dow returned 18.38 percent a year for the two decades since 1978, while the S&P 500 Index returned 17.75 percent. It's amazing what a single decade can do to a strategy's history—good or bad.

But what about three decades ago, when the market shed 40 percent of its value in the 1973–1974 bear market? This is where the Dogs of the Dow really shone (or howled?). While the market was running away from the big bad bear, the Dogs of the Dow barked their way to a profit in both years. That's right . . . a profit! I admit that a 5 percent gain over two years looks pretty anemic in isolation, but stand it up next to a 40 percent loss and I'd take it every time. And in the market crash of 1987? The Dogs of the Dow finished the year with a profit of 8.56 percent. (See Table 2.4 again for a full history of the Dogs of the Dow returns since 1960.)

For the 30 years since 1968, then, the Dogs of the Dow have returned an average gain of 15.58 percent a year. The S&P 500 Index, on the other hand, shows a return more in line with its very-long-term history, 11.51 percent a year. As the time horizon gets a little longer, we see more and more clearly the outperformance of the Dow Dogs.

If we extend the history a little farther back, to the arbitrary starting point of 1960 (my birth year), the Dogs of the Dow have averaged 14.57 percent per year. That's very close to my stated target of 15 percent annual gains that underpins the philosophies embodied in the *Money for Life* guidelines. If you can average 14 or 15 percent a year before taxes, you'll be able to live comfortably following the system I've outlined for your private foundation.

Let's look at the details now of the Dogs of the Dow—one completely mechanical system that may be all you ever need to get you to financial independence and keep you there.

The Dogs of the Dow is a strategy that requires all of 30 minutes a year, and can be used by anyone who can look at two numbers and determine which one is bigger. Here's the strategy in a nutshell:

- **Get a list of the thirty stocks in the Dow Jones Industrial Average.** *The Wall Street Journal* makes this easy for you. As the keeper of the index, the *Journal* groups the thirty Dow Industrials together in a single text box for you every day. All the information you need is right in that little box. It doesn't matter what day you choose; start whenever you're ready.
- **Find the dividend yield for each stock.** The dividend yield is the percentage return the company will pay in cash to its owners (the shareholders). For example, if you buy a stock at $40 per share and the company will pay you $1 per share over the next year in dividends, it is paying you a dividend yield of

2.5 percent. You don't even need to make those calculations, however. *The Wall Street Journal* contains a column called "Yield" with those numbers already calculated.

- **Circle the 10 stocks with the largest dividend yields.**   Just run down the list and grab those stocks sporting the highest yields. Those are the stocks you'll buy for the next year. If by chance there's a tie for the final spot on your list, break the tie by selecting the stock with the lower price per share.

- **Buy those 10 stocks in equal-dollar amounts.**   For the next year you want your money spread evenly over those 10 holdings. Don't worry if you own more shares of one than of another. What matters is that you've spread your dollars as evenly as possible.

- **Ignore them for a year.**   For the next year, don't even look at your stocks. (Okay, you can look, but don't touch.) This whole strategy is based on a patient and steady approach. If you're a nervous type and can't keep your hands off something that doesn't show immediate results, have someone do this for you and not let you get at the stocks.

- **Do it again.**   After at least a year and a day (for tax purposes), buy another copy of the paper, get the new set of rankings, and repeat the process. Sell your holdings that no longer make the top 10 list, adjust the weightings of the stocks you already hold that you'll hold for another year (if they're still on the list), and then buy the newcomers to the list. Bam! Thirty minutes and you're done.

It's really that simple. (And if you're interested in variations of the approach that have performed even better over time, let me direct you to my first book.) Some years you'll grow frustrated with this approach as your stocks sit idle, gaining very little while you witness other stocks zooming ahead. It's difficult to stay committed to something that's not working spectacularly in the short run. But there are countless examples of stocks that stayed "dogs" for months and months and then suddenly visit the groomers on their way to a "best in show"—

a marvelous rise in the stock price. This is a model that requires incredible patience at times. If you adopt it, stick with it.

Additional Models

Do I personally invest using the Dogs of the Dow approach? To be frank . . . no. But it's not for lack of faith in the approach. When I first began choosing stocks for myself, the Dogs of the Dow was precisely the investment strategy I favored. Since then, however, I've devoted many years of research into other models that I've grown to favor over the Dogs of the Dow. But for a first-time stock investor who doesn't yet have confidence or experience with individual stocks, it's hard to fault a simple system with a seven-decade proven track record of market outperformance. But as I learned when researching several models for *The Unemotional Investor,* there are many ways to skin the market's proverbial cat.

In recent years a number of books have been published that outline mechanical models similar to the Dogs of the Dow and my own "unemotional" models. Two authors who have done outstanding work are James O'Shaughnessy and Jon Markman.

Jim O'Shaughnessy is a money manager and author who has now written three excellent books championing what he calls *Strategy Indexing.* It's the same philosophy behind my unemotional models, where the investor uses a proven strategy to select a basket of stocks (rather than trying to make each single stock selection using intuition and/or individual financial analysis). The investor, in essence, builds his or her own stock index and holds all of the components a set length of time. Then when the time comes to renew the index, adjustments are made to the portfolio to reflect the current stocks meeting the strategy's criteria.

In his first book, *Invest Like the Best* (McGraw-Hill, 1994), O'Shaughnessy analyzes the factors in a series of profession- ally managed mutual fund portfolios in an effort to begin constructing a series of screens individual investors can use to pick potential winners out of a large universe of stocks. This factor analysis research led to his second book, *What Works on Wall Street* (McGraw-Hill, 1997), which details a study of several decades' worth of items from the massive S&P CompuStat database. Extending his work from his first book, O'Shaughnessy demonstrates just which factors really do lend themselves to accurate forecasts of a stock's promise and which data points are illusory. The book allows the reader to start looking at combinations of elements to develop individualized screens for choosing winning portfolios of stocks. In his third book, *How to Retire Rich* (Broadway, 1998), O'Shaughnessy turns to more practical advice for individual investors, building his research from his previous books into a user-friendly platform. All three books are worth reading, but for beginning investors, I'd actually recommend his latest book first and then point you later toward his two more research-oriented books as support for his theories.

Jon Markman is a former *Los Angeles Times* business jour- nalist who is now managing editor at Microsoft's MSN MoneyCentral Investor. His recent book, *Online Investing: How to Find the Right Stocks at the Right Time* (Microsoft Press, 1999), continues in the tradition of mechanical investment models. Markman leads the reader through a variety of tools, especially those linked to MSN MoneyCentral Investor's searchable data- base "Finder." By focusing, as O'Shaughnessy also does, on spe- cific financial criteria, Markman's models focus on the strategy rather than on the individual stocks—a winning combination.

And finally, before I left The Motley Fool, I wrote a num- ber of columns outlining my ongoing research into stock- selection strategies and models. Many of those columns are still available in the archives on The Motley Fool Web site (www.fool.com).

My own investment style has changed over the last several years as my research and business has taken me in new directions. I started out as a disciple of the Dogs of the Dow approach. That mechanical, entirely objective style of investing appealed to me so deeply (mostly as a way to take my second-guessing nature out of the equation) that my research into new models followed many of the same precepts built into the Dow high-yield approaches. Gradually my research pushed into far more aggressive models that focused on growth stocks that are far smaller than the Dow giants. (See my Unemotional Growth model, for example.)

As I began managing money professionally, however, my research pushed me in yet a different direction. My money-management firm's approach now is to focus on large-company stocks that are leaders in their industries. We focus on fundamental criteria such as long- and short-term earnings growth trends and also on stocks that are performing well on Wall Street. In other words, we want to buy blue-chip companies that are doing everything right and that are being rewarded for it by the marketplace. Nothing genius-caliber in the thinking here, believe me, but it's been a remarkably successful approach for decades.

By focusing on larger companies, we take some of the wildness out of the ride that accompanies investments in small-capitalization stocks. In addition, our approach allows us to commit to our holdings for at least a full year. Many of our clients simply can't justify the much higher taxes associated with short-term holdings, so we've developed an approach that balances the need for high performance with modest turnover and tax efficiency.

That style works for us, but I don't presume to claim it's right for everyone. Each investor needs to adopt a proven strategy (and there are many of them) that suits his or her investment needs and personal tolerance for volatility. A tremendously successful strategy that carries a lot of volatility won't do you any good if you're scared out of it the first time the portfolio takes a pounding. You need a strategy you can stick to. For example, I was asked to be one of six guest portfolio managers in Microsoft's MoneyCentral Investor's Strategy Lab from July through December 1999. Each of us was asked to delineate a strategy we would follow for the entire six months, and then our hypothetical portfolios were tracked publicly in the Strategy Lab pages at MoneyCentral Investor. I chose to employ an experimental mechanical 10-stock strategy I was looking into at the time, knowing that it might be a monumental success or an even more monumental flop. But it was paper money, and I disclaimed from the start that the trades in this mythical portfolio were not ones I was making for myself or for actual clients. Nevertheless, I was going to stick to the strategy regardless of the outcome. Part of my research has always entailed watching how a strategy performs in real time as opposed to relying wholly on back-tested results. Sometimes back-tested results obscure the fine points of an approach that turn out to be less appealing in reality.

For the first four months of the Strategy Lab round, the approach performed dismally. Of the six professional money managers, I was riding my mock portfolio into sixth-place ignominy and an embarrassing loss. Week after week the portfolio slipped or went sideways, but to a large degree that was also the case for the overall market indices (especially the S&P 500 Index, which I use as a standard benchmark). I stuck to the discipline, though, knowing that the only way to measure a strategy's effectiveness is to see how it performs in a variety of different markets. Late in October, though, things turned around for the strategy and it roared back to life. By the end of the year, not only had the portfolio recouped all of its early losses (more than 10 percent), it had posted an additional gain of better than 50 percent and pulled itself off the bottom of the Strategy Lab standings. At one point in the last week of the Strategy Lab, it actually surpassed all of the other portfolios, finally finishing third in the overall contest.

I'm not writing this to proclaim the strategy's genius. In fact, I'm not particularly happy with the strategy as a realistic approach because it has led to unnecessary trading on the fringes of the portfolio each month and has proven enormously volatile. My point is that all strategies will go in and out of favor as the marketplace changes moods. That's to be expected but can't be anticipated and avoided. If you're to be a consistently successful investor using such a mechanical strategy, you must be patient with the times when your approach is out of favor. The last thing you want to do is abandon a time-tested approach because it's failing to win the day-by-day contest. I all-but-guarantee that when you bail out on it, it'll come roaring back without you.

Think of your portfolio approach as if it were your favorite major league baseball team. Yes, it's fun to watch the team play every day (why else do they sell season tickets?), but unless you're the most fair-weather fan around, you're not going to abandon your team in favor of another on the basis of any single game's outcome. What's important is the outcome of the entire season—all 162 regular-season games and the playoffs. And even after the season's over, you're unlikely to abandon your favorite for another just because it hasn't won the World Series that year.

I know investing isn't exactly the same as team loyalty. After all, the latter is largely emotional (the portion that isn't regional, perhaps), and I've argued for years that investors should do everything possible to eliminate emotion from the investment process, but the long-term approach is the same in both contexts. Your investment strategy won't beat the market indices every single year (and certainly not every single quarter), but if it's a sound approach and you follow it with tenacity, you'll have more winning seasons than not. And a team that wins consistently typically fills the seats night after night and rakes in the best gate receipts. So don't be too hasty in abandoning a good strategy when it's out of favor. Look at the strategy's long-term history from time to time and you may be able to put any short-term weakness in a better frame of reference.

Sheard & Davey Advisors

What we do for our clients at Sheard & Davey Advisors is a hybrid strategy that developed out of my modeling research over the last five years. We are strictly large-company growth-stock investors. We limit our universe to America's largest companies and then focus on a handful of simple criteria. We want those companies that have consistently grown their earnings over the past several years and who are continuing to post top-flight earnings growth today. But we don't just want great earnings. We also want the stock to be getting rewarded for those earnings. So we also demand that these top earners have been going up in stock price. So in a sense, we are momentum investors, but we are dual momentum investors. We don't want stocks that are going up in price without the support of great earnings, too.

In other words, we want to buy the stocks of companies that are doing everything right fundamentally (solid earnings growth) and that are being rewarded for that performance by Wall Street (solid price performance).

It's a very simple combination, but one that has proven remarkably successful. This strategy allows you to buy stock

in America's premier companies and enjoy a strong investment return at the same time.

We're very concerned with tax efficiency in our firm, so
we set up portfolios so that we can hold our positions at least
a year to get the best capital gains tax treatment. When we
begin managing a new portfolio, we buy a collection of 20
stocks on day one. Then throughout the first year, we make
some transitional adjustments to separate the holdings into
four quarterly groups of five stocks each.

So if we buy 20 positions in January, the top five are considered fixed for the January quarter, while the other 15 are
considered a temporary holding pool. In April we'll fix
another group of five stocks. To do this, we look at our current
rankings and identify the top five stocks that aren't already in
the January five. In most cases, several of these stocks will
already be in our temporary waiting pool, so all we have to do
is list them in the April group; no trades are required. But let's
say two or three new stocks that we don't already hold have
appeared in the current rankings. In order to buy them for the
April group, we will sell the weakest performers in the temporary holding pool. They're not likely to remain high in our
rankings anyway, since we demand strong price performance
as one of our major criteria. Also, even though we generate
some short-term trades during the first transitional year, by
selling the weakest performers (sometimes even at a loss), the
tax consequences are greatly reduced.

Then again in July and October, we go through the same
process, pulling stocks into those quarterly groups either
from our temporary holding pool or from new purchases.
We always hold 20 distinct stock positions and then once the
four quarterly groups are established, every position is held
at least a full year thereafter so we don't generate any further
short-term trades. From that point on, our portfolios con-

tinue to be adjusted every three months. The group of stocks which is now one year old will be reevaluated and adjusted as necessary.

There's a dual advantage to this kind of rotation. First, by holding twenty stocks instead of a more concentrated group of five or ten, we're able to spread the individual stock risk across more positions to protect against a single event wiping out large chunks of our total portfolio value. And second, by adjusting the holding four times a year, we are able to have a dynamic portfolio that picks up changes in the investing climate more quickly than if we simply adjusted the entire portfolio once per year. For example, in 1999, one of our best-performing stocks for clients was Qualcomm (Nasdaq: QCOM). But it wasn't a stock we were buying for clients early in the year. If we had done a single annual update for the portfolios early in the year, we would have missed the stock's gains entirely. But by updating the portfolios each quarter, we were able to pick Qualcomm up during the course of the year, and our clients enjoyed a fabulous gain as a result. So even though we hold 20 positions (which might lead you to believe we water our returns down by holding too many positions), our portfolios actually mimic the performance of a much more concentrated five- or 10-stock portfolio, without as much risk.

That's what our firm does. We don't try to be all things to all people; we stick to a strategy that we know works very well, and we don't try to time the inevitable fluctuations in the popularity of different styles of management. Does that mean ours is the One True Path? Of course not. It works for us, but there are many ways to be a successful investor. Find the one that works for you the most consistently and then stick with it. Keep in mind that the purpose of learning how to invest isn't to turn you into a professional investor. Instead, it's to let you invest well and enjoy your financial independence. If you end up swapping one full-time career for another one and are still frustrated from achieving your life's goals, you haven't really accomplished anything helpful. You want your investing strategy to be a vehicle to get you to a destination, not have it become the destination itself.

In the next chapter I'll address some of the peculiar situations you'll face after you reach financial independence and need to manage your personal endowment to stay there for life.

8

MAINTAINING FINANCIAL INDEPENDENCE

Congratulations . . . you've made it! Or at least now you've got the tools to get you there, and you know that even if you live another 50 years you'll be able to support your current standard of living and stay ahead of inflation. Now what?

Once you've made that transition from the workforce to a life sustained by your own financially independent private foundation, very little will change in your approach to investing. You'll continue to stay fully invested in quality common stocks. You won't try to time short-term swings in the market. You'll stick to a proven portfolio strategy through thick and thin. But there are a few issues you'll want to address regarding the way you maintain your investment portfolio because your income now will be on a somewhat different schedule. For years you will have been paid weekly, biweekly, or perhaps monthly. Suddenly, your "salary" schedule is entirely up to you, and there are various ways you may wish to go about distributing your income.

Paying Yourself a Salary

If you're working with my suggested model where you will withdraw no more than 5 percent of your total portfolio value each year for your own salary, it's a fairly easy process to administer. The simplest of all plans is to determine how much you'll be withdrawing for the year, and at one of your regularly scheduled portfolio adjustments withdraw that much money in cash from your stock portfolio and deposit the cash into a money-market checking account. Then throughout the coming year, you can write checks against that money-market balance as you need to and you'll always know precisely how much you're spending versus how much is left for the rest of the year. It makes budgeting very easy, and you only have to touch your actual portfolio once per year.

Such a plan, however, has three minor drawbacks that you may want to avoid. First, by pulling out a large chunk of money all at once (your entire spending need for the year), you're not using your money as efficiently as possible. The majority of that money could well remain invested in your portfolio for much of the year, your hope being that it will continue to grow at a much greater than money-market rate.

Second, if you're trying to maintain a portfolio with more than one group of stocks, but you're always pulling money out at the same time of the year, you're drastically reducing one group of stocks over a few years while the other groups remain untouched. That skews your weightings across all of your portfolio positions. To pull money out of another group, then, would require you to switch withdrawal dates and could put you in a position to pay short-term gains taxes. So your plan of diversifying through multiple purchase dates is undermined if you pull money out of just one group year after year.

And third, the variable expense of income taxes on your portfolio gains is hard to predict if you're only pulling money

out once per year. It's true that you can make identical estimated tax payments each quarter based on your tax liability
the previous year and then settle up the difference in April,
but that's not necessarily the most efficient way to handle the
problem.

So despite the simplicity of pulling money out once a year
and dumping it in an easy checking account, it's not the
approach I would suggest. Rather, I'd suggest a somewhat
more complicated plan (not much, don't worry) that handles
these issues more efficiently.

Miniportfolios

By the time you reach financial independence, you will obviously have a substantial private foundation account. Given
that fact and my earlier argument about the level of diversification you should strive for (20-stock portfolios with roughly
equally weighted positions at the start of each cycle), it's a reasonable assumption that you will be managing more than a
single group of stocks, all updated on the same day each year.

A solid alternative might be to manage four groups of five
stocks each, with each group separated by three months. For
example, you might have one group that is adjusted every
January, another group in April, another in July, and a fourth in
October. That way you are managing a dynamic portfolio that
keeps up with changes in the markets throughout the year, but
without sacrificing the one-year holding cycle for each stock
which qualifies your profits as long-term capital gains.

In addition to those advantages, having four quarterly
miniportfolios allows you to take advantage of the savings
process in reverse. In the section of this book on savings I
explained that having multiple miniportfolios spread throughout the year allows you to add new savings regularly without a
lot of additional trading costs and without running up short-

term tax consequences. It works the same way (albeit in reverse) once you begin withdrawing from your portfolio to meet living expenses. Each quarter, as you perform your regular portfolio adjustment for that particular miniportfolio, you would withdraw one-fourth of that year's spending amount from your portfolio and deposit it into your money-market checking account.

Instead of a single payday each year, you give yourself four of them. That way each miniportfolio is drawn upon equally in your withdrawals, keeping the groups more balanced, and the bulk of your money you'll spend that year can remain invested longer, on average increasing your long-term returns.

Let's quickly look at an example. The private foundation accounts of Isaac Independent have a total portfolio value of $1.5 million. Sticking to his 20 Factor rules, Isaac will withdraw $75,000 in the coming year (five percent of $1.5 million). Isaac owns a 20-stock portfolio, split into four miniportfolios which he's staggered at three-month intervals. As each miniportfolio comes due for its annual adjustment, Isaac will withdraw one-quarter of his annual spending allowance of $75,000, or $18,750. Then for the next three months, Isaac will use that $18,750 to set up and administer his budget, at $6,250 per month.

By delaying the withdrawals until each new quarterly adjustment, more of Isaac's money is working for him longer. After withdrawing $18,750 in January, let's say, the remaining $56,250 Isaac has earmarked for this year's salary remains invested in his stocks. In April, when he pulls out another $18,750, the other half of his salary ($37,500) is still working for him. And so on. By the time he gets to October's withdrawal, that final $18,750 he already planned to spend has been at work in the market for him for an additional nine full months.

If Isaac's investments are averaging 15 percent a year, that's a monthly growth rate of roughly 1.17 percent. His April withdrawal, then, would earn him an additional $666 because he left it in the market for the extra three months instead of pulling it all out in January. His July withdrawal, because it remained invested an extra six months, would earn an additional $1,355. And his October withdrawal gains an additional $2,069 from its nine-month extra ride in the market. So simply by pulling his money out at three-month intervals instead of all at once, Isaac makes an additional $4,090 throughout the year. It doesn't alter how much he has to spend or when he was planning to spend it, but it's a more efficient use of his capital and makes rebalancing his mini-portfolios easier as well. Not a bad deal! Now of course if the market goes down, the money he leaves invested those extra months goes down, too, but I'm using long-term averages in making this suggestion. More often than not, Isaac will be better off leaving as much invested as he can throughout the year, only pulling it out when he really needs it.

Getting More Aggressive

For those of you who are more aggressive and want to maximize returns always, another alternative for your cash management plan is to use your margin leverage capabilities. Instead of selling enough stock each quarter to meet your spending withdrawals, you can manipulate your margin leverage amounts to withdraw money and rebalance your positions, just as you were doing while saving regularly. As you know, I'm already a conservative fan of margin leverage in that while you're continuing to save throughout your working career I recommend a maximum leverage amount of 20 percent on margin. I become even more conservative, however, once your savings stop and you begin to live on the growth of your portfolio. I believe that by the point you're living on the portfolio's proceeds, you shouldn't need the extra boost margin can give your returns.

You're supposedly already using a sound stock strategy that's beating the market and inflation, and by limiting your annual withdrawals to 5 percent of your net value you should see adequate portfolio growth anyway. So I don't see the urgent need to attempt to boost those returns further when you're already at your ultimate goal—financial independence. And lest you forget, margin leverage exaggerates your returns on the downside as well. When your portfolio suffers a rough patch, margin leverage will make it even worse, and since you no longer have the regular savings coming in you enjoyed while still working, I don't see that the added potential reward is worth the additional risk.

That said, I'm still a believer in a conservative level of margin as both a booster of your long-term returns and as a cash management tool (or personal slush fund). But if you opt for margin leverage even after you begin living on the proceeds of your portfolio, keep it very modest. I'd set an absolute limit in such a case of roughly 10 percent on margin. That gives you sufficient room to rebalance a miniportfolio that's fallen out of step with the other miniportfolios, and affords you a little boost to your long-term returns. Beyond that level, though, your increased risk doesn't justify the potential reward. Remember, at this stage—financial independence—your goals are indefinite maintenance and staying ahead of inflation. You're no longer trying to build your empire; you're there. The task now is not to muck it up.

Income Taxes

So how do taxes figure into this entire picture? After all, if your private foundation portfolio is earning 15 percent a year or so, up to roughly 20 percent of those profits will be due in capital gains taxes (less all your eligible deductions, of course). If you recall from my earlier discussion of why the 20 Factor Plan will work, however, I did not include incomes taxes as part of the annual 5 percent withdrawals you can make. Since taxes will vary from year to year, sometimes wildly, depending upon how well your portfolio performed the previous year, it's too difficult to budget a steady amount into a generalized formula for annual withdrawals.

Instead I built the issue of taxes right into the percentage breakdown so it would be assumed that you will pay taxes out of your portfolio growth before you calculate your 5-percent withdrawals. In other words, you'll actually withdraw five percent for spending throughout the year *plus* whatever you owe Uncle Sam in taxes. After all, you only owe income taxes when your portfolio has made money, so this option for accounting for that liability won't interfere with your regular budget planning. Let's look at an example to make the concept a little clearer.

Let's say your private foundation portfolio is $1 million. Over the coming year, if you earn 15 percent in growth, that amount will increase by $150,000. If your tax liability is 20 percent of that gain, you will owe $30,000 in taxes to the government the following year. That $30,000 should come out of your portfolio in addition to your 5 percent annual spending withdrawal. So after deducting $30,000 in taxes, your actual after-tax portfolio growth is $120,000. In other words, your 15 percent return is actually a 12 percent after-tax return. Your annual salary withdrawal the next year, then, would be based on the $1,120,000 after-tax value, which means you would be taking out $56,000 for spending over the following year.

Obviously you will be paying quarterly estimated tax payments each year, and the easiest way to calculate them is to pay an amount equal to the previous year's total tax liability (spread out in four quarterly installments) and then settle up the balance when you file your annual return. If you're managing four quarterly miniportfolios and withdrawing one-fourth of your annual spending allowance at each portfolio update, tax payments are then relatively easy to manage. At each quarterly update, you will withdraw both your spending allowance and your estimated tax payment at the same time.

Don't let the tax issue overly complicate your management techniques. What it really boils down to is that the 20 Factor rule about spending no more than 5 percent a year excludes your tax payments. The model is based on the assumption that your portfolio will grow enough after taxes to support that 5 percent annual withdrawal and keep you ahead of inflation indefinitely. So pull out the money you owe in taxes, then calculate the 5 percent salary you'll pay yourself and continue as normal. In years when your portfolio doesn't perform very well, of course, your tax liability is reduced, so it's not as large a burden. And in years when your portfolio does very well, your after-tax profit is so much larger that the extra tax amount you'll owe is no trouble to manage because your overall growth is still increasing.

No one likes to pay taxes, but I'm not in the camp that believes you should do everything possible to eliminate them altogether. Too many investors hurt their actual after-tax returns (the only real measure of growth that matters) in their blinkered pursuit of tax reduction. I look at it this way; if my maximum tax rate on long-term capital gains is 20 percent, I'm keeping four out of every five dollars my portfolio earns. I don't mind that I have to pay an extra $10,000 in taxes one year, then, because I know that means I've made an additional $40,000 for myself. Although it seems backwards, it's actually quite simple; the more taxes you're paying, the better off you are because it means you've made more for yourself too. Now if Congress decides to stop penalizing savings and investment and drastically reduces or does away with the capital gains tax altogether, so much the better for us (but don't count on it happening). So pay those taxes cheerfully as a sign of your success.

Commencement

Graduation ceremonies were always a source of mixed feelings for me (and I suspect for most graduates who were conscious through the ceremony and not nursing a Force-10 hangover). On the one hand, such ceremonies celebrate the completion of academic studies, but as the name of the ceremony and inevitably the commencement speaker's address imply, it is supposed to signal the beginning of something as well.

To a great extent, that's how I feel about this book also. Once you've worked this far through the book, you know the vast bulk of what you'll need to succeed financially. You've learned to pay down your bad debt while taking advantage of good debt. You've learned how to save and how to put those savings to the best advantage. You've learned how to think of yourself not as an individual facing "retirement," but as someone who is establishing a private foundation with a future that extends indefinitely. You've learned how to look at managing a portfolio while building the foundation to a key level and then how to maintain the portfolio once you've begun living on the proceeds. And along the way I've thrown my opinions, arguments, and prejudices at you on a variety of topics associated with the whole process of becoming financially independent. But reading this book, of course—or any other, for that matter—isn't enough to make you financially independent. You're still faced with the important task of making the information presented here work for you. It's time for you to take off your graduation gown and mortarboard and commence the next part of the journey.

It's important to remember, however, that your situation will be ever-changing, and so will the financial community. By the time you read this (or reread it) a new issue may have appeared to change your strategy or financial needs. Don't let that changing financial landscape keep you from making the journey with a guidebook in hand, however. Just be prepared (I wasn't a Boy Scout for nothing) for the inevitable contingencies and adjust to them. You have the basic information at your disposal now to work through whatever issues you will face. And if you need help, you'll know the right questions to ask of your consultants on taxes, estate planning, and investing. Now that I've beaten the analogy drum to death, let's move on to some practical help.

In the final chapter, I'll present a survey of a variety of resources you'll want to consult as you develop your private foundation plans. From the best investment books, newspapers, and Internet forums to database services and financial planning resources, I'll point you to some of the most useful and inexpensive (in most cases, free) tools available to you. Many of these entries will be World Wide Web sites, so if you're not hooked up to the Internet yet, all I can say is you're years behind the curve. Even for semi-Luddites like me, the Internet has become an indispensable tool. Whether it is for daily news, stock information, or simply the wonderful speed of e-mail communications, I use the Internet daily, and I suspect you will too. The Internet is changing how America does business. Be part of it.

9

TOOLS FOR TODAY'S MONEY FOR LIFE INVESTOR

If there is one advantage we have as investors today over previous generations, it is our overwhelming access to free or very inexpensive information regarding investments and all matters financial. And I intentionally used *overwhelming* in order to convey the dual sense of the word. The information available to us today is indeed marvelous and copious, but it can also be paralyzing. There's so much out there; where does one start and how much of it does one really need to wade through in order to make informed decisions? It's easy to fall into the "paralysis by analysis" syndrome, where the sheer volume of material begging to be read keeps the investor from actually making any decisions.

This chapter will help you cut through what's out there. It won't be an exhaustive survey of all that you can discover, but my intention here is to point you to some of the more useful and/or crucial areas you should become familiar with in your journey toward financial independence. As you get more comfortable with your own investing style

and systematic approach, you'll find (as I have) that a lot of
the information available to you is white noise you can tune
out. And you'll find out that much of it is redundant. (How
many different reports can you read about the latest brokerage upgrade of Intel before you reach the point of dimin-
ishing returns? How many market analyst predictions do
you have to see fall woefully far from reality before you
discover that they're just wild guesses dressed up in big
words?)

Be picky, then: Limit your reading and research time to
those areas that are most relevant to your own investment
style—and let the rest slip away into oblivion. Otherwise,
you'll find your research taking over your entire life, effectively ruining the beauty and simplicity of a mechanical
investment approach. Just to give you an idea of how the
information can swell to overwhelming proportions, when I
first began working with The Motley Fool, one could read
all of the new content (including all of the messages posted
to the boards) for any given day in a couple of hours. That's
still probably more time than is necessary for your own
practical purposes, but it was possible to do nevertheless.
By the end of my tenure at the Fool some four years later,
however, an eight-hour day wasn't enough to read half of
the new content and the two message folders (out of hundreds on the Web site) that I was closely associated with.
And that's just one financial Web site; there are scores and
scores of others clamoring for your surfing time. More information, however, isn't necessarily better information, and
what your goal must be as you start doing your own
research is to filter through all that's out there and lock onto
the sources you find the most useful—and then don't agonize over the fact that you can't get to everything else. It's
neither possible nor necessary.

Online Stockbrokers

If you're planning to manage your own private foundation accounts, making your own investment decisions, one of the first choices you'll have to make is from among the growing crowd of Internet-based deep-discount brokers. Each year a handful of new firms (or old firms branching out into electronic trading) join the field of possibilities, and as with most financial information, the choices can rapidly become more complicated than is necessary. If you're an investor as opposed to a trader, and if you're making your own decisions about which stocks to buy or sell and when to make those moves, then the functions your broker fulfills should be greatly limited in scope. For the individual investor, the days are gone when you had to rely on the advice of your personal, full-service broker. Also gone are the days when you had to pay upwards of $200 per trade. And gone are the days when you had to be a big-shot investor and trade in round lots (multiples of one hundred shares) or pay a hefty premium.

For the individual investor, today, there are only a handful of criteria that really matter. The role of the stockbroker today for involved investors has been reduced (rightfully so) to one of order taker. All you need from your broker is accuracy, efficiency, insurance through the SIPC, and inexpensive commission and margin interest rates. Almost everything else the brokerage industry uses as marketing tools to get you in their (virtual) doors is fluff; you can get it elsewhere for free.

Let's look at a typical transaction for the kind of investor I've described in this book—one who uses a mechanical model to adjust his portfolio a handful of times per year. Let's say it's time for a typical quarterly adjustment to a portfolio with 20 positions, five each in four quarterly groups. Of the five old holdings in this quarterly group, America Online

(NYSE: AOL), Dell Computer (Nasdaq: DELL), EMC Corp. (NYSE: EMC), Philip Morris (NYSE: MO), and FreddieMac (NYSE: FRE), your model has told you to hang on to one of them (EMC Corp.) and replace the other four. In addition, let's say you need to trim slightly the position in EMC Corp. to bring it back in line with the other four positions in that group. The four new stocks you will be buying are Qualcomm (Nasdaq: QCOM), Applied Materials (Nasdaq: AMAT), Computer Associates (NYSE: CA), and Home Depot (NYSE: HD). That means you'll have five stock sales and four purchases to replace the sold positions—a total of nine trades.

Depending on the type of full-service broker that you use, you could pay a wildly different commission on each of those nine trades. Some brokers charge a fee based on the dollar size of the order; others charge their commission based on the number of shares traded. So a stock with a high price per share (like Qualcomm) would cost more on a scale where commissions are based on the dollar amount invested than one where a fee is levied based on the number of shares. But for a stock with a fairly low price per share, where your dollar amount per stock will buy you more shares, you'll pay a higher commission. Either way, through a traditional full-service broker, these nine trades could run in the neighborhood of $2,000. If you're making this kind of adjustment four times a year, bam, there go $8,000 in profits a year out of your pocket and into your broker's. There's a good reason Fred Schwed's classic book is called *Where Are the Customers' Yachts?*

Why should your commission on a trade depend on whether the stock you buy is trading at $50 a share or $300 a share? The brokerage firm is still just fulfilling a single order. It doesn't matter, of course, and the flat-fee commissions schedules available through deep-discount brokers prove it. Today, with a deep-discount broker, you can make those same nine trades for as little as $45. That's $45 **total**, not per trade!

That's right, the identical trade that runs you $200 or so at those full-service brokers, with their marble-floored lobbies and their mahogany-inlaid conference rooms, can cost you as little as $5 to $20 at a deep-discount broker. The shares you buy of Applied Materials are exactly the same, the price you pay for the shares is almost always identical. The only difference is that you're keeping more of your money instead of handing it over to your broker, who in the old days was more than happy to convince you to churn your account regularly. But as you're the one who did the research, developed the strategy (or at least adopted a strategy you could understand and could implement without anyone else's help), and set up your portfolio, why should the broker receive a whopping fee just to execute the trade? For the individual investor who is making his or her own decisions today, the broker is no longer a consultant; he's a waiter, turning your order in to the kitchen and bringing it back out to you on a plate. As George Brown says in one of his self-deprecating commercials for the deep-discounter George Brown & Company, referring to its $5 commissions, "That's not a commission; it's a tip." And frankly that's how it should be.

For the kind of investing I've advocated throughout this book, then, a deep-discount broker is the best alternative. The costs are low enough that even a person with a modest portfolio can justify managing his or her investments through individual stocks rather than turning to mutual funds or a full-service broker. Let's look at three such brokers. I've had personal experience with all three of the following firms and feel that each of them represents a good value for the individual who is an investor rather than a short-term trader. For that kind of frenetic trading, a whole different set of requirements exists, and it's not an area I'm particularly interested in—so I'll save my pages here for the kinds of brokers that match the needs of the unemotional investor.

Ameritrade

Hands down, Ameritrade (800-AMERITRADE; www.ameritrade.com) has the coolest television commercials in the industry. From counterculture types teaching corporate suits how to buy stocks online to punk rockers embarrassing full-service brokers, Ameritrade has made it clear that the "common" person can now take control of his or her investments and leave the establishment in the dust. And as one who loves to root for the underdog, these commercials strike a chord with me. But let's get to the actual details; a lot of the full-service brokers have clever advertisements, too, and I'm not going to run out and open an account as a result of them.

Unlike many of the deep-discount brokers, Ameritrade allows a variety of methods for placing a stock trade. The cheapest and perhaps the quickest is to place the trade directly through their Internet site. At $8 per trade for market orders, Ameritrade offers one of the lowest commission rates around. (A market order means you place a trade to buy or sell a stock at whatever the current market price is; you're not specifying any limit on the price you'll accept.) For limit and stop orders, Ameritrade charges an additional $5. (A limit order is one where you specify a set price above which you won't pay when buying a stock. A stop order is a standing order for your broker to sell your position if it should ever trade at or below your set "stop" price.)

While I recommend using the Internet site, for some investors that's either uncomfortable or impractical, so Ameritrade offers two other options. For $12 a trade, you can place your orders over the telephone, through Ameritrade's automated touch-tone phone system. And if you absolutely must talk to a live broker over the phone, you can place trades that way for just $18 each. Even at that price, it's a huge savings over the full-service brokerage prices. In other words, the price is right at Ameritrade.

Another issue for beginning investors is the broker's minimum account requirement. Ameritade has among the lowest thresholds in the industry, requiring a minimum deposit of just $2,000 to open an account. (This can be met either with cash or with a transfer of securities from another investment company.)

One potentially important drawback to Ameritrade, however, is its margin interest rate schedule. Earlier in this book I discussed how the use of margin leverage can not only make your periodic rebalancing easier, but can also increase your returns over time. Of course, that depends to a large degree on what interest rate your broker charges you for margin borrowing. The lower the rate, obviously, the better the situation for you. Unfortunately, Ameritrade's rates aren't very attractive. On borrowed amounts of less than $25,000, Ameritrade charges an annual interest rate of 0.75 percent plus the prevailing prime rate. With the prime rate today of 8.5 percent, that equates to a margin interest rate of 9.25 percent—a little steep, frankly.

The rates do come down, however, as your margin borrowing crosses certain size thresholds. For amounts between $25,000 and $50,000, the rate is the prime rate plus 0.25 percent. For amounts between $50,000 and $100,000, it's the prime rate minus 0.75 percent. Between $100,000 and $250,000, it's the prime rate minus 1.00 percent. Between $250,000 and $1,000,000, it's the prime rate minus 1.25 percent. And on borrowed amounts above $1,000,000, it's the prime rate minus 1.75 percent (currently a rate of 6.75 percent). Let's face it, though: If your portfolio is large enough that you can borrow $1 million on margin and stay within the reasonable guidelines I've laid out in this book, you don't need my help. But for the rest of us, Ameritrade's margin rates are no bargain. Keep in mind, each percentage point you pay your broker raises the bar that much higher. You have to make another percentage point in total portfolio returns that year before the margin borrowing increases your returns. And if you lose that year, your losses are increased by the margin interest rate you're paying. A lot of the time in comparisons among deep-discount brokers, it's easy to get caught up in how much one broker charges per trade vis-à-vis its competitors, but if you use margin leverage, the interest rate you pay may very well be a bigger expense each year.

For example, let's assume a portfolio of $250,000 is spread across 20 stocks, each of which turns over once per year. That means a total of 40 trades per year. And if you're using a 20-percent margin limit, you'd be borrowing $62,500 on margin for the year. If Broker A charges $8 a trade and 7.75 percent margin interest, you'd pay only $320 a year in commissions, but an additional $4,844 in interest charges throughout the year. That's a combined total of $5,164. If Broker B, however, charges $20 per trade but only 6.75 percent in margin interest, your total costs would actually turn out lower—$800 in commissions and $4,219 in margin interest, for a combined total of $5,019. So when comparing brokerage costs, look beyond the simple rate per trade and factor in all the costs you're likely to have to pay. If it's an IRA (where margin is prohibited), of course go for the lowest commission rates.

When you make trades through these deep-discount brokers, you typically get rapid confirmations through e-mail or an automated phone-call service. And then within a few days after the trade, you'll receive an additional printed confirmation of your trades in the mail. Once a month you'll also receive an account statement, listing all of your positions and your account activity for the month. And then at year-end, you'll receive all of the forms and information you'll need to complete your annual income tax returns (just like the full-service brokers).

Finally, Ameritrade offers its account holders a variety of tools online to assist them in the research process. I generally don't consider these items all that important because virtually all of them and many more are available free on the Internet anyway. For my money, it's more crucial that the deep-discount brokers keep their costs low by streamlining their services. The more they try to look like full-service houses, with research and ancillary services, the harder it will be for them to keep the costs down. So don't worry too much about what research your broker can provide you. For the record, though, Ameritrade offers real-time quotes, reports and alert services (via e-mail or pager), customizable stock charts, and links to the latest news, earnings estimates, and stock profiles.

The downsides to Ameritrade? In my limited personal experience with this firm, I've experienced occasional problems in logging onto its Web site when the stock market had a frantic day, and sometimes its automated confirmation call-back service has been sporadic, but all deep-discount brokers have experienced similar growing pains as the demand for online brokers has swelled. Unless you're trying to day trade and need instantaneous feedback of your trades, this shouldn't be an issue for you. Overall, Ameritrade is a fine choice for an online broker. Now if they'd just slash those margin rates. . . .

Datek Online

The second of three online brokers I'll feature is Datek Online (800-U2-Datek; www.datek.com). Datek is exclusively an online brokerage firm, allowing you trading access only via your Internet connection. And while that may be a hindrance to investors who aren't quite comfortable yet using the Internet for financial transactions, don't let this prospect scare you. I've had nothing but good personal experiences with Datek in the past, and the firm offers some unique features that make it worth considering.

Like Ameritrade, Datek Online requires a minimum deposit of either cash or securities equaling just $2,000 to open an account. With such a small initial requirement, even the first-time investor who is funding an Individual Retirement Account is granted access to the stock market at a very low cost.

Unlike Ameritrade, though, Datek doesn't discriminate among different types of stock orders. All orders (market, limit, and stop orders) are charged the same flat commission rate of $9.99 per trade (up to 5,000 shares). What's more, Datek offers a guarantee that if it can't complete your trade execution in 60 seconds or less (for a marketable order, of course), that trade will not be charged a commission at all.

Where Datek shines over Ameritrade is in its margin interest rates. Datek doesn't have an elaborate schedule, breaking its rates down into a half-dozen different categories and then tying the rates to a floating benchmark (the prime rate). With Datek it's cut-and-dried. If you borrow less than $50,000, the margin interest rate is 7.5 percent. If you borrow more than $50,000, the rate is just 7 percent. That's it. Reasonably low rates and only two categories. Compare that rate of 7.5 percent for modest investors with the 9.25 percent top rate charged by Ameritrade, and Datek's slightly higher commission cost ($2 per trade more) becomes irrelevant. Let's say you have a portfolio of $50,000 and are borrowing the maximum 20 percent margin leverage that I claim is reasonable. That means a margin balance of $12,500. At Ameritrade, that margin balance will cost you $1,156 in interest over a year, whereas Datek would charge only $938. A $218 difference is meaningful on a portfolio of that size. Even though at Datek you'll pay $80 more in commissions (assuming 40 trades per year), you're still saving $138 by choosing Datek.

Going back to our larger-size portfolio example—a $250,000 portfolio borrowing $62,500 on margin and making 40 trades per year—a Datek Online investor would pay $400 in commissions and $4,375 in margin interest. That's a combined annual cost of $4,775. The same customer at Ameritrade, however, would pay $5,164 in total costs for the year. As I mentioned before, analyze how you trade and what kind of margin balance you're likely to carry to determine which broker will cost you the least in total fees.

Like all of the other online deep-discount firms, Datek Online offers gateways to charting features, individual stock and market news stories, and links to research reports. Not that it's relevant for the kind of investor I've been discussing, but Datek Online also provides unlimited free real-time stock quotes. If you're watching every tick of the market that closely, however, I'd suggest that you're on the wrong pathway. And finally, one feature offered by Datek that will undoubtedly bring in many short-term traders is access to after-hours trading of Nasdaq stocks. Through the Island ECN system, Datek allows its customers to trade Nasdaq stocks from 8:00 A.M. to 8:00 P.M. (Eastern) instead of limiting trading to typical market hours (9:30 A.M. to 4:00 P.M. Eastern). For short-term traders, I suppose, this is a vital feature. For the rest of us, this isn't an issue. But as Datek is the only one of the brokers I'm featuring that offers such a service, I feel compelled to mention it.

Overall, for those investors who are comfortable making all of their transactions over the Internet, Datek Online is a very good choice. Its fees are straightforward and very reasonable, and its minimum investment requirement is low enough to allow beginning investors with modest portfolios direct access to the stock market.

Brown & Company Securities

Of the three brokers I'm featuring, I've saved my personal favorite (Brown & Company; 800-822-2829; www.brownco. com) for last. And as a quick disclaimer, let me state up front that my personal account, my business partner's personal account, and all of our firm's clients' accounts are with Brown & Company, but we receive no compensation of any type from Brown & Company. (Perhaps I should have negotiated a fee before writing this book?) We've simply chosen Brown & Company because the firm offers us the best combination of service and value of all the brokers we've examined. Now if someone in Boston reads this and wants to put me on television to endorse Brown & Company for a fee, I'd probably consider it, but I do it here gratis because I think the firm offers the individual investor a terrific deal. Let's look at the details.

The obvious factor that sticks out with Brown & Company is its commission rate. For market orders placed through its Internet Web site (up to 5,000 shares) Brown charges a flat rate of $5 per trade. It doesn't matter if you're buying a single share of Dell Computer (Nasdaq: DELL) at $50 per share or 5,000 shares of Qualcomm (Nasdaq: QCOM) at $370 per share, you still pay Brown & Company just five bucks. That's a deal you just can't beat. Imagine what the cost would be for that Qualcomm purchase at a full-service broker! If for some reason you want to place the trade through a live broker over the phone, that's easy to do as well with Brown & Company because it has 12 regional offices fielding your calls, not just a single location that can be overrun at peak hours. And the cost to trade with a live broker is just $12 per trade—still a terrific bargain. For limit or stop orders, you'll pay $10 a trade online and $17 a trade through a live broker.

Brown also has among the lowest margin interest rates of all the deep-discount brokers. For margin balances up to

$50,000, Brown charges the prevailing "broker's call" interest rate, which right now is 7.25%. The rates then drop off as your margin balance increases. Between $50,000 and $100,000 the rate is broker's call minus 0.25 percent. Between $100,000 and $500,000, it's broker's call minus 0.50 percent. Between $500,000 and $1 million, it's broker's call minus 0.75 percent. And above $1 million, the rate is broker's call minus 1.00 percent, currently 6.25 percent.

Let's go back to our two comparisons. For a $50,000 portfolio, where the investor will borrow $12,500 on margin and make 40 trades per year, the total annual cost would be $1,106. That's $200 for the 40 trades and $906 in margin interest. By way of comparison, the Datek Online investor would pay $1,338 a year, and the Ameritrade investor would pay $1,476 per year.

For the larger portfolio example, borrowing $62,500 on margin and making the same 40 trades per year, the Brown & Company cost would be $4,575, the same $200 for the 40 trades and $4,375 in margin interest. At Datek Online the cost would be $4,775, and at Ameritrade it would be $5,164. So for both commission rates (especially if you're managing an IRA and can't use margin leverage) and for margin interest rates, Brown & Company offers the best package. In fact, in a recent survey, *SmartMoney* magazine ranked Brown & Company tops in the total cost category.

Just as important, however, in this age of online trading, the *SmartMoney* rankings also championed Brown & Company for Web reliability. While short-term slowdowns in Internet traffic aren't fatal to the long-term investor, it's nevertheless comforting to work with an online broker that is consistent in its service and accessibility.

Another feature of Brown's Web site that is of great help to the individual investor is that the online portfolio tracking service is updated immediately after you've made a trade. In other words, the cash balance the Web site lists for your account doesn't date back to the previous day's closing value; it's updated as each trade is made. This is particularly helpful in managing an IRA account, where margin is prohibited, and you must be careful not to overspend your available cash. Knowing exactly how much cash remains in your account after you've made all of your trades but one helps you invest as fully as possible without going over the line. Many online brokers don't have this immediate portfolio updating feature, making your trading days a little less convenient.

One of the reasons Brown & Company is able to offer such an attractive package for the individual stock investor is that it limits its field of operations. The firm does not accept bond investments or mutual fund investments, as some other deep-discount brokers do. In some surveys of deep-discount brokers, this has caused Brown & Company to be rated less attractively than it should be. But as I've argued that common stocks are the best pathway for the long-term investor, this isn't a real concern. If you're starting off in an index mutual fund, you're better off setting up your account directly with the mutual fund family. There are typically no costs associated with such a process, whereas if you were to invest in a mutual fund through a deep-discount broker, you might pay some unnecessary transaction commissions. So for index funds, go straight to the fund family. For stocks, go through a deep-discount broker.

Another factor keeping Brown & Company's costs so low is that the firm doesn't pretend to be a full-service firm, offering you investment advice and in-house research. On the Brown & Company Web site, you'll find a number of hyperlinks to financial news and research Web sites, but Brown & Company itself doesn't provide any of those services directly. Again, think of your stockbroker as a simple order taker. You're responsible for doing your own research (and I'll guide you to several resources where you can accomplish that) and making your own decisions. All you need from a broker is fast, reliable, accurate, and low-cost trade executions. Brown & Company fits that model perfectly. Everything else is a frill that will increase your costs.

Is Brown & Company too good to be true, then? Well, no. There *is* a catch. Not everyone is eligible to open an account with Brown & Company. As a way of focusing only on a certain type of independent investor who makes all of his own decisions (or hires a professional manager who then makes the decisions on his behalf), Brown & Company has a series of requirements (not overly strict, actually) that an investor must meet before opening an account.

First, a potential Brown & Company customer must have an annual income (from all sources) of at least $40,000. Second, he must have a total net worth (excluding his residence) of at least $50,000. Third, he must have a minimum of five years' worth of investing experience. Now that doesn't mean you have to have been a Wall Street trader for five years, but whether it's through mutual funds or individual stocks, a five-year investment history is necessary before Brown will accept your account. (If you meet all of the requirements except the five-year history, however, you can still open an account with Brown & Company if you've engaged a portfolio manager who meets that experience requirement.)

Fourth, Brown & Company has a much higher minimum investment requirement than the standard deep-discount broker. To open a regular taxable account (all such accounts at Brown & Company are margin-eligible accounts), you must deposit $15,000 in cash or securities. For an IRA, the minimum requirement is $5,000. Obviously, then, with the annual contribution limit of $2,000 for IRAs, the only way to have an IRA account at Brown & Company is to transfer an existing IRA that you've funded for a few years running.

Overall, if you meet Brown & Company's requirements, it's the broker I recommend as a first choice.

So which of the three brokers is best for *you?* Let's look at a few possible scenarios and make comparisons. The first one is simple: anyone qualifying for a Brown & Company account is best served by that firm's unbeaten combination of low per-trade commissions and low margin interest rates. But if you don't meet its restrictions, you'll have to decide which broker to select based on other criteria. For example, if you're starting a new IRA account with $2,000, you would be better served (ever so slightly) by choosing Ameritrade, because it charges less in commissions than Datek and its higher margin interest rates are irrelevant to your situation. For a taxable portfolio where you will be using margin leverage, however, Datek offers a better package. Even though it charges $2 per trade more than Ameritrade, Datek's margin interest rates are significantly lower than Ameritrade's and in a typical margined portfolio, the interest expense is significantly more expensive than the per-trade commissions.

Don't feel, however, that you have to place all of your accounts with the same broker. You may well decide to place your IRA at Ameritrade and your taxable portfolio at Datek, and then when they meet Brown & Company's requirements, you may transfer them. (Transferring an IRA from one financial institution to another is an easy process and does not constitute a withdrawal as far as the Internal Revenue Service is concerned. You're simply moving your IRA from one broker to the other.)

In just the past five years, the commission structure of deep-discount brokers has changed radically. The best rate to be found just a few years ago was $25 or $30 per trade. In that short time span, we've seen those costs slashed by 80 percent or more. It's my suspicion that within a few more years, trading commissions might disappear altogether.

Brokerage firms are already having to make up much of the revenue they have traditionally received through commissions from other sources, such as margin interest and by sending their order flow in more profitable directions. The actual process of executing a trade may become a freebie for the individual investor some day. Even as it stands now, though, it's a very modest entry barrier into the greatest investment arena available. Take advantage of it.

Stock Market Research

In keeping with my frugality theme (why pay for free information? and don't believe for a minute that you get what you pay for in the financial industries), let me begin with the free site that should launch all independent investors on their research journeys.

Yahoo! Finance

Yahoo! (www.finance.yahoo.com) is perhaps the largest and arguably the most successful of what we once called Internet search engines. They were sites where a "Web surfer" could start looking for other Web sites of interest, and the search engine would point him or her toward the addresses of the relevant sites. But as technology has stretched the Internet in such unforeseen directions in recent years, these sites have become much more than simple gateways to other places. They are destinations in and of themselves now. Yahoo! covers an enormous range of topics, but it's solely the financial section that I'll be addressing here. (For the main page for Yahoo!, go to www.yahoo.com.) And within just the Finance section alone, Yahoo! offers an amazing wealth of useful information.

Let me begin my Yahoo! Finance tour, then, with a brief summary of the major subjects covered there before I go into more specific detail regarding the investment sections.

In the **U.S. Markets** section, you'll find a summary of the major American stock indices, recent initial public offerings (or IPOs), a list of the most actively traded stocks that day, a market digest, and a mutual fund summary.

Under **World Markets,** you'll find similar information for overseas markets, with the major world stock indices, currency exchange rates, and a section specifically covering Canadian markets.

I'll return with more detail to the subject of the **Research** section shortly, but by way of summary now you'll find information there arranged by industry, a stock-screening vehicle where you may enter certain criteria and the database pulls up those companies meeting them, a summary of recent stock analyst upgrades and downgrades, earnings reports and estimates, links to individual companies' Securities and Exchange Commission filings, financial statements, and historical price quotes.

In the **Loans** section, you can visit the Loan Center (an informational center), check current home mortgage interest rates, get access to credit reports, and browse for automobile loan interest rates.

The Investment Challenge allows you to pit your stock-selection skills against those of other visitors, in an online stock market simulation.

The **Reference** section is comprised of two areas of information. The first includes a company and fund index as well as a glossary of terms. The second includes a series of calendars, including economic events, company earnings releases, and scheduled stock splits.

The **Yahoo! Bill Pay** section is a new addition to the finance area and allows users to set up electronic bill paying.

The **Editorial** section includes links to some of the major financial commentary sites on the Internet, including The

Motley Fool, TheStreet.com, Individual Investor, and Online Investor.

The **Financial News** section is a clearinghouse for the major business newswire services where you can get up-to-the-minute stories from the Associated Press, Standard & Poor's, PR News, BizWire, and others.

In the **Taxes** area, in addition to an information center, you will find an online tax filing refund estimator, a tax organizer, and a message board where you can exchange questions, answers, and opinions with other readers.

The **Insurance** section also includes an information resource center, as well as providing links where you can obtain price quotations for auto insurance, life insurance, health insurance, home insurance, and renters' insurance.

And the **Community** section is where Yahoo! users come together. There is a series of message boards arranged by topics, a stock chat area, a listing of Internet events, an ongoing marketplace poll, and access to finance clubs.

One of the amazing things the Internet has afforded us all is access to each other. I have received e-mail from around the world over the last few years, and through my columns and message-board postings I've been able to converse with a variety of savvy investors I'd never have had the privilege to meet without the assistance of the digital media. It's a double-edged sword, however. It's vitally important that you verify information you come across online in chat rooms and message boards. The downside of complete democratic access to these media is that anyone can post comments and opinions—and you don't need me to tell you that not everyone in the world is a nice guy. You'll find patently false information, and rumors proliferate in some places on the Internet as unscrupulous or just plain malicious posters try to manipulate the flow of information. Check out your sources well, and

you'll find the Internet a fabulous resource. But if you buy or
sell stocks based on hot tips from anonymous sources online,
someone will be along in a day or two to clean your remains
from the Internet Superhighway—because you *will* get run
over.

I'll mention two other elements you will find on the
Yahoo! Finance main Web page, and then, as promised, I'll
delve a little deeper into the information most relevant to
stock investors. In addition to all the sections of information
I've catalogued already, there are links to several related
resources, including an instant stock alert service, Yahoo!'s
"companion" service, a news ticker, and sections on real
estate and small businesses. Happy browsing.

The other element, which I've saved for last (because it
will serve as a transition into the material oriented toward
stocks specifically), is the stock quotes service that Yahoo!
provides. At the top of each page in the Finance section you
will find a window where you may enter one or more stock
symbols and get a price quote in a variety of formats. (If you
don't know a stock's ticker symbol, a lookup function is also
available.) This is where the real research can begin on an
individual company's stock.

Rather than simply list all the possible features, let's walk
through a scenario and follow the trail for a single stock,
EMC Corporation (NYSE: EMC). To get a straightforward
price quote, then, just type "EMC" into the Quotes window
and leave the default setting on "Basic." What's provided is a
window showing you the time and the price of the last trade
on the stock (Yahoo!'s quotes are 15- to 20-minute delayed
quotes, not real-time); today's change in price and the percentage move that represents; and the number of shares
traded so far today (the trading volume). At the bottom of the
quote page you'll also find a list of links to the latest news stories for that company, a quick and easy way to track the

progress of a stock you already own or one you're considering purchasing.

If you want more information, you'll find a variety of
links next to the quote information that you can pursue. They
include a chart function, news stories about the company, the
company's Securities and Exchange Commission filings, a
company message board, a profile of the business, a summary of research analyst opinions on the stock, and a summary of company insider transactions.

Let's say you want more information than the Basic Quote
provided. Change the Quote feature setting from "Basic" to
"Detailed." In addition to the basic last trade information you
saw in the Basic Quote, you'll now see the day's trading
range, the current bid and ask prices, and the opening price
for the day. You'll discover that the average day's trading volume for EMC Corp. has been 5.7 million shares; that it
doesn't pay a dividend but that it last split two-for-one on
June 1, 1999; that its 52-week price range is from $35¾ to $90¾;
that the company has earned $0.99 per share over the previ-
ous year, which gives it a Price/Earnings Ratio of 88.38; and
that its market capitalization is $89.032 billion.

With the stock trading near the high end of its 52-week
trading range, and given that the range is pretty large, it's
safe to assume that EMC Corp. has had a pretty good year,
but how has it done compared to the overall market index?
Let's look. Click on the Chart link and up pops a one-year
chart of the stock. At the bottom of the chart, you'll find a
number of links that will allow you to customize the chart to
make it smaller or larger to fit your monitor better, to change
the period (from daily charts all the way up to five-year
charts), and to incorporate features such as the stock price's
moving average or a comparison line for the S&P 500 index.
Let's click the S&P 500 line and the chart reconfigures, showing EMC Corporation's progress over the last year with a

blue line and the S&P 500 Index's progress with a red line. Hmm, over the last year the S&P 500 Index gained roughly 20 percent while EMC Corp. gained about 135 percent—not a bad relative comparison, you'd agree.

So, EMC Corp. has been a good stock over the past year, but what are its prospects for the future? What do the analysts who follow the stock full-time think of it? Click the Research link for the stock and Yahoo! provides you with a summary of the professional analysts' opinions, courtesy of Zacks Analyst Watch. For example, you'll see that of the 26 analysts with ratings on the stock, 15 give it the highest rating, a Strong Buy. Another eight rate it a Moderate Buy, and the remaining three rate it a Hold. None of the analysts rate the stock a Moderate Sell or Strong Sell. So on a scale of 1 to 5, with 1 representing a Strong Buy and 5 representing a Strong Sell, the current average recommendation is 1.46. Last week the average was 1.32. So over the last week, someone has lowered a rating on EMC Corp.

If you want to follow the earnings numbers and estimates, you'll see that EMC earned $0.29 per share in the September 1999 quarter, which was 7.41 percent higher than analysts had expected. You can also see the range of analyst estimates for the current quarter and fiscal year, and the estimated growth rate for future earnings. In addition you can see the recent trend of these earnings estimates as analysts have revised their forecasts.

The research section also includes an earnings history for the stock so you can compare the growth for EMC Corporation with its industry group. And finally, Yahoo! makes available links to the actual research abstracts from the brokerage firm analysts (again courtesy of Zacks Analyst Watch). So if you want to see what Hambrecht & Quist, for example, had to say about the company in its October 29, 1999 call, it's just a click away.

Now that you've seen how the company and the stock have been performing, maybe it's time to discover what the company actually does. (It's hard to tell with some of the high-technology companies today, I know.) Click on the Profile link, and the page that loads will include a list of recent corporate events (such as earnings announcements), the firm's location, and if there is one, a link to its own Web site. In addition, you'll find a summary of the company's business, a list of the corporate officers, and then a slew of financial statistics about the firm. In addition to the stock-related items you've already seen, you'll also find a series of fundamental ratios for the company, such as book value, price-to-book ratio, price-to-sales ratio, after-tax income, profit margin, return on assets and return on equity, the current ratio, long-term debt-to-equity ratio, total cash and the short interest (the number of the company's shares that have been sold short). If you're not familiar with short selling, it's simply playing the stock market in reverse. When you believe a stock will fall in price, you may borrow shares of the stock from your broker (if you have a margin account), sell them on the open market, and pocket the proceeds of the sale. At some later date, you will have to purchase those shares back in order to return them to your broker. Obviously you hope to purchase them at a lower price than you sold them.

Okay, now that you've seen what Wall Street thinks of the stock, what about what the folks inside the boardroom think? Some investors view insider buying and selling as potential signals about the company's future. In most cases, insider buying can be taken as a vote of confidence by the company's officers—but insider selling may not mean the reverse. Because many corporations reward their corporate officers today by using stock options as incentives rather than remunerating them with a strictly salary-based package, a sale by a corporate officer may mean nothing more than that he or she is cashing a form of a paycheck. It doesn't necessarily mean the officer believes tough times lie ahead. Another word of caution about using insider trading as a signal: Corporate officers aren't necessarily great predictors of stock prices. It's very often difficult to be objective about a company's stock when one's compensation and future are so closely tied to it. I've seen a lot of rosy forecasts from corporate insiders end up dead wrong.

But if you want to watch the trends of insider movements, you can watch them to a delayed degree by clicking the Insider Trades section. All corporate insiders who hold a certain percentage of the company's shares have to file their purchases and sales, and these records slowly become public knowledge. Yahoo! lists them for you, telling you who the insider is, the date of the transaction, the number of shares (or options on shares), and the value of the transaction. More information for your mill.

And finally, the Upgrades/Downgrades History section will list the most recent brokerage house rating changes on the company. For example, on November 19, 1999, SoundView Tech downgraded EMC Corporation (the nerve of them!) from a Strong Buy to a Buy. (Do you remember my mentioning that the brokerage average rating dropped slightly? Here's the reason why.) This section also reveals that on November 11, 1999, J.P. Morgan started coverage of the stock with a Buy rating. On November 4, 1999, PaineWebber started coverage of EMC Corporation, but with a Neutral rating. And so forth, all the way back to the February 25, 1998, notice from Deutsche Morgan, starting coverage with a Buy rating.

Just as you should be cautious about insider buying and selling, however, you should be equally skeptical about analyst ratings. Analysts take first prize in the Meaningless Euphemism contest. Their ratings can be so obfuscating as to make it impossible to tell what they really believe about a stock's future. For example, when a Wall Street analyst really hates a stock, he or she will typically rate it a Hold rather than some form of Sell. The research firms are invariably linked to investment banking divisions and no firm wants to alienate a potential banking client by publicly declaring that the stock is a dog, so they opt for the more tame Neutral or Hold rating. But everyone watching the analyst game knows that's code for "sell this puppy before it bites you in the butt—if it hasn't already." The research analyst/investment banking conflict of interest is one of the biggest shams in American financial markets, so take everything you hear from analysts not just with a grain of salt, but rather tie yourself to the whole salt lick. My favorite rating is "Source of Funds." Now how's that for telling you to sell without actually uttering the dreaded S-word?

Believe it or not, this has only been a cursory glance at all that Yahoo! Finance has to offer you. There are many other features and links to information sites you'll undoubtedly discover in your research process. One such feature I must mention is the ability to set up your own portfolio on Yahoo!, where stock prices and values and returns are calculated for you automatically. It's not a real-money portfolio tied to any brokerage firm, of course; it's strictly an information resource where you can track either your actual holdings or perhaps a group of stocks you're considering for future investments. Whatever way you ultimately use Yahoo! Finance, it's a marvelous place to come up to speed on any given stock in a very brief amount of time. This information simply wasn't available to the average investor a decade ago, let alone for the cost of an Internet connection. The revolution made possible by the Internet has handed a lot of control back to average investors by opening the information vaults for all to see. Take advantage.

Value Line Investment Survey

Breaking from my survey of free services, I do want to discuss one particular service I use and have written about extensively, despite its being a fairly pricey subscription service. The *Value Line Investment Survey* (800-833-0046; www.valueline.com) is a weekly publication covering 1,700 stocks that represent the majority of the trading volume on the major exchanges. Value Line also publishes an expanded version that includes 5,000 stocks, but for investors focusing on industry leaders and large-company stocks like I do, the original publication is sufficient.

In addition to providing a complete array of fundamental and historical data on each of the 1,700 companies, Value Line's usefulness lies in its proprietary ranking system. Each stock is ranked for Timeliness over the following 12 months on a scale of 1 to 5. On the surface, this isn't terribly different from the scale that traditional Wall Street analysts use. But there are some vital differences for the Value Line reader. First, Value Line doesn't have a conflict of interest with an investment banking consideration. Second, Value Line actually uses the 4 and 5 rankings with regularity. In fact, their ranking system is completely objective, based on a series of quantifiable criteria, and after these tests have been applied, then the stocks are ranked accordingly. The top 100 companies receive a 1 ranking. The next 300 receive a 2 ranking. The middle 900 receive a 3 ranking, and then the symmetry is repeated on the other side of the curve, with 300 stocks carrying a 4 ranking and the worst 100 carrying a 5 ranking. Third, what's so remarkable about Value Line's Timeliness ranking system is that it has consistently outperformed the S&P 500 Index for decades, dating back to the mid-1960s. Anyone using these rankings as a starting point in picking stocks is way ahead of the game. Any mechanical system that regularly beats the stock market is something to take seriously, and since 1965 Value Line's system has done so.

Using the Timeliness rankings, then, allows the individual investor to screen the enormous universe of stock possibilities down to a much more reasonable list of candidates using a time-tested system. Much of my own research has incorporated the Value Line ranking system into my mechanical screening systems. It's a wonderful resource.

The one drawback is the cost. A year's subscription to the *Investment Survey* runs $570. The good news, however, is that a great many public libraries subscribe to the publication and you may have free access to it. Be prepared, though, to wait in line on Friday afternoon, when it comes out. It's a very popular resource for individual investors.

A couple of years ago, Value Line also began offering an electronic edition of the *Value Line Investment Survey*, and if you use the publication regularly, it's decidedly worth the few extra dollars ($595 a year) to subscribe to the electronic edition. In addition to electronic versions of all of the printed materials one gets with the standard edition, subscribers get a variety of extremely useful screening tools. Perhaps foremost among them is a customizable database including hundreds of data points for each stock. This allows the user to screen the database in a matter of seconds based on whatever fundamental criteria the user chooses. For those of you who use mechanical screening routines like I do, this is an indispensable device. To perform a typical screen using the electronic edition might take 30 or 40 seconds, but if I wanted to perform the same operation using the print version, it would take hours and introduce human error into the process.

Another advantage of the electronic version is that the weekly edition and database update is always available for downloading at noon (eastern) on Friday. Depending on your local post office, the print version can arrive anytime from late Thursday to Tuesday of the following week. The consistency of delivery through the electronic downloads alone is worth the $25 extra.

Microsoft's MoneyCentral

MoneyCentral (www.moneycentral.com) is one of the Internet's all-purpose investing sites. You can follow your stocks in an electronic portfolio there. You can read the latest market and stock news. MoneyCentral sports a wide variety of columnists who cover an equally wide variety of topics, from short-term trading to personal finance. In their Investor section, they run a full-time Strategy Lab where you can follow along with the thought processes of six professional money managers as they invest a mock portfolio for six months, demonstrating a range of strategies in real time. (I was honored to be one of these managers in the second half of 1999 and used the opportunity to experiment with a model strategy I hadn't previously used. There's nothing like a real-time test to put a strategy through its paces.)

One of the best features among many at MoneyCentral, however, is its own screenable database. Previously the Finder was a feature only available to paid subscribers, but Microsoft has recently opened up the entire site for free access, making it an even more useful resource for the individual investor. Like the Value Line database (except that it's free), Finder allows the user to specify fundamental criteria that he or she feels are useful in choosing stocks, and the database points out which stocks meet the criteria. So, for example, if you're interested in stocks with a market capitalization of greater than $5 billion, with an annual earnings growth rate of better than 15 percent, and a price-to-sales ratio of less than 1.5, plug those variables into the Finder and up will pop any stocks in the database meeting your criteria.

If you've developed a screening routine that has proven itself over time, using Finder is a very economical and quick way to begin your research process.

If you're still searching for a screening model of your own, but like the ease and convenience of MoneyCentral's Finder, pick up Jon Markman's book, *Online Investing.* Markman will walk you through a range of screening strategies with the Finder database. In no time you'll be comfortable with the tool and will have learned a variety of powerful strategies as well. You may well develop the next best mechanical strategy.

Other All-Purpose Sites

Each month additional investment sites spring up on the Internet. Some are terrific, some are weak, and a great deal of their content is redundant. To keep from becoming a news and investing junkie, you'll have to begin discriminating among them for the few you enjoy the most, and let the others go. The following is a brief list of some of the best of what is currently available among general investing sites. Give them a read and find your favorites.

The Motley Fool

I'm obviously going to be biased about The Motley Fool (www.fool.com), given that I got my start writing about investing while wearing a jester's hat. The Fool has been described as the world's largest investment club, and that's a pretty apt description. Because the site has always encouraged a high level of reader participation, the lines sometimes blur between content provider and customer. And as Martha Stewart would say, "This is a good thing." In fact, many of the site's staff writers began (as I did) as readers of the site. From news, columns, and research reports to games, fun merchandise, and wildly active message boards, the Fool has become something of the standard for online Investment education sites. And the best feature of the Fool is its cost to readers— nada.

CBS MarketWatch

A more mainstream media outlet and less personal than the Fool, CBS MarketWatch (www.marketwatch.com) nevertheless provides good news coverage, a stock screener, and some charting utilities, as well as data from Zacks and Hoover's. Like the Fool, MarketWatch is a free service.

Morningstar

Long recognized as the premier tracker of the mutual fund industry (especially for professional investors), Morningstar (www.morningstar.com) has made a great deal of information available to individual investors. Morningstar's Quicktake reports will provide you with a summary of a mutual fund's or stock's fundamental and financial statistics. The site also includes feature articles on general investing as well as specific current news stories. Morningstar offers a premium service that gives the user access to analyst reports on mutual funds as well as an e-mail service that provides market and portfolio news directly to the user.

Quicken

While the Quicken site (www.quicken.com) offers many of the same stock-oriented features available elsewhere, its aim is a bit wider reaching. More of a full-service personal finance site, Quicken covers areas such as mortgages, banking, and retirement planning (including a Roth IRA calculator). In addition, Quicken offers portfolio tracking, news reports, a stock screening engine, stock quotes and a mutual fund finder.

TheStreet.com

Offering many of the same features found elsewhere, TheStreet.com (www.thestreet.com) has tried to separate itself from the pack by riding the personality of its founder, Jim Cramer. A frequent guest on CNBC's Squawk Box, Cramer has become something of a trader's guru. Never short of an opinion, Cramer is willing to stick his neck out, both as a writer and as an actual money manager in an industry that cowers in homogeneity at times. Cramer's columns and those of his staff writers are intended to be cutting edge instead of run-of-the-mill, and as a result, TheStreet.com is a subscription service. (There is limited access at no charge.)

SmartMoney

Like CBS MarketWatch, SmartMoney (www.smartmoney. com) is a site run by a mainstream media company, the publisher of *SmartMoney* magazine. Geared toward a wide variety of personal finance issues, the SmartMoney slant is often toward the mutual fund industry, and for that reason I find it less useful than some of the others. But that aside, the site does offer many of the same attractive features that make the best stock sites so useful: news, a portfolio tracker, market reports, charting features, quotes, a fund finder, analyst recommendations, and feature articles.

The list of similar sites continues to grow, and by the time this book finds its way into your hands, there may be a half-dozen more sites that have moved into the top echelon. As you become a more experienced investor, you will undoubtedly find that you'll need to scour fewer and fewer of these sites. You'll find the features you need in one or two sites and will return there again and again for all your research needs. And if you become a mechanically inclined investor as I am, using objective and rigid analytical screens to assist your stock-selection process, you'll find that you read the intricate news stories less and less.

I find that at some stage, the more one reads, the harder it becomes to make a decision. An unemotional investor short-circuits much of that anxiety created by information overload by ignoring the analyst reports and the news stories (often rumors) that swirl around each company and focusing instead on tangible data that can be compared objectively. In other words, don't ask me if Dell Computer (Nasdaq: DELL) is a buy, sell, or hold today. Without a context, that isn't a question with a good answer. Compared to what? But when you ask me which stock looks better, Dell or Compaq (NYSE: CPQ), then I can sit down with real numerical comparisons and give you a more useful answer. If you rely on analyst opinions or news stories, you can be too easily swayed by the wrong types of information. For that reason, you may find that you'll only use a handful of the many features available to you. Don't feel as a result that you're somehow not doing everything you can as an investor. Find what works for you and stop worrying about what your neighbor or colleague is doing.

Technical Analysis Sites

Investment analysis techniques are usually classified in one of two camps: *fundamental* or *technical*. Fundamental analysts look at a company's business and try to determine the financial outlook for the individual company, its earnings prospects, and a fair value target for the stock price. They often decide between companies based on which business is likely to generate the best profits or which is most undervalued by the market. The theory is that the best business will also produce the best stock results. Pure technical analysts, however, ignore the company fundamentals and look at the stock as a simple commodity. They evaluate the stock based on how it is being traded in the open marketplace. As such, they examine charts of the stock's trading action and look for patterns or situations they believe will lead to a rise in the stock price. It is very much a psychological approach to investing in which the analysts attempt to determine how investors will behave based on how they've behaved in similar situations with other stocks in the past.

Investors in both camps tend to be dogmatic about the validity of one method and the utter absurdity of the other, but of course, as in most things in life, it's never that simple. In recent years I've held the stance that since I am not a chartist, I'm really a fundamental analyst. But that's not entirely accurate either. The fact is, I'm a quantitative analyst, and some of the criteria I examine are as much technical as they are fundamental. For example, if I'm using a model focusing on earnings growth rates (a decidedly fundamental factor), but I'm pairing that with a screen based on a stock's price performance relative to the rest of the market over the last year (relative strength), that adds a purely technical factor into the mix.

So in recent years, I've softened my stance on the technical analysis camp, although in my personal case, I'm not looking for particular patterns on charts, but rather, using some price-performance criteria within my quantitative, objective mod-

els. Nevertheless, there are many successful technical investors out there, and if you're interested in becoming one
(and technical analysis does not by definition lead to day
trading, although most day-traders are technical analysts),
start with a quality book that surveys the major theories
behind technical analysis: John J. Murphy's *The Visual Investor: How to Spot Market Trends* (John Wiley & Sons, 1996).
Murphy is recognized as a leading teacher of technical analysis techniques, and his book will make the seemingly arcane
world of charting a little less bizarre.

Another technical analysis book worth browsing is
Thomas J. Dorsey's *Point & Figure Charting: The Essential
Application for Forecasting and Tracking Market Prices* (John
Wiley & Sons, 1995). Point and figure charting is an ancient
method of tracking the trading of a stock (or other commodity), and as such can actually be carried out using old-
fashioned paper and a pencil. In this age of high-tech
everything, the charting technique is extremely simple to
understand and use, and also takes much of the subjective
nature of interpreting charts out of the process. If there is
such a thing as an "unemotional" approach to charting, the
point and figure method may be it.

It should be no surprise to you that charting sites on the
Internet are extremely popular. With the ability to get access
to large volumes of data and get them updated constantly
(not to mention quickly and without cost), the computer and
the Internet are an obvious boon to individual investors using
technical analysis. In the past, only institutional analysts had
the wherewithal to gain access to these kinds of tools. Now
they're available free on the World Wide Web. The following
two sites are among the more popular such sites and are
worth visiting if the charting arrow is in your investment
quiver.

ASK Research

Let's say you want to see how Microsoft (Nasdaq: MSFT) has been doing over the last six months. No hype, no rumors, no marketing, just the actual stock's price performance. Head to a site like ASK Research (www. askresearch.com) and click on its Daily Charts feature. This is a customizable charting center where you can determine the layout and the type of chart you wish to view for stocks, mutual funds, or stock indices. Among the features you can adjust are the size of the chart (to fit your computer configuration and printer), the time span the chart will cover (from one month to four years), the type of chart (bar, line, or candlestick), the chart colors, and the price scale (linear or logarithmic). A linear chart treats the gaps between dollar amounts equally. That is, the same distance is covered on the chart between $10 and $20 per share as it is between $110 and $120. For short time periods, a linear chart is very clear, but for longer time periods, a linear chart can distort the picture because, on a percentage basis, the move from $10 to $20 is a 100% increase while the move from $110 to $120 is only an increase of 9%. On a linear chart, they would appear the same when in fact, they are vastly different moves. To compensate for the different scales in percentage movements as a stock prices rises, a logarithmic scale should be used. This is important to keep in mind, too, when you're listening to an analyst or a reporter telling you a stock has soared uncontrollably high. "See, look at this chart! It goes straight up." On a logarithmic chart, however, the angle of ascent for a successful growth stock will be more realistically displayed. But I digress.

Back to the chart features at ASK Research. Once you've laid out the basic chart configuration, you may choose from two different kinds of overlays. That is, in addition to the daily price information for the stock, you can also have one, two, or three different exponential moving average lines (measuring the average price of the stock over the last 10 to 200 days); or you can use Bollinger Bands as an overlay.

In addition, ASK Research lets you examine a number of technical indicators to "read" right alongside with the price chart. These indicators use the raw technical information in different ways to help you generate theoretical "buy" and "sell" signals. The indicators available at ASK Research include volume, on-balance volume, stochastics, Williams%R, Wilder's Relative Strength Index (RSI), M.A.C.D. (moving average convergence/divergence), price rate of change, and a money flow index. (If you're unsure of what those indicators are, head to Mr. Murphy's book for a tutorial.)

For short-term traders (frown on the practice though I may), ASK Research also offers intraday charts with price intervals of anywhere from 5 to 30 minutes. Keep in mind that these quotes are delayed 15 to 20 minutes, however. If you need information more quickly than that, you'll have to subscribe to their real-time service. Again, unless you're day trading, this isn't necessary. Have I made it clear that day-trading is a losing proposition for nine out of ten who try it? I have? Good. Just checking.

You can also set up your own portfolio on ASK Research to track how your positions are faring. You can get the standard news and commentary, courtesy of CBS MarketWatch, and information on any of the major market indices. Also, you can establish a Watch List of 6 to 10 stocks at ASK Research. Each of your Watch List stocks appears on a single page, allowing you to rotate quickly among the charts for all of the choices as the day's action progresses. Just as with real-time quotes, though, I can't imagine anyone but a short-term trader needing this.

For a quick visual perspective on any stock, ASK Research is a good place to begin. As I'm not a chartist, though, I can't judge the effectiveness of the tools available on the site other than from a very rudimentary standpoint, but I've found the site useful when I want a simple snapshot of a stock over a certain period.

BigCharts

Perhaps better known and institutionally supported is BigCharts (www.bigcharts.com). It offers the same kind of snapshot views (BigCharts calls them *Quick Charts*) and customizable charts (Interactive Charting) provided by ASK Research. But BigCharts goes beyond that service and provides some other useful tools for technical analysts. In addition to the standard fare of stock quotes, news stories, and the like, BigCharts lists some potentially useful information regarding industry groups. You may rank the 10 best and 10 worst industries (based on aggregate price performance) over a period as short as one week or one as long as five years. If you are a top-down analyst who works from the larger economic picture down toward your individual stock choices, this information may be particularly helpful.

In the Market section, BigCharts provides a stock-screening tool based on technical factors. You can check stocks on the New York, American, and Nasdaq exchanges as well as bulletin board stocks (don't bother with these) for a list of stocks matching the following criteria:

- Largest percentage price gain or loss
- Largest net price gain or loss
- 52-week highs (or lows) by percentage price gain (or loss)
- Most active by volume
- Most active by dollar-amount traded
- Most active by price, up or down

In the BigReports section, you will find snapshots of the day's big movers, stocks in the news, stocks reporting earnings, and the like.

One of the best features of the BigCharts site (and one I find myself using with regularity) is its Historical Quotes section. In my research, I often need to check a list of stocks to see how they performed between specific dates. With BigChart's tool, it's very easy to do.

Let's say you need to check the closing price for Dell Computer (Nasdaq: DELL) on Wednesday, January 12, 1994. You simply plug the ticker symbol and date into the slots and up pops the information. You'll find that Dell closed that day at $25⅜, which is also where the stock opened for the day. Its lowest price was $25. That day 788,600 shares of the stock traded hands. In addition, you'll see a two-month daily price chart for the focus period, with an arrow indicating the precise day you've entered. And perhaps as useful as anything, BigCharts includes split adjustment information from the date specified to the present. In Dell's case, for example, a split adjusted price for January 12, 1994, would be $0.396484. That represents a split factor of 64:1 from that date to the present. Split-adjusted prices are crucial if you're checking the performance of a stock over a period that includes splits. For example, if you bought 100 shares of Dell that day in January of 1994, you actually now hold 6,400 shares because of the several stock splits. And if you wish to calculate the gain per share from the purchase date to the present, you'll need that split-adjusted price rather than the actual price at which it traded back in 1994. So if Dell trades at $42 a share today, your gain isn't the difference between a $25 purchase price and today's $42 price; it's the difference between the split-adjusted 40 cents a share and today's price—a mammoth 10,493 percent gain in just under six years. Any complaints? Didn't think so.

If you're doing any kind of historical research, for strategy planning or even just for tax-basis calculations, the Historical Quotes feature at BigCharts.com is one to bookmark.

APPENDIX

Annual Income Requirement Worksheet Example

Expense Categories	Annual Expenses
Housing	$7,000
Insurance	2,000
Healthcare	2,000
Transportation	1,000
Food	7,000
Clothing	2,000
Travel/Entertainment	5,000
Hobbies	1,000
Home Maintenance	2,000
Charity	4,000
Furnishings	5,000
Pocket Money	7,000

Annual Income Requirement	**$45,000**
the 20 factor	**× 20**

Financial Freedom	**$900,000**

INDEX

AUTHOR BIOGRAPHY

Robert Sheard is an internationally recognized investment writer. He was a senior writer for The Motley Fool for several years before opening his own money management firm, Sheard & Davey Advisors, LLC (sheard-davey.com). His research has been profiled in *SmartMoney* magazine, the *Los Angeles Times*, *The Miami Herald*, the *San Jose Mercury News*, the *Houston Chronicle*, *The South China Morning Post*, and a number of other newspapers and Internet forums. His first book, *The Unemotional Investor* (Simon & Schuster, 1998) was a *New York Times* and *BusinessWeek* best-seller, a number one nonfiction bestseller at Amazon.com, and was named one of the Best Business Books of 1998 by the editors at Amazon.com.

Sheard's money management firm opened in June of 1998 and has since been ranked among the "World's Best Money Managers" by Nelson Information. The firm follows the same unemotional philosophies set forth in Robert's writings—the use of a mechanical, time-tested strategy and no attempts at market timing. Through December 31, 1999, the firm's composite annualized return has been 74.8 percent (net of all fees) versus a 20.7 percent annualized return for the S&P 500 Index.

He lives in the Sandhills of North Carolina, where his handicap is still his putting.